BUILDING THE YELLOW WALL

Uli Hesse works for the Berlin-based award-winning *11Freunde*, the bestselling football monthly in Germany. He has written nine books about the game, among them *Tor! The Story of German Football*, the first extensive English-language history of the game in Germany, *Who Invented the Stopover? And Other Crucial Football Conundrums* and *Bayern: Creating a Global Superclub*. He has been contributing to *FourFourTwo* and *When Saturday Comes* since the mid 1990s, and has penned more than 500 columns for ESPN about German football. He was born less than two miles north of Borussia Dortmund's ground.

BUILDING THE YELLOW WALL

*The Incredible Rise and Cult Appeal
of Borussia Dortmund*

ULI HESSE

WEIDENFELD & NICOLSON

A W&N Paperback

First published in hardback in Great Britain in 2018
This paperback edition first published in 2019
by Weidenfeld & Nicolson
an imprint of Orion Books Ltd

1 3 5 7 9 10 8 6 4 2

© Uli Hesse 2018

A CIP catalogue record for this book
is available from the British Library.

ISBN   978 1 4746 0625 7

Typeset by Input Data Services Ltd, Somerset

Printed and bound in Great Britain by Clays Ltd, Elcograf S.p.A.

MIX
Paper from
responsible sources
FSC® C104740

The Orion Publishing Group Ltd
Carmelite House
50 Victoria Embankment
London, EC4Y 0DZ
An Hachette UK Company

www.weidenfeldandnicolson.co.uk

PROLOGUE

Lars Ricken had never seen such desperation on the faces of football fans before – and although he was only nine years old, he would never do so again. He turned around to look at the South Stand. It was not yet the massive, imposing, world-famous terrace it would become later, when Borussia Dortmund defiantly preserved the standing area and even added a second tier to this giant slab of concrete while everybody else went plastic and all-seater. But it was already one of the most renowned stands in the German Bundesliga, noted for the electric and – depending on whose side you were on – either exhilarating or intimidating atmosphere generated by the passion of the people who stood there.

Not now, though.

From where Ricken was – on ground level behind the goal, slightly to the right, his small hands grasping the fence that separated the pitch from the spectators – it looked as if there were some empty spaces on the terrace. How strange. The game was sold out and although there was not more than a minute to go, he wondered why people had left. Then he realised they hadn't. They had sat down. Ricken let his gaze wander across the stand, trying to count the fans that were slumped down on the steps, unable to watch any longer. There were dozens. Some were staring at the ground, others had covered their heads with flags or scarves. He could see heaving shoulders and realised people were sobbing.

Although he was just a boy, Ricken knew why these people had been gripped by utter dejection. The team everyone here simply called Borussia badly needed a goal. At half-time, local television had reported as fact that Borussia were relegated from the Bundesliga for the second time in the club's history. That announcement proved slightly premature because a second-half penalty converted by local boy Michael Zorc kickstarted the team and the players in yellow had thrown everything forward, incessantly attacking the goal in front of the South Stand despite the stifling heat. But time was ticking away. In more ways than one.

Ricken was dimly aware that Borussia were having such severe financial problems that the German FA had threatened the club with the deduction of points due to their debts. The members had made a young lawyer by the name of Reinhard Rauball the new president, hoping he could stave off bankruptcy. However, getting the finances in order would be an almost hopeless task with the team in the second division. Some people felt that if Borussia went down now they would never come back.

With 30 seconds left on the clock, Dortmund's goalkeeper hurried to take a goal-kick and start the last attack of the game. The ball was still in motion when he knocked it to a teammate, but the referee turned a blind eye and didn't blow his whistle to have the goal-kick retaken.

Unusually for the time, the game was shown live on commercial television. While Borussia hurriedly built from the rear, the commentator welcomed Dortmund's opponents to the top flight. Yet there was still time for one final, desperate cross. Ricken could make out Zorc's curly head as the player flicked on the ball towards the left-hand post, not far from where the nine-year-old boy was standing. Through the wire mesh, he saw someone in a yellow shirt make contact with the ball and try a first-time shot from a very tight angle. He heard sharp intakes of breath all around him, as if the air was being sucked out of the stadium. Ricken quickly turned his head to follow the flight of the ball, but all he could see was a confusing clutter of white and yellow shirts, tired players manically stabbing at a loose ball. Then he heard the loudest cheer of his life.

People were jumping up and down, their eyes still misty with the tears of anguish they had been unable to hold back. While the men around him were beginning to scale the fence, others were already running onto the pitch to celebrate.

Ricken had never seen such joy on the faces of football fans before – and although he was only nine years old, he would never do so again.

'Obviously, when we won the Champions League eleven years later, I was on the pitch instead of in the stands,' he says. 'So I don't really know how happy they were when I scored the winning goal against Juventus. But they can't have been any more jubilant than we were on that day in 1986.'

Then he falls quiet to reflect on what a roller-coaster ride it has been.

INTRODUCTION

Borussia Dortmund have not lifted a European trophy since 1997, when the Bundesliga side upset a Juventus team starring Zinedine Zidane, Christian Vieri and Didier Deschamps in the final of the Champions League. And they have not won a league title since 2012, when a young team coached by Jürgen Klopp denied mighty Bayern Munich for the second year in a row.

And yet Dortmund are nothing short of a global phenomenon – a magnet for football enthusiasts from all corners of the world and, as the *Guardian* put it, 'everyone's second team'. In October 2014, the BBC reported the club was 'attracting more than 1,000 fans from England to every home match'. (This should read Britain rather than England, as fan groups such as the 'Edinburgh Borussen', the members of which are always conspicuous by their kilts, will hasten to point out.) One month later, in November 2014, Ryanair announced that the airline had now 'scheduled London–Dortmund matchday specials for UK fans'.

One reason for this irresistible draw is certainly that the football is good. In fact, Dortmund were the only team aside from Barcelona that boasted a positive record against Real Madrid over eight encounters between 2012 and 2016. Another reason is that the club managed to stay competitive at the highest level while still being owned by its members rather than Russian oligarchs, Arabian oil magnates, Chinese conglomerates or, indeed, German car manufacturers. However, the primary reason so many people from abroad regularly flock to an industrial city in Germany's Ruhr area that can hardly be called picturesque is the atmosphere.

As early as 2009, *The Times* named Dortmund's ground – officially the Signal Iduna Park, after a local insurance company, but commonly still called Westfalenstadion by most fans – the number-one stadium in the entire world, saying: 'This place was built for football and for fans to express themselves. Every European Cup final should be held here. The best atmosphere on the Continent on a game-to-game basis.' Shortly before Christmas 2015, the *Daily Mirror* published a video on its website that showed Dortmund fans belting out what the paper called 'the most amazing rendition of Jingle Bells you'll ever hear', calling the team's support 'Europe's finest fans'. Beneath the video, there was a poll: 'Are Dortmund fans the best in the world?' Seventy-three per cent said yes.

Echoing these sentiments in April 2016, the *Telegraph* voted the place some locals simply refer to as 'the Temple' the greatest stadium in European club football. The newspaper said: 'No wonder Jürgen Klopp cried when he left Borussia Dortmund. The German knew that he was leaving behind the most spectacular arena that European football has to offer: the old Westfalenstadion is not only vast (over 80,000 pack in most weeks), but delivers an awe-inspiring carnival of sound and colour, most vividly expressed in the giant murals that rise, with ominous grandeur, from within the famous "Yellow Wall" terrace. A sight every football fan should experience once before they die.'

Indeed, the ground is an impressive sight when full. And it's never empty. According to the specialist magazine *Sports Venues 2016*, Borussia Dortmund are the second-best-supported sports team on the entire planet (only the NFL's Dallas Cowboys draw more people per home game). Which begs two very obvious questions: why and how? Why and how have Dortmund become a club whose fans make the covers of international magazines almost as regularly as their star players do? After all, when Real Madrid travelled to Dortmund in September of 2016, *Marca* did not announce that they were up against World Cup winners André Schürrle and Mario Götze or flamboyant star striker Pierre-Emerick

Aubameyang. Instead, the magazine's cover said: 'La BBC Contra El Muro Amarillo' – Gareth Bale, Karim Benzema and Cristiano Ronaldo against the Yellow Wall. Put differently, why and how have Dortmund become so popular, both in Germany and abroad?

Well, that is a somewhat longer story. Normally, one would start at the very beginning. In this case, though, it might be helpful to start at the point when people began to realise something out of the ordinary was happening.

CHAPTER I

'The first time ever?' Jürgen Klopp wanted to know.

'Yes,' I said. 'So far, it's only been teams from Spain, Italy or South America. And England, of course.'

He let this piece of information sink in, seemingly oblivious to the commotion around us. Mario Götze and Marco Reus, close buddies, were goofing around and doing their worst to distract star striker Robert Lewandowski, who was posing for the camera. Sebastian Kehl, Borussia Dortmund's captain, was calling his kids back home via Facetime and was walking around the room with his iPhone held aloft, so that they could see what the surroundings looked like. Stefan, the photographer, was shaking his head and rolling his eyes, giving me a glance that was meant to say: 'See? I told you they would be totally sweet if alone, but a bag of fleas if we try to shoot them together.' Meanwhile, the editor of *FourFourTwo* magazine was retreating into a corner, his hands dripping with sweat. It's not that it was unseasonably hot in La Manga, southeast Spain, on this Tuesday afternoon in January 2013. Rather, he had just been told that the Hasselblad lens Stefan had handed him for safekeeping was worth as much as a nice car, if considerably more fragile.

Suddenly, a deep voice came booming through the room, stopping everybody dead in their tracks.

'All right, boys,' Klopp announced. 'We're going to be the first German team on the cover of the biggest football magazine in the world. That is an honour. So let's focus and give it all we got.'

The brief speech didn't exactly turn his exuberant charges into docile choirboys, but it instilled enough discipline in the players for them to get down to work. Ninety minutes later, we had what would become the cover photo of the March 2013 issue. It was indeed the first time that a German team was going to stare out at unsuspecting customers from newsstands not just across Britain but also in places as far away as Australia, Egypt and Malaysia.

This was no accident. In the previous seven years, starting with the 2006 World Cup, people's perception of Germany and German football had undergone a dramatic change, especially in Britain. As early as September 2010, Nick Harris, soon to be named chief sports news correspondent of the *Mail on Sunday*, had written a glowing piece for his Sporting Intelligence website headed 'What has Germany ever given its football fans? (Except cheap tickets, tasty beer, good governance and international success)'. The London Olympics had proved that you could be an outstanding sportsperson without being overpaid, pampered and out of touch with reality. It was time for a breath of fresh air and the Bundesliga, where you could go and watch the best team in the land for less than £10, seemed the most logical candidate to provide it.

But why not Bayern? After all, the Munich giants had just reached two Champions League finals in three years, were running away with the 2012–13 Bundesliga title and boasted international stars such as Arjen Robben, Franck Ribéry, Bastian Schweinsteiger and Manuel Neuer. The people in London who briefed me couldn't quite put their finger on why exactly they wanted Dortmund instead. They said Klopp was more charismatic than Bayern's Jupp Heynckes. They liked the fact this Dortmund team was young and exciting to watch, their aggressive style known in Germany as *gegenpressing* taking your breath away. They found it fascinating that only a single player in the entire squad had cost more than £4 million. Also, from a business point of view, Dortmund's yellow shirts would really jump out at people walking past the newsagent's at Grimsby Town railway station on a drab February morning. Finally, and crucially, there were the fans.

Like most big German teams, Bayern drew an awful lot of people, but their support didn't capture the imagination in quite the same way as Dortmund's black-and-yellow army did, mainly because Bayern didn't have what Dortmund had – a massive terrace that seemed like a throwback to football's golden age. The South Stand, now widely referred to as the Yellow Wall, holds 24,454 people for domestic games, more than twice as many as Celtic's fabled Jungle did in the 1960s and only slightly less than the maximum capacity of the Kop at Anfield during the 1970s.

Unlike Jungle or Kop, the term Yellow Wall is not very old. In fact, the Nick Harris piece mentioned above may very well have been the first English-language article to use it. Even the German original, *Gelbe Wand*, is of fairly recent origin. It didn't appear on the pages of *Kicker* magazine, the twice-weekly bible of German football, until the first week of May 2009. Asked about the fact that no fewer than 10,000 fans had travelled with Borussia to a game at Eintracht Frankfurt, Dortmund goalkeeper Roman Weidenfeller told the magazine: 'It is incredible. Even when we are playing away from home, the yellow wall will be there.' It would be another 21 months before Kicker began to capitalise the expression, indicating it was now an established term.

While we were shooting the magazine cover on the first floor of Dortmund's posh team hotel in La Manga, the man who is more or less responsible for coining the name Yellow Wall was a mere stone's throw away, taking care of the sizeable group of fans who had followed Borussia to this winter training camp in order to combine keeping an eye on their team with escaping an increasingly harsh winter at home. Daniel Lörcher, born in 1985, was working for Dortmund as one of the club's four Supporter Liaison Officers (SLOs). (Today, five years later, that number has risen to nine. Yes, Borussia Dortmund employ no fewer than nine men and women who, according to UEFA's definition, 'are a bridge between the fans and the club and help to improve the dialogue between the two sides'.) Going to La Manga was Lörcher's first official engagement, as he had become an employee of the club only a few weeks earlier. Before that, he was a leading member of Dortmund's largest ultras group, The Unity.

In early December 2004, The Unity produced a tifo (a mosaic or mural) that paraphrased an Oscar Wilde aphorism. It read: 'Many walk through dark alleys, but only few are looking at the stars.' (The German words for alley and gutter, which is the term used in Wilde's original, are almost the same.) These were very trying times, as Borussia were technically bankrupt and there was a distinct possibility that the club could go out of business, hence the reference to dark alleys and looking at the stars.

The tifo was impressive, but Lörcher felt the South Stand, being so huge, offered the potential to display something even more stunning and uplifting, providing the ultras – who, despite their high visibility, only numbered a few hundred – could get the regular fans on the terrace to participate. What he envisaged was a vast number of those two-stick flags characteristic of ultras, in bright yellow and distributed all across the stand, not just in the area behind the goal where the members of The Unity are to be found. It would look like a wall.

'We called a Danish retail chain that has stores all over Germany, because we needed a massive amount of fabric that had the right shade of yellow,' Lörcher recalled. 'They sold us more than three miles of this cloth and we produced four thousand flags. We rented sewing machines for weeks on end and then had to learn how to use them. It was hard work, but we had a lot of fun!'

The resulting tifo was spectacular beyond The Unity's wildest dreams. As the players of Borussia Dortmund and Hansa Rostock walked onto the pitch for the last game of the season on 21 May 2005, ten weeks after the club's demise had been averted, the flags bathed the entire stand in yellow. A large banner at the bottom of the stand read: 'At the end of the dark alley shines the yellow wall.' And a sign mounted under the roof declared: 'Yellow Wall South Stand Dortmund'. (It should be noted that Yellow Wall – like the club's marketing motto *Echte Liebe*, real love – is rarely used by older local fans, who simply call the stand *Südtribüne*, the South Stand, or just *die Süd*. The ultras, meanwhile, have their own reason for feeling ambivalent about the expression, but more about that later.)

It is tempting to say that Lörcher has changed sides, from leading the chants for the ultras to working for the club. But that's not how Borussia look at the people who support them. Lörcher's predecessor as chief SLO, Jens Volke, is another former ultra. The two men were headhunted because the club was and is honestly interested in how the fans feel and what they want. It is not mere lip service, as the number of SLOs indicates. Involving the supporters has a history at the club that dates back to the 1990s and is, in fact, one of the reasons why the South Stand could become the Yellow Wall in the first place – why it was never converted into an all-seater area in the wake of Hillsborough and the Taylor Report.

The close relationship between the club and its support can produce some strange results, though. On most days during Dortmund's 2013 winter camp in La Manga, there were two training sessions scheduled, at ten in the morning and four in the afternoon. The pitch was not far from the Hotel Principe Felipe, a popular golf resort surrounded by condos and bungalows for less-well-heeled holidaymakers. This is where the fans were staying. Every day, when the coach took the players to a local club's training pitch, you could see them coming out of those buildings, following the team like moths flocking to a lamp. With the difference that moths don't carry six-packs of beer and cheap wine in Tetra Pak cartons.

It was truly a bizarre sight to watch the reigning German league champions – a team that had just remained unbeaten in a tricky Champions League group, finishing first ahead of Real Madrid, Ajax and Manchester City – conduct a training session on a pitch lined by dozens of fans, perhaps as many as one hundred, sipping wine while slouching on folding chairs and exposing beer bellies to the Spanish sun. Klopp and his players acted as if this was perfectly normal, though it's probably not a coincidence that his successor would conduct his first winter training camp, three years later, in Dubai, 4,000 miles away from Dortmund. (Still, a few fans would make that trip, too.)

I could see why so many fans decided to spend their holidays in a professional football club's winter training camp, though. It's not just that they were close to the players. It's also that the training sessions were truly fascinating and totally different from what usually happened during the season. In Germany, many regular training sessions are still open to the public, so supporters are used to seeing players running laps with that casual gait peculiar to athletes, doing a few stretching exercises and then ending the session with some sort of game. But in La Manga, the sessions were intense drills. In fact, they were so taxing that Klopp interrupted them every fifteen minutes so that the players could catch some breath and briefly relax the mind.

The team was working on its pressing game, especially on moving forward as a unit – instead of retreating – immediately after having lost possession deep in the opponent's half. Klopp referred to this as *gegenpressing*, counter pressing, because it was the best way to nip counter-attacks in the bud.

'The only problem with gegenpressing is that you cannot train it as a tactical measure,' Klopp explained to me in La Manga. 'You can't tell the players: you stand here and if this happens, you run there. Instead, you have to train the impulse. It has to be an impulse to move into a ball-winning position immediately after losing the ball. You don't teach a situation, you teach the impulse until it becomes a natural action.'

It is a complex approach to the game. If one player fails to do his job, be that putting the man with the ball under pressure or closing down passing lanes, you are flirting with disaster. And so you have to keep teaching the impulse. However, there is normally very little time to do so, because as a coach you are always analysing the last game or preparing for the next while giving your players ample time to recuperate between matches.

'It's almost impossible to work on the finer points of the game during the season,' Klopp said. 'What should be training is more like talk therapy, where you explain to the players what they are doing wrong and ask them to change it. We just don't have the time for anything else. So you have to work on these things during the pre-season preparations. However, whenever there's a big tournament in the summer, your internationals will only join you for the last two weeks before the new season begins. That's why I'm so grateful for the German winter break. It changes everything.'

Klopp's teams, especially his Dortmund sides, indeed had a history of doing better in the second half of the season. That would also be the case in 2013. Although Borussia had waltzed through Europe, they found themselves off the pace in the Bundesliga after the first half of the season, trailing both Bayern and Leverkusen. Borussia had thrown away a two-goal lead in Frankfurt, conceded a late equaliser against Hannover and lost the derby against Schalke at home. (Only four days before beating Real Madrid!) It seemed the players were struggling to stay mentally alert, and so Klopp worked on the gegenpressing impulse during those seven days in Spain.

In the first week of February, *FourFourTwo* hit the newsstands with a cover that showed Lewandowski, Götze, Reus and Kehl flanking a typically mischievous Klopp, while the tagline declared Dortmund to be 'Europe's hottest club'. Eight days later, the team travelled to Ukraine to play Shakhtar Donetsk in the Champions League's round of 16. The hosts had a good team, smartly assembled by coaching legend Mircea Lucescu, that featured some very talented players, including the elegant Armenian midfielder Henrik Mkhitaryan. Still, Europe's hottest team went into the tie as favourites and seemed to feel comfortable in this role. The inevitable Lewandowski goal and a late Mats Hummels header earned Dortmund a 2–2 draw away from home and the second leg was something of a formality, although the 3–0 scoreline was a bit harsh on Shakhtar.

In the next round Dortmund were drawn against Spanish side Málaga, bankrolled by a Qatari businessman. A few months earlier, the CNN website had reported: 'Over the last decade, Europe's football clubs have become the new must-have accessory for any billionaire itching to blow a significant chunk of their wealth. European champions Chelsea, English title winners Manchester City and French team Paris Saint-Germain have all been transformed by benefactors willing to splash out on world-class players. Another example is Spanish team Málaga, which has gone from La Liga also-rans to European Champions League qualifiers in just two years thanks to the riches of Sheikh Abdullah Bin Nasser Al-Thani.'

However, as Málaga were preparing to meet Dortmund, their story had turned from a rags-to-riches fantasy to a cautionary drama. For some reason (the English reporter George Prior told CNN it might have had something to do with Málaga not getting 'the TV rights they wanted') the Sheikh had come to the conclusion he should, in the words of the American news channel, turn off the tap. The club's entire future hung in the balance and the best players, veterans such as Javier Saviola and Martin Demichelis and youngsters like Isco, would soon jump ship.

It was another reason why the *Guardian*'s minute-by-minute coverage of the first leg in Spain quickly turned into a collection of what the newspaper called 'paeans to German football'. It began with a statement from economics professor Stefan Szymanski (Simon Kuper's co-author for the book *Soccernomics*), who called the tie 'a metaphor for the economic and political fault lines of Europe' in which 'Dortmund represents solid German values, a profitable club from the tightly regulated Bundesliga'. Then, with the game in progress and Dortmund dominating the proceedings, many readers began to leave comments that touched upon broader issues than the match itself. A man named Julian Menz wrote: 'I miss seeing my PL team play regularly, but I would recommend German football to anyone tired of the lame atmosphere at many Premier League grounds. I get to Fortuna Düsseldorf (struggling) and they regularly get over 50,000. The atmosphere is cracking. Non-stop singing. Plus you can stand. And have a beer and a fag. Oh, and it costs between 15–20 quid.' Someone called Stewart Todd said: 'I've been to games in Munich and Cologne. And the experience was superb. From the basic things like affordability to the atmosphere at the ground, ability to get a beer and food.' One Mahyar Shami added: 'I have gone to a match in Dortmund and it was a brilliant experience. The city has a major buzz before it and there is great chants and banter. I personally thought it was a better atmosphere than going to United v Liverpool or Arsenal v Tottenham and this was just an average Bundesliga match against Hoffenheim.'

The game in Spain finished scoreless and although Dortmund should have been disappointed with the outcome, it was still a good result, so optimism reigned supreme among the support. The atmosphere for the return leg was electric, even by the standards of the Westfalenstadion. As the teams stepped out of the tunnel, they were treated to a truly impressive tifo. For UEFA games, the South Stand loses more than half of its capacity, as seats have to be brought in. It means there were only 11,131 fans in the stand, but they all played their part in the ground's first *Wendechoreo*, flip-over or turn-around choreography.

This term refers to a tifo where all the fans in a stand hold coloured cards over their heads to create a pattern. At a given moment, some of them turn their cards around to display a different colour and thus change the pattern into something else. Before the Málaga game, most fans held up yellow cards, only those around the edges of the stand brandished black ones. A banner was unfurled that said 'On the Trail of the Lost Handlecup', referring to the Champions League trophy which Dortmund had last won sixteen years earlier. (Due to the trophy's peculiar shape,

Germans call it *Henkelpott*, which translates as cup with handles, but evokes a chamber pot.) As the players were nearing the centre circle, the giant image of a cartoon character was hoisted over the backdrop of the coloured cards, a grinning man wearing a Dortmund cap and looking through a pair of binoculars. While this was rising into the air, some fans at the heart of the stand turned their yellow cards around to create the black silhouette of the European cup.

It was a truly amazing sight, and to this day the choreography is regularly mentioned when football fans discuss the most dazzling tifos. But for Dortmund supporters, this piece of art has been overshadowed by the 90 minutes that followed. Or rather, by 70 seconds of them.

At first there was no inkling that this would turn out to be one of the most magical nights in the club's history. On the contrary, Dortmund seemed gripped by nerves and never really found their rhythm. The visitors scored on 25 minutes and although Götze, Reus and Lewandowski linked up for an equaliser of rare beauty with five minutes left in the first half, Klopp's team now faced an uphill struggle, as they needed at least one more goal to go through.

In the early stages of the second half, Weidenfeller made a string of good saves to keep his side in the game. But eventually Dortmund gained the upper hand. The players in black and yellow were attacking the goal in front of the South Stand, as they always try to do after the break, and created some good opportunities. But on 82 minutes and against the run of play, they were hit on the break. Isco set up Julio Baptista, whose shot would have gone wide if hadn't been for Eliseu, who poked the ball into an empty net at the far post. He was blatantly offside, but the goal was allowed to stand and neither Dortmund's players nor the fans protested too much. A feeling seemed to permeate the stadium that this was just one of those nights.

Only it wasn't. It was a night unlike any other. Half a minute into injury time, a loose ball in Málaga's penalty area fell to Reus, who knocked it in from eight yards. The Spaniards were still through on the away-goals rule, but they lost possession almost immediately after kicking off. Lewandowski crossed into the box, Dortmund's Brazilian defender Felipe Santana headed the ball into the path of Reus, who tried a shot at goal but mishit the ball so that it became more of a cross into the goalmouth. There was a chaotic scramble for the ball until Santana, also offside, bundled it across the line from close range. Again the referee gave the goal and Dortmund were among the four best teams in Europe.

'That's one of the faces of football,' a slightly dishevelled Klopp told Sky Sports after the game, groping for the right words to describe his feelings in English. 'There is one very disappointed team now and one very lucky team. It was unbelievable. It was our worst game in the Champions League in the first half. We showed nerves. We were better in the second half, but they were clever and ran down the clock. What happened then was . . . crazy.'

On 12 April 2013, the draw for the Champions League semi-finals was made. It paired Borussia Dortmund with Real Madrid and Bayern Munich with Barcelona. For almost every observer, it looked as if the stage was set for a showdown between the Bundesliga and La Liga in the biggest club competition in the world. However, even at this point, Real and Barça were merely supporting actors. Behind the scenes, a drama was unfolding that was only about Bayern and Borussia and the future of the German game.

The relationship between these two clubs is a lot more complex than people think. Today, they are invariably referred to as 'rivals' and their matches have been dubbed 'the German Clásico'. There is a Wikipedia article called 'Der Klassiker' entirely devoted to the antagonism between the two sides. Look closer, though, and you'll find that this Wikipedia entry was created as late as 2014 – and that it still doesn't have a German version. That's because the supposed Bayern–Dortmund rivalry is a very recent phenomenon.

Germany is unique – certainly in Europe, perhaps in the world – in that even though they were a major footballing nation, they did not have a nationwide, professional league until well into the 1960s. Once professionalism was legalised, new powerhouses began to emerge, as the historically most successful clubs – Nuremberg and Schalke, but also Hamburg and Dortmund – found it hard to adapt. Gradually, Bayern Munich and Borussia Mönchengladbach emerged as the leading teams and those two clubs dominated the 1970s. At the end of this decade, Mönchengladbach fell by the wayside – and ever since, Bayern have ruled the roost alone, regularly but only temporarily annoyed by a challenger like Leverkusen, Bremen or, indeed, Dortmund.

Which is why Dortmund supporters who grew up before the mid-1990s still consider neighbours Schalke the one team you must beat. They dislike Bayern with the same intensity (some sort of natural instinct) and for the same reason (because they always win) as any other German football fan – but that's not the same as a passionate rivalry. Perhaps the situation was best summed up by Hertha Berlin fans. When Bayern lifted the 2014 league title in Berlin, the home supporters sang: 'You win the league, you win in Europe, you win the cup – we don't give a fuck!'

Bayern, meanwhile, find themselves in the perverse situation that they try to keep all Bundesliga opposition down while at the same time being acutely aware how much they need a proper domestic rival to stay sharp and alert in order to be competitive in Europe. A few months after the events described in this chapter, I talked about this paradox with Bayern striker Thomas Müller. He told me: 'Competition is good for business, as they say. If you have strong competition, you've got to try harder. And that always helps you to develop and improve.' Then he added: 'Dortmund have been very consistent. I think both the club structure they have built and the squad they have assembled over the past years make them a rival you have to take seriously in the foreseeable future. That's a good thing for us, as a club, because having a strong opponent means you have to be more attentive.'

However, it also means you are suddenly fishing in the same pond as someone else. Bayern had always prided themselves on the fact that the best German players wanted to wear their colours. Which is why Christian Nerlinger, then Bayern's director of football, declared in December of 2011 that his club was strongly interested in Mönchengladbach's Marco Reus, adding confidently: 'If Bayern want to sign a player, Bayern will sign him.' Two weeks later, Reus signed for his hometown club, Borussia Dortmund. A few months after that, Klopp's team won the Bundesliga for the second year in a row – and humiliated Bayern in the cup final.

That is the backdrop to the events which unfolded in the build-up to the 2013 Champions League semi-finals. On 19 April, five days before the first leg against Real, and one day before news broke that Bayern president Uli Hoeness was at the centre of a tax-evasion scandal, Jürgen Klopp sat down for a regular press conference ahead of Dortmund's league game against his old club, Mainz. Suddenly, a reporter asked a question that had nothing to do with the match at hand. 'There has been a lot of talk during the last days about "Spanish conditions" in the league, with Bayern and Dortmund at the top,' he said. 'Is this really something we should be worried about?'

The Bundesliga was indeed resembling a two-horse race again, as those training sessions in La Manga had clearly paid off for Dortmund. Klopp's side had lost only two league games since January, which was more than enough to climb past Leverkusen and into second place. That is why Hoeness had recently expressed concern about the fact that Bayern and Dortmund were so much better than the rest of the league that they had become the German version of the Real–Barcelona duopoly. Klopp could have replied that, yes, it might look like that at the moment. Or he could have evaded the subject altogether. But evasion is not his strong suit.

Klopp rolled up his sleeves and took a deep breath to gain some time. 'This is one of the cases where I have to be extremely careful of what I say,' he replied. 'Let me put it this way: unfortunately not.' Then he looked at the journalists. 'Is there a league where just one team dominates and the rest are left behind?' One of the writers suggested Scotland and Klopp nodded in agreement. 'Since Rangers were demoted, yes. OK, so what I much rather fear are Scottish conditions. I think that when the new Bayern squad is announced in the summer we will find that what Hoeness has said isn't altogether supported by the team that has been assembled.'

Klopp is often rightly criticised for letting his emotions get the better of him, but in this moment he displayed almost superhuman self-control. Like everyone else in the room, he knew that Bayern had signed Pep Guardiola, widely regarded as the best coach in the world, to take over the following season. It was also common knowledge that Bayern were interested in the services of Dortmund's Robert Lewandowski. But Klopp was the only person in the room who knew that Bayern had just robbed him of his most talented player, the silky-skilled Mario Götze, a 20-year-old who was born an hour west of Munich but had been playing for Dortmund since the age of nine.

Just a few days earlier, on the morning after the legendary Málaga game, Klopp had been approached by Michael Zorc, a former player and now the club's director of football. According to Klopp, Zorc 'walked in like somebody had died' to inform him that Götze was going to activate a release clause in his contract and join Bayern. There were only losers in this story, because the transfer would turn out to be a disastrous career move for Götze, while Klopp was so shocked by losing a player who was obviously enamoured of the club, his teammates and Klopp himself that he later compared the moment to a heart attack. It was certainly a major reason why Klopp, who had already memorably compared the Munich club to business pirates – 'Bayern go about football in the same way that the Chinese go about industry. They look at what the others are doing, and then they copy it with other people and more money. And then they overtake you' – would soon tell writer Donald McRae that Bayern resembled the villain in a James Bond film, evoking the image of a mentally unstable billionaire plotting world domination.

For the time being, though, Klopp had to bite his tongue. He could only drop vague hints during the Mainz press conference, because too much was at stake. With the Real Madrid game coming up, he couldn't afford to break the stunning news and cause a commotion. So it was somebody else who did it.

Thirty-two hours before Dortmund met Real, a tabloid 'exclusively' disclosed what it referred to as a 'sensational transfer'. The news sent shock waves through the team's support. It's not that Dortmund fans are naive or blind to the realities of professional football. They have had their fair share of teams made up of highly salaried mercenaries without any emotional ties to the club or the city. But that was precisely the reason why there was a widespread feeling that this Klopp side was different. Some of the players, such as central defenders Mats Hummels and Neven Subotić, were genuinely close friends. The same went for Poles Jakub Błaszczykowski and Łukasz Piszczek. Midfielder Kevin Großkreutz, like Reus a local lad, used to support the team from the South Stand, for which he still had a season ticket. Weidenfeller was in his eleventh season with Borussia. Of course there were players in the squad, Lewandowski most prominent among them, for whom this was basically just a job. But skipper Kehl told me: 'This team is like a band of brothers.' (We know each other so well – we have sung karaoke together on a mutual friend's stag night – that there was no reason for Kehl to feed me a line like that if he didn't really mean it.)

Klopp called the timing of the news 'a nine on a scale from one to ten', with ten being the worst possible moment. It was patently not in the interest of the club or the player to leak the transfer, so most fans immediately assumed that someone at Bayern had informed the tabloid in order to cause turmoil in Dortmund (and divert attention from the Hoeness tax scandal). How the fans would react was now the most pressing problem.

Klopp had barely sat down for the pre-match press conference later that day when an out-of-town journalist spoke up. 'How is the team dealing with the news?' the man asked. Then he added: 'And please refrain from using the cliché that the players have to be professional about it.'

Klopp shot the man a look that could have withered an oak. 'It's the first time I see you here, but you're already making demands,' he replied. 'What's your department? Wildlife films?' Then he steered the discussion away from the squad and towards the support.

'We have always said that this is an extraordinary club, now we have the chance to prove it,' he began. 'If somebody has forgotten how much we wanted to reach this semi-final, how much blood, sweat and tears we put into it, then I suggest he should stay away from the ground tomorrow. But the people who understand this will support us no matter what. In extreme situations, our fans have always responded in an outstanding manner. I think tomorrow will be no exception.'

And it wasn't. At least not in the stands, where hardly a voice was raised against Götze. On the pitch, though, it was an exceptional evening. The fans knew that Klopp's teams had always felt comfortable playing against sides with a lot of individual class but little tactical discipline, yet nobody could have been prepared for a 4–1 mauling of mighty Real. Or for the fact that Lewandowski became the first player in the history of the European cup competitions to score four goals in one match against the proud Spanish team. For once, even visiting coach José Mourinho was forced to eat humble pie. 'Dortmund were the best team by far,' he said. 'They deserved it. They were stronger collectively and in every individual duel. We had so many difficulties. They were better physically and mentally.'

With biblical inevitability, Bayern had thrashed Barcelona in the other semi-final and it now seemed a foregone conclusion that the season would culminate in the first all-German final in the Champions League or the European Cup. At, of all places, Wembley. However, first there was the nail-biter of a return leg at the Bernabéu for Borussia. After riding out an early storm, Dortmund appeared to be cruising into the final until Benzema found the target with eight minutes left. Six minutes later, Sergio Ramos made it 2–0. Real threw everything forward, but the Germans held out.

Until that night, Dortmund had been the only undefeated team in the Champions League, but they could live with being stripped of this distinction. What was a lot harder to take was the fact that Götze had hobbled off the pitch with a thigh injury after less than a quarter of an hour. German legend Lothar Matthäus, now working as a pundit for television, argued that the injury was some sort of psychosomatic reaction to the pressure the young man found himself under due to the controversy triggered by his move. In any case, Götze would miss the final against his future team, a heavy blow for Klopp, whose squad was nowhere near as deep as Bayern's.

Some 150,000 football fans from Germany, two-thirds of them without tickets, made the journey to London for the final on 25 May 2013. One of them was Lars Ricken. Born in Dortmund, Ricken spent nineteen years as a player with Borussia and is best remembered for his stunning lob from thirty yards out that put the 1997 Champions League final beyond doubt. Since 2008, he had worked as Dortmund's youth coordinator, but that was not the capacity in which he travelled to England.

'Each team in a Champions League final is represented by a so-called final ambassador,' Ricken says, looking back on his very own, very strange Wembley experience. 'These are usually people who have a special relationship with this competition. For the 2013 final, Bayern's ambassador was Paul Breitner, while I was appointed Borussia's ambassador.' He hesitates. 'It was not a problem as such and I was happy making all sorts of appearances in the build-up to the final. While still in Dortmund, I had also heard that I was supposed to take part in some kind of opening ceremony before the game. But that was all. I had no idea what exactly had been planned.'

They didn't even tell him on the eve of the game, when he was called to the stadium 'to try on the costume'. It consisted of a medieval soldier's breastplate, a shield, a sword and a helmet. Ricken was aghast. He still had no idea what the ceremony would look like, but he had no intention of representing a German club on English soil dressed in armour and wielding a weapon. Not even in jest. He told the UEFA representative: 'I'm sorry, I'm not going to wear that. And I can assure you that when Mr Breitner arrives, he will tell you the same thing.'

It would seem Paul Breitner had considerably fewer qualms about making a fool of himself. Because when Ricken, dressed in a simple black jacket with a yellow sash, stepped out of the tunnel before the Champions League final, he saw Breitner striding towards him wearing the breastplate. And that wasn't even the worst part. The two men were surrounded by two armies of extras, who were obviously about to begin fighting each other with bows and arrows, sticks and swords.

'It's moments like these when you wonder what has gone wrong in your life,' Ricken says drily. 'But I could hardly throw down my costume and run away. So I told myself to stop thinking about it and just follow the instructions I was given over my headset.' What the *Independent*'s Michael Calvin called 'the toe-curling pretensions of an opening ceremony [that] would have been an embarrassment had it been staged before 200 people on a village green, rather than in front of a TV audience in excess of 200 million' was so bizarre that the Dortmund ultras turned around en masse and, with their backs to the pitch, gave the spectacle the finger.

Thankfully, the game was infinitely more entertaining, full of flair and skill, highly intense, with plenty of goalmouth action and all sorts of controversy. Bayern were lucky to finish the game with eleven men, as Ribéry should have been sent off for elbowing Lewandowski midway through the first half and the Brazilian Dante, who had already been booked, could have seen another yellow card when he clumsily kicked Reus in the penalty area on 68 minutes. At least the foul led to a penalty, which İlkay Gündoğan converted to make it 1–1 after Mario Mandzukić had given Bayern the lead on the hour.

The reason Dortmund lost this final was probably that they failed to score during the first half-hour, when they ran their lungs out and by and large played the overwhelming favourites from Munich off the park. But goalkeeper Manuel Neuer denied Dortmund on numerous occasions and eventually Bayern settled down, overcame their nerves and gained the upper hand. With the benefit of hindsight, Klopp should have made one or two substitutions in the final quarter of an hour, because his courageous team was fading fast. However, while Heynckes had internationals such as Luiz Gustavo (Brazil), Xherdan Shaqiri (Switzerland) and Anatoliy Tymoshchuk (Ukraine) on the bench, Klopp felt none of his substitutes was quite on the level of the players who had started the game. In the final minute of normal time, Dortmund paid the price when Robben left many tired legs in his wake and scored the winning goal.

Although the trophy went to Munich, Dortmund won a few things on that day in the English capital. The team certainly won the respect of everyone watching, while the fans won admiration. Bayern's fans had been more actively seeking attention – they presented a tifo before the game and later illuminated the night with Bengal lights and flares. Yet Borussia's support left the more lasting impression. Michael Calvin reported: 'Dortmund, rescued from bankruptcy and reinvented as a people's club, had the vibrancy and optimism of the artless newcomer. Their fans provided the soundtrack to a stirring contest. They formed a sea of yellow, which lapped against the landmarks of the capital before sweeping, in a flood tide, across the east end of the Stadium. They sang incessantly to the co-ordinated rhythms of four drummers. It was authentic, and mesmerising.'

Such was the wave of attraction to the team in Britain after the final that Ben McFadyean, an Aston Villa fan who grew up in Germany, started a Dortmund supporters' club in London that now numbers more than 400 members. I experienced a little bit of that fascination myself a few hours after the final whistle, when I was sitting in a pub near East Finchley tube station, nursing a pint. Suddenly, I heard a loud cheer. A few customers had stood up and were about to leave. The colour of their scarves gave them away as Dortmund fans and when the pub staff realised, they formed a line to salute them. Which in turn prompted the regular punters to join in the applause. All around me, British men and women rose from their seats to pay tribute to a few Borussia Dortmund fans who felt in equal measure embarrassed and proud.

Not bad for a club whose beginnings are insufficiently described by the word 'humble'.

CHAPTER 2

When Michael Calvin said in the *Independent* that Dortmund had been 'reinvented as a people's club', it sounded like a throwaway line – but it was actually astonishingly clear-sighted for someone who only followed the team from a distance. Why he used the verb he used ('reinvented') will be the subject of a later chapter. What he meant by 'people's club' is that Borussia Dortmund, despite their rapidly growing international following, are still firmly rooted in their community.

To understand this community, we have to look at geography and demographics. In late 2016, Dortmund's population climbed above 600,000 for the first time in two decades, which meant it was the eighth largest city in the country. Dortmund belongs to an urban area that Germans call Ruhrgebiet – the Ruhr region, after the river which serves as its southern boundary. The demarcation lines to the north and the west are also rivers, Lippe and Rhine, respectively. (The eastern border of the Ruhr area is less easy to define; most people point towards the city of Unna, twelve miles east of Dortmund.) The Ruhr area is so far in the west of Germany that when the people who live here say they spend their holidays at the sea, they don't mean one of the classic German spas but the Dutch coast, as the Netherlands is only a short drive away.

The Ruhr region comprises almost a dozen larger cities plus many smaller ones. They are all independent municipalities, but you will often go from one town into another without realising you have done so because the area is so densely populated that the different places all blend into each other. More than five million people live within 1,700 square miles, which means the region is not unlike Greater London – the difference being that seven major motorways cut through the Ruhrgebiet. For this reason, everything feels really close together. For instance, Schalke's arena is twenty miles away from Dortmund's stadium, more or less the distance between Loftus Road and the old Upton Park in London. But thanks to the ubiquitous Autobahn, you can go from Schalke to Dortmund by car in barely twenty minutes. (Admittedly, not on a matchday.)

This also explains why the region is one huge urban sprawl in which people are commuting all the time. They live in Duisburg but work in Essen and have family in some place along the way, perhaps in Witten or Bochum. This state of affairs – somehow separate, somehow welded together – goes a long way towards explaining why the football rivalries are so heated here. While people from the Ruhr area have a strong sense of regional pride and often define themselves as being from this area, rather than being from one particular city, closeness can foster resentment. The authoritative book about the local game is called *In the Land of a Thousand Derbies*.

While the word Ruhrgebiet refers to the area's geography, another name for the area tells you how it came into being: Revier. This is short for Kohlerevier, coal district, and hints at the region's industrial past. As late as the middle of the nineteenth century, the Ruhr area was still a cosy, tranquil rural region. In 1840, only 7,000 people lived in Dortmund, yet it was considered one of the biggest towns in the area. Gelsenkirchen, by comparison, had a population of 624 and Schalke (today a borough of Gelsenkirchen) was literally a smattering of farm buildings. The Industrial Revolution changed all that. Ten years later, in 1850, there were almost 300 coal mines in operation in the Ruhr area, giving work to 12,700 people and producing almost two million tons of coal. And only two generations after that, in 1903, 250,000 miners were toiling away here, producing 65 million tons of what was dubbed the black gold. The Ruhr region had suddenly become the largest metropolitan area in the whole of Europe. Dortmund had a population of 157,000, while 139,000 people lived in Gelsenkirchen.

Where had all these people come from? Obviously, many of them were migrant workers from neighbouring regions or even countries (the first statistical breakdown of the workforce in the mines, conducted in 1893, found a considerable number of people from Austria-Hungary, the Netherlands and Italy). However, the majority of immigrants came from the eastern territories of the country, places like Silesia, Posen, and East and West Prussia. These people were technically Germans, but their homes were historically Polish. (These regions had become German between 1772 and 1795, when Prussia, Austria and Russia swallowed up the Kingdom of Poland.)

This explains the proliferation of Polish names in the Ruhr area. Schalke's golden age is inseparably linked with people called Szepan, Kuzorra and Tibulski. When Borussia Dortmund beat Liverpool in 1966 to become the first German club to lift a European trophy, the goalkeeper was Tilkowski, the right back went by the name of Cyliax and the man who scored the winning goal was called Libuda.

Living together was not always easy for the various ethnic groups. One of Dortmund's greatest early icons was Max Michallek, known as 'Spider' for his long limbs. It was not until I was working on an oral history book about the club and talked to a man who had grown up in the same street as Michallek during the 1930s that I learned this wasn't his real name. He had been born as Michalski and later changed his name, in all likelihood to disguise his Polish origins.

By and large, though, the Ruhr area was (and still is) a functioning melting pot. The hard work and the often dangerous conditions bound people together and formed the characteristics typical of coal-mining and steel-working communities the world over: a no-nonsense approach to life, a strong work ethos, a sense of solidarity and an aversion to fancy talk and pretensions. If a person from the Ruhr area likes you, you have a friend for life. If he doesn't like you, he will tell you so to your face. If this hurts your feelings, you should get yourself a thicker skin. Life wasn't meant for the faint-hearted.

Although Dortmund did have its share of mines, the city became more famous for steel. In 1871, the steel company Hoesch opened a plant in the northern part of the city, not far from what is today Borsigplatz square, which was named after a man who had founded a local factory that produced machine tools. (Like many towns, Dortmund was divided by the railway line into a more affluent part – the south – and a poorer, blue-collar area to the north. This division is still acutely felt in the city.) For the next one hundred years, Hoesch became the borough's lifeblood. During its peak, the company employed 25,000 people. Those steel workers formed the community that would spawn Borussia Dortmund.

In 1899, Dortmund's port opened, which meant the city could now export its goods all over the world. And it was not only steel or coal. There was a third pillar on which Dortmund's economic boom rested – beer. The pale lager that made Dortmund a household name in pubs around the world was called Export, for its long shelf-life. In the years leading up to the First World War, Dortmund was home to thirty breweries whose annual beer production rose to more than 150,000 barrels. In fact, as late as the 1980s, people who entered Dortmund were greeted by street signs that read 'Welcome to Europe's Beer City Number One'. Only Milwaukee produced more beer than Dortmund. This beverage would play another crucial role as Borussia came into being.

Football was not very popular in Germany around the turn of the century. The game was frowned upon because of its English roots and – an element that should not be underestimated – the fact that it encouraged competitiveness. In fact, almost any sport that was essentially a game aroused suspicion. The major athletic activities in Germany were track and field or boxing, rowing, fencing and, especially, gymnastics. Not coincidentally, these were sports that centred around discipline and drill. Sports that would prepare people for military life and war.

However, some Germans liked football. They tended to be either educated, anglophile public schoolboys or people who didn't mind a bit of rowdiness and had a rebellious streak. The former were in very short supply in the north of Dortmund, but you could find a few of the latter.

One of those was Franz Jacobi. His family lived just off Borsig-platz square and only a short walk away from Trinity Church, which had been built for the predominantly Catholic workers who had come from Silesia to stoutly Protestant Dortmund. In 1902, at the age of thirteen and while training to become an office clerk at the Hoesch steel mill, Jacobi joined a Catholic youth organisation called Young Men's Sodality. One of its major attractions was that it gave its members opportunities for physical recreation, partic-ularly track and field and gymnastics. By all accounts, Jacobi was an excellent runner.

Four years later, two things happened that would have far-reaching repercussions for Jacobi and his city. The first was that a chaplain called Hubert Dewald took charge of the Sodality. The second happened far away from Dortmund. Curiously, near White Hart Lane in London. That's where a truly cosmopolitan German by the name of Reinholt Richter was living at the time. Richter, who originally hailed from the Dresden region, was working in England – as a butler, no less – when he heard that the lease on a fine pub-cum-restaurant in Dortmund called 'Zum Wildschütz' ('The Poacher's') was supposedly available. Richter was one of those people who never let an opportunity to travel pass by (he also spent parts of his life in France, Egypt, Switzerland and Jerusalem). On the spur of the moment, he grabbed a few belongings and set off for Dortmund. One of those belongings was a football.

When Richter walked into the 'Wildschütz', he realised he had been misled. Heinrich Trott, the landlord, had no intention of giving up his public house. While Richter didn't find the job he was hoping for, he did find a soul mate. One of Heinrich Trott's daughters – Lydia, commonly known as Lilly – was romantically involved with Franz Jacobi, which is why you rarely went into the pub without finding him there. Jacobi and Richter quickly struck up a friendship that was destined to last a lifetime.

By this time, there were some football clubs in Dortmund, most notably Dortmunder SC 95, based south of the railway line. But it was Richter who introduced Jacobi and his friends to the game and they became enthusiastic players. There was one problem, though. Chaplain Dewald was vehemently opposed to what he called 'the crude and savage hustle' of the footballers. He even railed at them from the pulpit, infuriated by the fact they would play on Sundays. 'It's not a simple day of recreation we can spend as we may see fit,' Dewald lectured his congregation. 'According to God's will it's meant to refresh body and soul. The body through rest from work, the soul through occupation with its eternal salvation.'

Crossing an institution like the Catholic Church the wrong way was no trifle in the first decade of the twentieth century. But Jacobi and his friends, most notably a young man called Heinrich Unger, loved the new game so much that drawing the wrath of the chaplain seemed a small price to pay. During the following years, the boys would continue to kick a ball about on local paddocks and meadows, while Dewald continued to grouse and scold, even more so because the footballers never met in the parish hall right next to Trinity Church and instead preferred the 'Wildschütz', near Borsigplatz square. A pub run by a Protestant.

The matter finally came to a head six days before Christmas 1909. During meetings of the Young Men's Sodality, Dewald had regularly singled out Jacobi and Unger for criticism. Now he went a step further. The chaplain used the festive season to condemn football once more during a morning sermon. Then he announced that Sunday afternoon mass was now compulsory for members of the Young Men's Sodality and that failing to attend was sinful. A few hours later, around noon, seven football lovers were debating this turn of events in Jacobi's parents' flat when suddenly an old friend walked in. Reinholt Richter, still a compulsive traveller, was working in Paris at the time but had come to Germany to spend Christmas in Dortmund. He understood that the chaplain's announcement amounted to a ban on football, because Sunday afternoon was the only time of the week working people could play with any intensity. Richter suggested a solution that was as simple as it was radical.

Many decades later, Jacobi would tell Dortmund's club historian Gerd Kolbe: 'Reinholt Richter was a true friend. He played a crucial role in Borussia's formation when he all but urged us to break away from the Young Men's Sodality and create our own club. He was our backer and helper when it came to founding Borussia. He became something like the driving force behind the club.' Encouraged by Richter, the budding club founders scheduled a meeting for the same evening, of course at the 'Wildschütz', and invited everybody they knew who liked the game and wasn't afraid of the Church.

By seven o'clock, about fifty young men, all members of the Sodality, had come together in an assembly room known as the Hall of Mirrors, on the first floor above the pub. Jacobi and Unger explained their plan, which meant leaving the church association and setting up a rival organisation. About two-thirds of their listeners got cold feet and left the room when they realised what this meeting was all about. Some went home. Others informed chaplain Dewald about a dangerous development down at the 'Wildschütz'.

Dewald was still a fairly young man himself, only six years older than Jacobi. Boiling with anger and indignation, he hurried over to the pub to stop what he would later refer to as 'a parish schism'. He never even made it into the Hall of Mirrors. Jacobi gave him a push on the stairs, or perhaps even a proper punch, and the man of faith went tumbling down the steps. There was no turning back now. After Dewald had left the building, a group of eighteen young men formed their own club. They elected Heinrich Unger their first president, while Franz Jacobi became the club secretary.

'Borussia's foundation on the fourth Sunday in Advent 1909 was almost a revolutionary act for us young lads and it took a lot of pluck and moral courage to see it through,' Jacobi later said. 'After all, next to the government, our holy Catholic Church was the most important institution of all for us.' It was indeed a serious conflict. A week later, during his Christmas sermon, Dewald even threatened the footballers with excommunication. But gradually, the two sides made peace with each other, especially once Dewald was transferred to a different parish in another city in 1917, where he unexpectedly died only a year later.

But the fact that Borussia Dortmund owes its existence to an act of rebellion against the Church has never been forgotten in the city. In 1975, Borussia's Old Boys played a game against the Trinity Church XI which was billed, with tongue firmly planted in cheek, as 'the Reconciliation Match'. Borussia, led by a 53-year-old Max 'Spider' Michallek, won again, 6–3.

For the most recent generations of Dortmund fans, retracing their club's formative steps is not easy. The cities in the Ruhr area were an important target for allied bombers during the Second World War and most suffered heavily. (Which is a major reason why many of those cities are so unattractive today – they were hastily rebuilt in the 1950s.) In March 1945, 1,069 British bombers dropped 5,000 tons of explosives on Dortmund, by and large reducing the city to rubble in less than an hour. It was the largest aerial attack on the Continent during the war and the building that housed the 'Wildschütz' wasn't spared.

After the war (and extensive reconstruction jobs), Heinrich Trott's descendants kept the pub going until 1987, although the first floor was converted into flats. Then a chip shop moved into the restaurant's former premises on the ground floor. Until well into the twenty-first century, there wasn't even a plaque on the building to inform passers-by that football history had been made here. But now it's different. In November 2013, a bustling, committed Dortmund fan by the name of Jan-Henrik Gruszecki noticed that the former Hall of Mirrors was being auctioned off by court order. He bought the flat and restored the first floor to something approaching its former glory. His ultimate plan is to open a restaurant downstairs and recreate the original 'Wildschütz'. Gruszecki would also like to brew his own beer – for a very good reason.

After the eighteen renegades had formed their club, they realised something crucial was missing: a name. According to German custom, two elements were obvious, the name of the city (Dortmund) and the year of foundation (1909). That left something descriptive, an abbreviation that would inform people what sort of club this was, plus a memorable moniker.

When you look at any German football table these days, you'll notice that – unlike in England – there are only very few teams that call themselves FC. That has to do with the traditional German club model. German clubs do not exist to make money, to entertain or to foster exclusivity. They are set up to serve a local community, anyone can become a member and then have a say in how the club is run. Jacobi and Unger wanted their own club because they wanted to play football, but that doesn't mean they wanted a club that would only play football. Quite the contrary. Both men still liked track and field. And what if one of the members would one day suggest opening a swimming or a bowling division?

Bayern Munich, for instance, decided to call themselves FC when the club was formed in 1900 and indeed only played football for many decades. But when the club became bigger and more diverse, other divisions were created, from gymnastics to ice hockey. In the 1980s and 1990s, Bayern boasted the best chess team in the country. Incongruously, it was known as Football Club Bayern Munich.

To avoid such a scenario, most athletic clubs in Germany carry more general names such as Sportverein (SV) or Sportclub (SC), both of which mean sports club. When Jacobi and his friends founded their club on 19 December 1909, they settled on Ballspielverein, ball sports club, or BV for short. (Besides football, the club today has a handball and a table-tennis division.) What was missing now was a pithy name people could call the club, preferably something that sounded Latin, like Fortuna or Union.

Shortly before his death in 1979, Jacobi recalled what happened next in the Hall of Mirrors above the pub: 'As we discussed the formalities of setting up the club at Trott's place, we noticed we hadn't yet thought about a name for our club. Rather by accident, I looked around Trott's lounge room and discovered on the walls large images of the Borussia Brewery, which stood on Steiger Street, fairly close to us, until 1901 or 1902. I liked the name, Borussia, and said it completely spontaneously. It was met with general approval. My brothers Julius and Wilhelm, who were also among the club founders, liked it, too. They later told me one reason they agreed to the name was that our father, who had died early, used to work for the Borussia Brewery for a while. They felt they were somehow building a small family memorial in his honour.'

Borussia is neo-Latin and means Prussia. There are about one hundred clubs in Germany that are called either Borussia or Preussen (Prussia). Apart from Jacobi's club, the most famous is the one from Mönchengladbach, or simply Gladbach. Their success in the 1970s is probably the reason why English speakers tend to reserve the name Borussia for Gladbach and will refer to Borussia Dortmund only as Dortmund. It used to be very different. When Gladbach representatives travelled to Geneva in 1971 to convince UEFA that their European Cup game against Inter should not be annulled (a can thrown from the stands had hit an Inter player), they were in for a reality check. The reporter for *Kicker* magazine told his readers: 'You could tell that Borussia Mönchengladbach is still a nobody on the European stage from the fact that the UEFA people referred to the team as "Borussia Dortmund".'

In fact, calling the club just 'Dortmund' carries a faint undertone of rudeness. At the very least, it marks you out as an out-of-towner. When the fans chant this word, they do so in praise of their city rather than the team. Most will refer to the club as Borussia or by an abbreviation: BVB – for Ballspielverein Borussia. In fact, this is probably one of the four most popular abbreviations in German football (the other three being HSV for Hamburg, KSC for Karlsruhe and MSV for Duisburg). When you come to the city for a game, you should make a point of referring to the team as Borussia or BVB, not Dortmund.

Borussia's first kit was blue and white, as these were the colours of the Sodality and the nascent footballers still had those shirts. To distance themselves from the church organisation, they added a red sash to the kit, as a working-class symbol. The colours which are now so readily associated with Borussia Dortmund, black and yellow, arrived a few years later.

At the time, it was not easy for new clubs to be admitted into the league pyramid, as the German FA (*Deutscher Fußball-Bund*: DFB) and its regional associations were cautious. Too many teams formed and then folded again a few months later. But BVB had managed to be allowed into the western German branch of the DFB by using the track-and-field division as a sporting Trojan Horse. (Said branch also oversaw other athletic competitions and originally admitted BVB as a track-and-field club.) That is why three local clubs who were still banned from organised football were eager to join Borussia in 1912. One of them, Britannia Dortmund, was quite big and led by a young, brash and forceful man called August Busse, who worked as a fitter for the Hoesch steel company. During a general meeting at the 'Wildschütz' on 4 January 1913, Busse raised his voice. 'Borussia Dortmund is no longer a Catholics' club,' he said. 'Most members are protestants. So I bring forward a motion to change the club colours. I suggest Britannia's old colours: black and yellow.' The motion was backed by Jacobi, so the other members went along with Busse's idea.

For Franz Jacobi, his club was always a surrogate family. 'We were a very jolly bunch, we liked to laugh and sing,' he said. 'We were always up for mischief and knew how to party. People who laugh and sing together, become close – they feel as if they are in a family.' But Borussia were also a family in a very literal sense. Among the eighteen founders were three Jacobis (the brothers Franz, Julius and Wilhelm), two Ungers (brothers Heinrich and Robert) and two Brauns (brothers Franz and Paul). What's more, everybody came from the same social background and nearly all members lived in one of the streets leading towards Borsigplatz square.

If anything, the ties between the club's members became even stronger during the First World War. 'Many of our players were sent into combat,' Jacobi told club historian Kolbe in 1977. 'We wrote each of them one letter per month, to stay in touch. We looked after the parents, wives and children of our soldiers, actively involving them in the club's social life. That was the beginning of the Borussia Family.'

Before the war, football in Germany was a sport for players and their friends or family members, not for spectators. In April 1914, almost 73,000 people, among them George V, followed the FA Cup final between Burnley and Liverpool. But when Fürth defeated Leipzig in the final for the German championship one month later, barely 6,000 curious onlookers saw the match. The title was decided by a one-game play-off rather than through a league system because there was no nationwide top division in Germany. Under the rules of the DFB, professionalism was illegal and so the game was played by amateurs who couldn't afford to travel around the vast country all the time in order to play a game.

It was in the years following the war that football became the workingman's game in Germany, partly because of the introduction of the eight-hour day, and thereafter a mass-spectator sport. The place where Borussia played their games, a pasture known as White Meadow, was no longer viable. It was too small and had no perimeter fence. The club decided to expand the White Meadow into a proper stadium, which would come to be known as the Borussia Sports Ground. The idea was to lease the piece of land from the city and then build a wall around it. This would cost almost 50,000 Reichsmark, which was an enormous sum for a small, local club like Borussia Dortmund.

'It was only possible because all our members donated their free time and lent a hand,' Jacobi recalled. 'From drawing plans and obtaining permissions to the actual construction – we did it all ourselves. Some 10,000 hours of work had to be put in. Free of charge, of course! The opening was planned for Sunday, 17 August 1924. But the new enclosure was blown away: there was a gap in the stadium wall that was sixty-five yards wide. We rose to the occasion, working nonstop until Sunday afternoon. At 3 p.m., as scheduled, the Lord Mayor could inaugurate our Borussia Sports Ground.'

The ground now held 12,000 people, perhaps more, as there were no stands but simple terraces that were basically grassy knolls. It was a daring endeavour to build something this big, because Borussia played lower-division football and were not even the best team in their own city. In the season just past, BVB had finished behind local Dortmund teams like VfL Hörde or Merkur Dortmund in what was technically the second level of the league structure but in practice was a very humble division. (At that time, the western part of the country alone had eight regional divisions at the top level. Their respective winners played a tournament to determine the western German champion who would then play the champions from the country's other regions in knock-out rounds for the national title.) One year later, though, in 1925, Borussia topped their division and earned themselves the right to play against two clubs from neighbouring cities for the district championship. One of those two clubs was Schalke.

It was a chaotic time for the Ruhr area. After the Weimar Republic ceased its reparation payments in the aftermath of the war, French and Belgian troops had occupied the region in January

1923 and would continue to do so until the summer of 1925. When BVB met Schalke for the first time, on 3 May 1925, foreign soldiers were still a common sight on the streets of Dortmund and Gelsenkirchen.

The Schalke team that played Borussia at a neutral ground that day in May, in a city just east of Gelsenkirchen called Herne, included a 19-year-old miner by the name of Ernst Kuzorra, destined to become a club icon and one of the best players in the country. But the difference between the two sides was not just individual class. Schalke were in the process of perfecting their very own take on what was then called the 'Scottish passing game' – think tiki-taka as opposed to the more direct English style favoured by most German teams. Ironically, it had been two Dortmund lads who were responsible for Schalke's inimitable style that would come to define an entire era: Hans and Fred Ballmann.

The brothers were born in Dortmund but grew up in Britain and worked there as miners until they were interned during the war and then told to return to their native country. When they arrived back in the Ruhr area, without a job or a place to live, they spoke English much better than German but would soon do most of the talking with their feet anyway. An acquaintance, who happened to be a Schalke member, alerted his club to their talents. In return for a flat and an occupation, the Ballmanns taught Schalke's players what they had learned in Britain. Kuzorra would later say that they introduced elements he had never seen before – 'things like one-twos or even bicycle kicks'. Above all, they introduced combination football.

And so BVB found themselves thoroughly outplayed on this day in early May 1925. 'Schalke's close-meshed play tired out Borussia,' a local newspaper report said. 'Dortmund fell victim to the tempo of Schalke's passing.' Although Schalke finished the game with only ten men on account of an injury, they won this inaugural encounter 4–2. It would be more than eighteen years before Borussia could finally win a match against the team from Gelsenkirchen.

That tells you more about Schalke than it does about Borussia, though, as the men in black and yellow were slowly improving. By the time of the 1925 derby, BVB already knew a player in their ranks who would eventually change the club's fortunes. In fact, there are people who argue that Borussia would today be nothing more than a small, nondescript local team like one of the dozen or so other Dortmund clubs they eventually managed to eclipse if a twelve-year-old kid called August Lenz had joined, say, DSC 95 instead of BVB in 1922. But Lenz chose to play for Borussia, first as a goalkeeper, then later as a centre-forward. He would wear the yellow shirt for more than thirty years and play more than 1,000 games for the club. In 1935, Lenz became Borussia Dortmund's first international when he represented Germany in a game against Belgium, scoring twice.

Lenz was so important to Borussia that for all practical purposes he became the club's first semi-professional player. Needless to say, he was employed by the Hoesch steel company, like almost everyone else in the north of town and connected to Borussia. But his direct supervisor was a football fan and he turned a blind eye whenever Lenz failed to report to work. The man's lenience was rewarded in 1936, when Lenz helped Borussia finally win promotion to one of the sixteen regional leagues that formed the top level of the German game at the time, the Gauliga Westfalen. (Even if you have never heard the name August Lenz, you might have seen his image, because The Unity, Dortmund's largest ultras group, uses one as their logo.)

But even though Borussia were climbing up the league pyramid and now boasted a true star player, they couldn't hold a candle to Schalke. Well, hardly anyone could. In the 1920s and 1930s, the team from Gelsenkirchen became first a sensation, then living legends. With their quick passing game – dubbed *Kreisel*, spinning top, because it left opponents reeling – Schalke thoroughly dominated the game in the Ruhr area and then the entire western part of the country. In 1929 and 1930, they reached the quarter-finals of the national trophy, raising hopes among fans all across the industrial heartland that a team which represented the working class could at last break the dominance of the middle-class sides from Nuremberg, Fürth and Hamburg. Then, in August 1930, the empire struck back.

The regional football association for western Germany announced that Schalke's first-team players had been paid expenses far in excess of what was permissible. Thus they qualified as professionals and were banned from participating in organised league football. There was more than just a grain of truth to the accusation, but few fans in the Ruhr area could figure out what was wrong with honest pay for honest work. Schalke drew good crowds and were earning good money, so why couldn't the players benefit from their popularity? What's more, the ban was widely interpreted as a deliberate attempt to keep Schalke, the big workingman's hope, down and cement the status quo. Such was the outcry in the western part of the country that the ban was lifted less than a year later. The incident also triggered a public debate about professionalism that came close to ending the German obsession with amateurism. However, just when the DFB was about to change the rules, the Nazis seized power in 1933 – and because they considered professional sports an English disease, they maintained the ban on professionalism.

Schalke, meanwhile, never looked back once the ban was lifted. The team in royal blue won the German title for the first time in 1934, defeating Nuremberg in the final in Berlin. On their way back to Gelsenkirchen, the team's train stopped in Dortmund. Cheered by countless football fans, the players signed their names in the mayor's 'Golden Book', the traditional way for guests of honour to document their stay in a city. The enthusiasm surrounding the side in the entire Ruhr area grew into adulation and finally awe when Schalke won five more national championships between 1935 and 1942. Put differently, they were amazing – and not just by German standards. In May 1937, Schalke wiped the floor with

Brentford FC, a fully professional team that had just finished sixth in England's top flight, winning 6–2.

For modern fans, who have grown up with the Dortmund–Schalke rivalry as the most intensely felt in the German game, it is very hard to understand how different the situation was before the war and even in the years leading up to the formation of the Bundesliga in 1963. Imagine pre-war Schalke as some sort of Harlem Globetrotters of the working class. The club regularly staged important games not at their own ground but played in Bochum and quite often in Dortmund, where 40,000 would come out to support Schalke against teams such as Hertha Berlin.

A football fan in the Ruhr area in the 1930s and 1940s supported his local team – and Schalke. Alois Scheffler, the only man in the history of Borussia Dortmund who was honoured for seventy-five years of membership, told author Gregor Schnittker in 2011, when he was 96: 'Back then, a lot of *Borussen* rooted for Schalke. For many, Schalke were the pride of the region. They said: what counts is that one of us, from the west, wins the title. It's hard to imagine that today. Which is a pity.'

Another reason why Schalke were quite popular in Dortmund in those days was that the city had not yet produced its own major team. People from Dortmund still tended to support the club that catered to their local community. If you lived in Hörde, in the southeast of town, and worked at the Phoenix steel mill there, you would watch one of the local clubs, possibly VfL Hörde, who played at the same level as Borussia for the larger part of the 1930s. If your home was Marten, in the west of Dortmund, chances were you worked in the coal mine Germania and supported Arminia Marten, who would play in the Gauliga Westfalen alongside Schalke and BVB for four years between 1937 and 1941.

Unwittingly, the Nazis changed all that. The German Labour Front, a Nazi organisation that had replaced the independent trade unions, was planning large recreational areas, usually parks, close to major factories. The idea was that the workers should have a place to relax and get some fresh air to stay in shape and remain productive. The Borussia Sports Ground, which the members themselves had built in 1924, was not far from the Hoesch steel mill. In 1937, the Nazis informed the club that BVB would have to leave the stadium, because the land was needed for a public outdoor swimming pool. Franz Jacobi recalled: 'With a heavy heart, we had to vacate the ground that had become our second home, after Borsigplatz square. And we didn't get a penny in compensation!'

Borussia Dortmund were suddenly homeless. And there was only one place they could go.

CHAPTER 3

When you come to Dortmund to take in a game, you should begin what today seems to be called 'your matchday experience' on a city-centre square known as the Old Market, just off the city's major shopping street. That's because there is a place called Wenker's on the southeastern corner of the square. It is a historic place, as beer has been brewed here since at least 1517. In 1729, a man called Johann Wenker purchased the building and founded the Kronen Brewery, which would be owned by the family for the next 270 years and sponsored Borussia Dortmund during the crucial first seasons under Ottmar Hitzfeld in the early 1990s, when the club finally recaptured its former glory. In 1843, Johann's great-great-grandson Heinrich Wenker invented *Export* here, the beer Dortmund became famous for.

It was in this very building, in the restaurant, that Borussia were admitted into organised football in 1910. Of course, the house looks very different today, like most houses in Dortmund, because it, too, was almost completely destroyed by the Royal Air Force on 12 March 1945. But it's a good place to begin to understand what makes the city tick, not least because one of the smaller Borussia fan stores is right next to it. Just in case you need a scarf or a shirt. And you may want one because Dortmund is one of those places where people will look at you disapprovingly if you don't sport something yellow on a matchday.

This has to do with the enormous, almost absurd importance of football in the Ruhr area, most notably in Dortmund and Schalke. The cities here have gone through so many coal crises, steel crises and beer crises that a good deal of their identity has eroded. The mines are gone. The breweries were sold. The steel mills have been consigned to history. Generations of children in Dortmund used to stare at the night sky turning a glowing red over Hörde and were told angels were baking cookies, when of course it was the massive blast furnace of the Phoenix steel mill. (This mill was dismantled and shipped to China, where it was rebuilt piece by piece.) Where once steelworkers and their families lived in tiny digs, breathing dirty air, there is now a man-made lake lined by tasteless but expensive bungalows, some of which belong to BVB players.

For decades, the lives of the people living here and elsewhere in the Ruhr area were defined by coal, steel, beer and football. Now, there is football, football, football and football. It is understood that out-of-towners do not come to Gelsenkirchen or Dortmund for the culture, the architecture, the landscape, the nightlife, the sights or whatever it may be that draws people to Hamburg, Cologne, Munich or Berlin. If you don't live in Dortmund and sit outside Wenker's on a Saturday, having a pint, it's taken for granted that you are here for the football.

There are some subtle differences, though, between Dortmund and Gelsenkirchen. One is that Schalke's shiny domed stadium is more than twice as far away from the local main station as Dortmund's ground. It is four and a half miles from Gelsenkirchen's old quarter to the Veltins Arena, along a route that is not very scenic, dominated as it is by the A42 motorway. In Dortmund, however, you can walk to the stadium from the city centre, for instance along Lindemannstrasse, a street lined by pubs and bars. That's why it is impossible to be in Dortmund on a matchday and not realise Borussia are playing at home.

If you do want to walk from Gelsenkirchen's old quarter to the Veltins Arena, halfway between the two, you'll pass a small football ground. It's nondescript. There is only one stand, with the rest of the pitch surrounded by grassy knolls. And yet this is sacred ground for anyone interested in the history of football in

Germany. This is the mythic *Glückauf-Kampfbahn*, the place where Schalke used to play between 1928 and 1973. It seems totally impossible, but when the team played their first game here after the ban mentioned in the previous chapter was lifted, in June 1931, more than 70,000 people filled this tiny place.

But you can't linger for too long, because you still have three miles to go until you reach the modern, domed stadium. When you do so and look past the arena, you may notice a single old-fashioned floodlight pylon in the distance. It marks the remnants of yet another old ground. This is where the Parkstadion used to be, which was built for the 1974 World Cup and served as Schalke's home until 2001. Soon, it will be all but unrecognisable, because the club are planning a small stadium for their youth teams here.

Although Schalke have a reputation for being a lot more romantic, sentimental and backward-looking than Borussia, you can breathe history a lot better when you watch your football in Dortmund. As you walk up the Lindemannstrasse in a southerly direction, you'll soon see the massive Westfalenstadion (Signal Iduna Park). Right next to that, slightly overshadowed by the East Stand's second tier, which was added in 1995, is Stadion Rote Erde – Borussia's ground from 1937 to 1974. It is virtually unchanged. In fact, it now resembles its original state more closely than it did when BVB moved out and into the stadium next door. That's because a wooden grandstand built in 1965 opposite the main stand (which is the West Stand) was taken down again in the mid-1970s.

Rote Erde (red soil, an ancient name for Westphalia) was built as an athletics stadium by the city between 1924 and 1926. Football was only an afterthought, because the stadium, which could hold over 30,000 people, was way too big for the small local clubs. This was underlined when Wacker Munich, a decent but hardly overpowering Bavarian team, played a select Dortmund XI at the opening of the new stadium on 6 June 1926 and won 11–1. For the next couple of years, Rote Erde hosted various track-and-field events and a large Catholic festival attended by the future Pope

Pius XII. Big football games were rare. Schalke made a handful of appearances here, and Germany (with August Lenz) won a friendly against Ireland 3–1 in 1935.

Two years after this game, Borussia were told they had to turn over their own ground to the Nazis. The only place where BVB, who had just been promoted to the regional but top-level Gauliga Westfalen, could possibly play was Rote Erde – a stadium on the other side of the railway tracks, in a middle-class neighbourhood in Dortmund's south, a three-mile walk from Borsigplatz square. It's not an exaggeration to say that BVB's members hated the ground and deeply resented having to move there. In fact, there are accounts which suggest that many within the club suspected they were being punished by the fascists for representing a historically left-wing community.

It's difficult to appraise Borussia's role during the Nazi years correctly. As a general rule, German clubs did not cover themselves in glory. Many expelled their Jewish members and handed the running of the club over to stalwart Nazis long before it became a simple question of survival to please the party. But it would seem that Borussia, in the words of club historian Gerd Kolbe, 'went through those years with their heads held high'. Peter Paul Elisko, a Social Democrat born in 1924, told him: 'The BVB family, the people who were actually club members, were anything but Nazis. After all, their background was in Trinity Church. There were very few Hitler supporters. Look at [the pub landlord] Trott. At times, he would be so outspoken about how he felt about the Nazis that we feared they would take him away.'

There was one high-ranking Nazi at the club, Willi Röhr. He even joined the notorious SA (*Sturmabteilung*, the party's paramilitary wing) in 1935. But it wasn't until 1939 that he was voted onto Borussia's board and his sons always maintained that Röhr used his reputation to protect some of the club's renegade members. And there were a few of those. Franz Hippler and former groundsman

Heinrich Czerkus were not just communists, they were active resistance fighters. Both spent time in concentration camps and were murdered by the Nazis during a massacre in spring 1945. A BVB supporters' club named after Czerkus keeps his memory alive. Since 2004, these fans have organised an annual event – the Heinrich Czerkus Memorial Run – which starts at Rote Erde and ends in a botanical garden in the south of the city, the place where Hippler and Czerkus were executed together with hundreds of other dissidents.

Borussia's strained relationship with the Nazis is also apparent from a number of statements to be found in a 1939 publication, compiled on the occasion of the club's thirtieth birthday. The most delicate passage begins with the sentence: 'There is one point, though, which tarnishes our festive feelings.' That point was, of course, the ground. The club repeated their complaints about having been told to leave their beloved home without receiving any form of compensation. You could understand the anger, especially since the Nazis' swimming pool still hadn't been built. (In fact, it would not be constructed until 1951.) But it was daring indeed to criticise the city openly, and thus the party, in such an official publication.

Then again, perhaps Borussia Dortmund just weren't important enough in 1939 to really come under fascist scrutiny. After all, the first team had just been beaten 7–0 at home by Schalke and would lose the return leg 9–0 in the Gauliga Westphalia. And yet there were the first subtle signs that something was stirring. Borussia's Under-19 team, led by Max Michallek, did very well, reaching the final of the Westphalia championship that year. The game was played in Münster, thirty-five miles north of Dortmund. The opponents were – who else? – Schalke. Michallek, not yet seventeen years old, scored two goals and Borussia sensationally won 4–2. It was the first time at any level that a BVB side had defeated a team representing Schalke. Three of the kids who secured this precious win would not survive the war.

Borussia's first proper victory came four years later, in November 1943. In deepest wartime, some 12,000 people came to Rote Erde to watch what was not yet called the Ruhr derby. Only three days earlier, Dortmund had suffered the fifth major bombing since the beginning of the war, so the size of the crowd is nothing short of astonishing. Both teams were missing a number of players who were fighting on one of the various fronts, yet most of the stars were present. Schalke fielded Otto Tibulski and the 36-year-old Fritz Szepan, already a living legend. But it was August Lenz who scored the only goal of the game, after just eight minutes. Three months later, things were back to normal as Schalke won the return leg 4–1. It would be the last competitive game between the two budding rivals for almost three years.

When the war ended, Dortmund was so thoroughly demolished (at least 70 per cent of all living quarters were gone) that there was a short-lived plan to not rebuild the inner city at all. But as early as June 1945, just weeks after Germany's capitulation, the mines opened again, producing much-needed coal. And on the very last day of that fateful year, the first blast furnace at the Hoesch steel mill was back in operation.

Even football returned, though slowly. In the immediate aftermath of the war, all sporting clubs had been dissolved by the occupying forces, in this case the British Army of the Rhine (BAOR). But on 4 December 1945, the British allowed the formation of new clubs and the reformation of the old ones. For the next half-century, a British presence would leave its mark on the city. There were half a dozen barracks in Dortmund, three of them sitting side by side to your left when you approached the central part of town from the east driving along Westfalendamm, one of the city's major roads. (On the other side of the road, opposite those camps, a rugby field was built for the soldiers.) Napier Barracks, meanwhile, was in Brackel, a borough four miles east of the Borsigplatz area. It closed in October 1995. Ten years later, Borussia Dortmund built their training centre on the same site. The two stone lions that stood by the barracks' Officers' Mess have been preserved and today greet the people who want to watch BVB train.

In January 1946, Schalke and Dortmund met on the field of play again, but it was just a friendly, won 3–1 by the side from Gelsen-kirchen. However, it wouldn't be long before the teams played each other with something at stake.

For the 1946–47 season, the twenty best teams in Westphalia (the eastern part of the Ruhr area plus neighbouring regions) were put into two groups, the winners of which would play a final for the local championship. Borussia finished first in their group, three points ahead of Erkenschwick, a team that had until recently been coached by Schalke icon Ernst Kuzorra, who found it hard to wind down his stellar playing career even though he was 41 years old. Schalke, meanwhile, didn't lose a game and very comfortably topped the other group. This seemed the natural order of things. Schalke had won the regional championship of the Ruhr area or Westphalia in every single season since 1927. Although the best years were obviously behind the wonder team, Schalke went into the final against BVB in Herne as odds-on favourites.

The ground in Herne was fourteen miles west of Borsigplatz square, but only seven miles east of Schalke. This small difference was important in 1947, as barely two years after the end of the war, the infrastructure in the area was still chaotic and travelling constituted a massive problem. What's more, 18 May 1947 was a re-lentlessly rainy day. Yet a large number of people made the journey from Dortmund to Herne nonetheless. A newspaper report read: 'If military terms weren't frowned upon, you'd have to say there was an invasion of football lovers from Dortmund.'

A few years ago, I appeared on a local radio show in Dortmund and asked the listeners if they knew anyone who had been at that historic game more than six decades ago and was still alive. To my great delight, we found three.

Winfried Pawlak was ten years old at the time and travelled to the game with his father and some of his parents' friends.

Pawlak did so because he was a Borsigplatz boy. Although Borussia had been playing south of the railway tracks for a number of years, they were still considered a club for a very specific community – and that's also how the club defined themselves. Pawlak knew all the first-team players, because they lived just around the corner. His father was a club member and Pawlak himself played youth football for BVB. There was never any question that they would go and see the biggest game their club had been in so far. 'One of our neighbours was a scrap dealer,' Pawlak recalled. 'He had a platform lorry with a wood carburettor. We gave him some money and he drove us to Herne through the rain.'

Most people, though, rode a special kind of train. Erwin Pfänder, also a small boy at the time, told me: 'We travelled on a hoarding train and of course we were soaking wet before we even got to Herne.' Hoarding train was the nickname given to trains that would take hungry city slickers to farms in the countryside, where they could hoard food. These trains were so overcrowded that most passengers stood on the footboards outside and hung on to metal handlebars that ran along the carriage. That's how Pfänder rode to the game with a 22-year-old friend of his elder brother, who had died on the Eastern front. Although Pfänder lived on Borsigplatz square, he wasn't a BVB member. He went to the final because it was an exciting adventure to travel past the mountains of rubble and ruins towards what seemed like an exotic place to see a game of football.

Helmut Bojahra, the son of an East Prussian miner, also rode one of those trains. He was twenty years old and although he came from Dortmund, he didn't yet consider himself a Borussia supporter. 'I used to go and see Arminia Marten play when they were in the top division,' he says. 'I would always go when they played Schalke. You have to remember, Schalke were something akin to a religion in the Ruhr area at that time. So we went to Herne because we were interested in football and this was an important game – and also because we hoped to see Kuzorra or Szepan. They were still idols then.'

The record books list the attendance figure for the final as 30,000 – but only because that was the ground's official capacity. Most observers maintain that at least 38,000 people were on hand when the game kicked off at four in the afternoon. My three interviewees couldn't remember too many details after all those decades, but they all agreed that it was very crowded (and wet). 'What I do recall is seeing August Lenz,' Pfänder said. 'He had such a physical presence and was so powerful.'

To nobody's surprise, Schalke took the lead. But on 53 minutes, Lenz set up Max Michallek, who equalised from distance. Ten minutes later, the favourites regained the lead thanks to a penalty. But still, Schalke were struggling. Their combination game, the famous *Kreisel*, depended in no small part on the mobility of centre-half Tibulski, who distributed the ball. That is why Dortmund coach Ferdinand Fabra, a noted chess player, had told his centre-forward Lenz to put pressure on Tibulski, thus stopping Schalke from building from the rear. Jürgen Klopp would have mightily enjoyed the sight of this early form of his pressing game.

The rain-soaked pitch also worked in Dortmund's favour, because Borussia fielded the much younger team. Eventually, Schalke's ageing stars began to tire. With twelve minutes left, BVB defender Heinrich Ruhmhofer went on a rare foray deep into the opposition half and made it 2–2 with another long-range shot. Then, on 85 minutes, came the goal that would stand as the most momentous in the club's history for the next twenty years, perhaps even for the next forty. Michallek moved through midfield, elegantly despite his long legs, and tried a shot. Schalke's veteran goalkeeper Hans Klodt, a former international, dived to his left and parried the strike. But before he could scramble to his feet, an 18-year-old kid by the name of Herbert Sandmann got to the loose ball first and put it away.

The 3–2 result was so stunning that even many people in Dortmund suspected a mistake when carrier pigeons, hugely popular among workers in the Ruhr area, spread the news about the outcome. Instead of drawing attention to Dortmund's triumph, the newspaper *Rhein-Ruhr-Zeitung* headlined: 'Schalke no longer champions of Westphalia!' The players from Gelsenkirchen were so shocked themselves that they beat a hasty retreat and refused to attend the victory ceremony. A Schalke fan called Josef Schröder, an eyewitness, told author Gregor Schnittker: 'We just couldn't understand we had lost the game. It was a heavy blow we would feel for years to come. It was a turning point, a changing of the guard. BVB went from strength to strength and produced star player after star player. They would win the first three seasons of the *Oberliga West*.'

Oberliga was the name of the new top level of the German game. Or more precisely, the West German game, as communist East Germany introduced a single, nationwide league as early as 1949, decades before the West. There were five of those leagues: *Oberliga Nord* (covering the north of the country and usually won by Hamburg); *Oberliga Süd* (for the southern clubs, most powerful among them Nuremberg, VfB Stuttgart and Eintracht Frankfurt); *Oberliga Südwest* (featuring Kaiserslautern and other sides from the southwest); *Oberliga Berlin* (made up of the teams in the western part of the now divided city); and the notorious *Oberliga West*. Notorious because it was normally more competitive than the other leagues and jam-packed with strong teams – not just Dortmund and Schalke but also Essen, and especially Cologne, who would soon be considered the most efficiently run club in the land. At the end of the league season, the best teams from these five leagues were distributed among two groups, the winners of which contested a final for the national championship. Between 1949 and 1963, eleven finalists were *Oberliga West* clubs.

And there was another novelty after the war: money. The question of professionalism was still dividing the German game and some people feared the controversy could result in a hostile split, not unlike fifty years earlier in England when rugby split into rugby union and rugby league over the question of player compensation. There were rumours that a leading VfB Stuttgart official, Gustav Sackmann, was going to start a breakaway professional league if the DFB insisted on its amateur rule. All of which led, as happens so often in politics, to a half-baked compromise. Less than thirty years after unequivocally stating 'We oppose the professional game for ethical reasons, it would be a sacrilege against the youth of this country', the DFB grudgingly allowed something approaching semi-professionalism. From the late 1940s on, West German players were allowed to receive payment for their football services, provided a) their basic wages did not exceed DM320 per month (in the early 1950s, that equalled £27) and b) they could prove that they held down a proper job. It was far from true professionalism, of course, but it meant that good German footballers no longer had to work in the mines or in steel mills. They could concentrate on the game while their clubs would help them find a nice day job – running a sporting goods store, say, or a petrol station or pub.

Borussia thrived during those Oberliga years. As Schalke fan Josef Schröder suggested, the timing was perfect. While it took Schalke a couple of years to rebuild, BVB had a lot of talented youngsters waiting in the wings, thanks in no small part to one of the club's most unsung of heroes, an old man with a wooden leg called Emil Heuser. I had never heard this man's name, let alone read about him in one of the many German books about the club, until some of the veterans I interviewed for the oral history project told me how he would knock on people's doors after the war and ask parents: 'Do you have a boy? Is he interested in football? If yes, don't send him to Arminia Marten or any of those teams, send him to us, send him to Borussia.'

Another factor was the formerly unloved Rote Erde ground. The Oberliga system was a tremendous success, as the fans lapped up those games against famous clubs from the Rhineland, such as Cologne or Aachen, and, of course, the regular Ruhr area derbies against Schalke or Essen. Borussia were lucky to have a ground big enough for such matches. And the fact that this ground was not north of the railway line, in the rough part of town, or way out in the east or west but just off Westfalendamm, within walking distance from the city centre, turned BVB from a club that catered to a tightly defined community into a club for the entire city within a single generation. One day in July of 1949 would prove this beyond doubt.

That season, Borussia finished first in the Oberliga West (while, amazingly, Schalke only avoided the drop through relegation play-offs) and then disposed of an old but now obscure Berlin club called SV 92 and Kaiserslautern to reach the final for the national title against VfR Mannheim. This club should not be confused with the better-known Waldhof Mannheim. In fact, the 1948–49 season would be VfR Mannheim's single moment of glory. The team never again finished at the top of the Oberliga Southwest, didn't qualify for the Bundesliga when that league came into being in the 1960s and is today an amateur club playing at the sixth level of the league pyramid.

The final was held in Stuttgart on 10 July 1949, such a sweltering day that the game came to be known as the 'Heat Battle of Stuttgart' (which suggests that military terms were not quite so frowned upon any more). Borussia were widely expected to dominate the match and win the title for the first time. The team's biggest star was Alfred 'Adi' Preissler, a 28-year-old striker who had easily won the Oberliga West's Golden Boot (ahead of a young man called Alfred Kelbassa, who would one day play alongside him for Borussia). Preissler was born in Duisburg, but on his way back home from the Russian front during the war he met his future wife. She was a Dortmund girl and so Preissler moved to Husen, a borough on the northeastern edge of Dortmund.

Another excellent player on that 1949 team was Erich Schanko, who cut a strange figure because he was prematurely balding and moved about on pencil-thin legs. Schanko was extremely popular with both his teammates and the fans and would become the first Borussia player to be granted a testimonial match (for which Manchester City and Bernd Trautmann came to Dortmund in 1957). Schanko would never be allowed to forget the 1949 final, because early on he collided with an opponent and lost four teeth. Yes, it was a painful day for Dortmund. Playmaker Michallek had been suffering from a ligament problem in his left ankle. Over the course of the game, the joint swelled until it became impossible for Michallek to wear a boot. With fifteen minutes left, he took off his shoe and – this being a time before substitutions – played in his sock.

The final was watched by a gigantic crowd that numbered 90,000 people, many of them sitting so close to the pitch that the players found it difficult to take corners and throw-ins. BVB twice took the lead, both goals scored by right-winger Herbert Erdmann, but the Mannheim players ran up and down the pitch like men possessed. Borussia's goalkeeper Günter 'Bubi' Rau was one of his team's best players and even saved a penalty in the first half. He was the main reason why BVB came very close to winning the tight, tense game. But five minutes from time, a Mannheim forward tried a distance shot that was powerful and desperate in equal measure. Rau dived to his right and fully extended his body, but the ball went in off the post.

Extra time it was – and one of the men watching from the sidelines perhaps now understood why he wasn't playing. August Lenz had started every league game (and scored ten goals) but was not selected for the final. The striker was deeply hurt, putting a strain on his relationship with the club for a long time, but he was 38 years old and even players much younger were now fading fast in the relentless Swabian heat. After 108 minutes, Rau left his line to block a shot and the ball fell to Mannheim's centre-forward who fired it into an open net before Rau could get back. Immediately,

dozens of fans invaded the pitch to celebrate, circling the Dortmund players who hung their heads as if they knew they lacked
the strength to come back.

Despite the defeat, the team was given a hero's welcome upon
their return to Dortmund the next day. There were certainly tens
of thousands of people lining the streets, some reports even speak
of 200,000 – and judging from the photos, this may well be true.
People carried the players on their shoulders from the main station to the town hall and then to Borsigplatz square, several miles
away, across debris and past countless buildings destroyed in the
war and not yet rebuilt. On some of the pictures taken that day,
you can see how the hardships of the war and the years of hunger
had left their traces. And yet people's haggard, emaciated faces
were beaming with joy and pride. Borussia were the second-best
team in the country – and they were now clearly seen as the team
that represented the entire city of Dortmund.

Maybe even a larger region. Hans Dieter Baroth, who would
go on to write many books about life (and football) in the Ruhr
area, was twelve years old at the time and came from a family
of devoted Schalke fans. On the Sunday of the final, though, his
father and his uncle listened to the radio coverage of the game
and celebrated Borussia's goals. It took Baroth a while to figure out
what was happening. 'Your own club comes first,' he noted. 'Then
the Ruhr area. Then the west of the country. Only then Germany.
Dad and his brother suffered with the black-and-yellows for the
sake of the Ruhr area.'

Preissler supposedly said that he and his teammates weren't
too depressed about losing the 'Heat Battle of Stuttgart', because
they knew that their best years were still ahead of them, that the
future belonged to Borussia. In a way, it was true, as the club had
entered its first Golden Age, a period of sustained success that
would last for more than fifteen years. Yet Borussia had to wait a
bit longer until they finally lifted a trophy than they might have
thought. Preissler himself left the club for two seasons, lured to

Preussen Münster in 1950 by promises of silverware and glory (and a handsome signing-on bonus). In 1953, BVB won the Oberliga West again but then failed to reach the final because of a single goal, having finished level on points with VfB Stuttgart in their group. Suddenly, it seemed as if there was a very real danger that the club's golden generation – epitomised by Max Michallek, now well into his thirties – would hang up their boots without actually having won anything.

But in 1956, it all came together. The heart of the team was an attacking trio: Alfred Preissler (centre-forward), Alfred Kelbassa (inside right) and Alfred Niepieklo (inside left). Collectively, they were known as the 'Three Alfredos'. If that conjured up images of a circus act, it wasn't far from the truth, as the three were a major attraction, combining for sixty-three of Borussia's seventy-three league goals during the thirty-game Oberliga West season.

Franz Jacobi, who founded Borussia and always liked to think of the club as a family, would have been very proud when, in 2009, a German reporter went to interview an 82-year-old Niepieklo. Upon ringing the doorbell, the journalist noticed that the nameplate above Niepieklo's read 'Kelbassa'. When he asked Niepieklo for an explanation, the old man smiled and replied: 'Borussia was a big family. We always spent time together. I guess that's how and why Alfred Kelbassa's son married my daughter.'

Incidentally, there was another pair in that 1956 team linked by more than just football: veteran Erich Schanko and midfielder Elwin Schlebrowski. The two knew each other before they became teammates, because they had met in Oxford, of all places. Both men had been taken prisoner of war by the British and were sent to POW camps near that city, probably Harcourt Hill Camp in North Hinksey and Shotover House Camp in Wheatley. In May 1946, the two camp teams played a game against each other and Schlebrowski noticed an excellent footballer in the other side, a prematurely balding man with pencil-thin legs.

Now, ten years later, Schlebrowski and Schanko were on the

same side as BVB finished yet another group stage level on points with a big club. This time it was Hamburg, but Dortmund had the better goal difference (and the better goal average, which was the system used then). Seven years after the 'Heat Battle of Stuttgart', Borussia were in the final again – and this time it would be a very different experience.

For starters, the weather was the exact opposite. 'Oh, the rain! The rain!' was the first thing Ilse Schmidt told me when I asked her about the journey Dortmund's support made to the site of the 1956 final, the Olympic Stadium in West Berlin. She was the daughter of one of the original BVB players. Her father, Karl Hagedorn, appears in a team shot taken on 15 January 1911, when Borussia played their first-ever competitive match. In addition, Ilse and her mother were well-known to many BVB fans because they had been working in the ticket booths at the northern entrance of Rote Erde since the mid-1940s.

Ilse Schmidt and her family went to Berlin in one of several small buses organised by the club. There were also special trains, but – in marked contrast to 1947 or 1949 – many fans now travelled by car. After all, this was *Wirtschaftswunder* Germany, the term used to describe the economic miracle that turned the country into an affluent, industrial superpower only a few years after the end of the war. The A2, the motorway between Dortmund and West Berlin, was littered with Volkswagen vehicles and you didn't have to look at the licence plates to know where they were coming from. 'It was like a colourful car parade,' one fan told me, 'because all those black-and-yellow scarves were hanging out of the windows.' At least 5,000 fans made the six-hour journey to West Berlin.

Borussia's opponents on 24 June 1956 were Karlsruhe. They had won the German FA Cup the previous season (and would go on to defend it, although the final wouldn't be played before August). Still, most people considered BVB to be the favourites. So it came as a bit of a shock when Karlsruhe took the lead after all of ten minutes. But Borussia had the Three Alfredos. Niepieklo, Kelbassa and Preissler all put their names on the scoreboard, and right-winger Wolfgang Peters added a fourth before an hour was up. Even though Karlsruhe pulled one back, Dortmund's players were so sure of victory in the final half-hour that Michallek began to showboat, clearing a cross by backheeling the ball out of the danger zone.

It was BVB's first championship (in fact, their first proper title) and the image of captain Preissler holding the dish-like trophy aloft would form the central element of the gigantic tifo the Dortmund ultras prepared for the club's centenary in December 2009. The day after the 1956 final, some 250,000 people welcomed the team back home, although it was raining again. The team travelled around town on a lorry, with a band leading the way. However, the cheers drowned out the music. A paper wrote: 'But those celebrations paled into insignificance when the team reached Borsigplatz. The square was one mass of people lined by a sea of flags. One cannot imagine the scenes of joy that were taking place.'

Borussia Dortmund's most immediate reward for the championship was a date with Manchester United in the 1956–57 European Cup, the competition's second season. It was not, however, the club's first meeting with a British side. That dated back to May 1950 when Tottenham Hotspur, having just won promotion to the first division, went on a short tour of the continent and played four games in West Germany. Spurs defeated Arminia Hannover, Tennis Borussia Berlin and Wacker Berlin before travelling to Dortmund to face Borussia.

This was only the third time that BVB had played foreign opposition (after a match with Austria Vienna in 1949 and a friendly against Belenenses from Lisbon in April 1950). It was a special game for Dortmund's goalkeeper Bubi Rau, because Spurs had expressed serious interest in his services the previous summer. On this day, though, he and his teammates were no match for Tottenham. Winger Sonny Walters opened the scoring. Len Duquemin,

Eddie Baily and Harry Gilberg were also on target as Spurs won easily, 4–0.

The two teams met again only one year later. The occasion was the so-called Festival of Britain, a nationwide exhibition that ran from May to September 1951. It was meant as a celebration of British industry, arts, science – and sports. Many teams from the continent received invitations to play British sides. No less than 154 individual games were staged across the nation during the second and third weeks of May. West Germany sent three teams, one of which was BVB.

Borussia met Derby County, then Spurs at White Hart Lane and finally Swindon Town. It was the first time the German club played football outside of Germany. (Which means that Spurs not only hold the distinction of being the first British side to face Borussia, they are also only the second team Dortmund ever faced abroad.) It seems this time the Germans weren't quite so overwhelmed by the occasion. They managed to draw with Derby and kept the score against Spurs down to a creditable 2–1.

The match programme noted: 'The hospitality and kindness extended to all our party on our visit to Dortmund was such that in offering the heartiest of welcomes to our visitors we express the hope that their memories of their visit to Tottenham will be as pleasant as ours are of our visit to Dortmund.' There were even nine lines in German on the front page.

A few months later, in May 1952, Scottish champions Hibernian came to Dortmund and won an excellent game 2–1. So Borussia were still without a win against a British team. The spell was finally broken in May 1954 at, of all places, Soldiers Field in Chicago, Illinois. BVB were on a tour of the United States that would see the club cross the continent and play in places as far apart as New York City and Los Angeles. In Chicago, Borussia met Plymouth Argyle and beat the English team, then in the second division, 4–0. Two weeks later, on Randalls Island, New York, Dortmund took on Chelsea, who had a strong team at the time. Yet the Germans won

6–1. One assumes the stunningly one-sided scoreline owes something to the fact that Chelsea's Scottish goalkeeper Bill Robertson was in a New York hospital, getting his appendix removed, and an American by the name of Phil Hannaby replaced him between the sticks.

The match in Chicago against Plymouth Argyle was also Borussia's first under floodlights. That's noteworthy because you sometimes read that this distinction belongs to the match away at United in the European Cup on 17 October 1956. It was played at Maine Road, as Old Trafford didn't yet have floodlights, and an amazing crowd of 75,598 came out to watch the West German champions. In their history of United in Europe, David Meek and Tom Tyrrell note that Matt Busby's team 'jumped firmly into the driving seat', leading 3–0 at half-time. They add: 'But German teams are invariably made of stern stuff and sure enough they did not give up. A rare error by Roger Byrne was punished by Kapitulski and then Preissler scored to pull the score back to 3–2. The recovery put the tie back on a knife's edge for the second leg and was a sharp reminder about counting chickens before they were hatched.'

But the next day's headline in the Dortmund paper *Westdeutsche Allgemeine Zeitung* did not mention United's strong first half or BVB's recovery. In fact, it didn't even mention the score. Instead, it read: 'Borussia in golden shirts!' On their trip to England, the club had acquired a set of special, fluorescent floodlight shirts produced by Watson & Mitchells in Manchester for Umbro. Although they weren't very comfortable, they looked dazzling under artificial light and are fondly remembered to this day because Borussia would later play one of the most famous games in the club's history in them.

That was not, however, the return leg. According to Meek and Tyrrell, 'Mark Jones, Bill Foulkes and Roger Byrne had to use every trick in the defender's armoury to peg back the speedy Germans. United were lucky to finish the match 0–0 and so go through on the first-leg result.' Borussia's very first European adventure had come to a rather early end. But the club wouldn't have to wait long for their next chance to shine on the international stage. Because almost exactly one year after the match in Berlin against Karlsruhe, the exact same XI in black and yellow contested another final for the national championship. That was great news for the club. Less good news for Dortmund's most rapidly rising new star.

CHAPTER 4

On a sunny but cold Wednesday morning in February 1997 I was watching Borussia Dortmund train. It was long before the club had built the state-of-the-art training centre where Napier Barracks used to be. At the time, BVB's first team trained on a small pitch behind what was then still called Westfalenstadion. And I do mean 'small'. It beggars belief, but the team that would win the Champions League a few months later was training on a pitch that wasn't regulation size, which is why coach Ottmar Hitzfeld couldn't properly practise corners and other set-pieces.

I was used to watching training sessions, because in Germany it's a very recent phenomenon that teams train behind closed doors. Until Jürgen Klinsmann took over at Bayern Munich in 2008, it was almost unthinkable for a Bundesliga club to close training sessions to the general public. When you wanted to get a player's autograph, you went to a training session and then, when the team walked back to the dressing room after working out, you just approached him with something to sign.

However, on this particular day I was attending the training session because I had an appointment with one of the players. I was watching them so intently that I didn't notice an older man ambling up to me. Well, he wasn't really old, barely 61 years of age, but his hair was greying and so I presumed he must be one of the pensioners who regularly attended Borussia's morning training sessions. Suddenly, he addressed me.

'Excuse me, are you a journalist?'

'Er, yes and no.'

He flashed me a warm smile. 'Why, that's an interesting answer. Are you or are you not?'

'It's like this,' I said. 'I am here because I have an interview scheduled with Paulo Sousa. So I guess that makes me a journalist. But I'm not working for a newspaper. I'm working for a fanzine.'

He raised an eyebrow. 'A fanzine? What exactly is that?'

'It's a magazine produced by fans for other fans.'

'That's fascinating,' he said, breaking into another smile. 'You have to tell me more about it.' Then he straightened his back, extended a hand and introduced himself. 'My name is Alfred Schmidt. This is my first day as Borussia Dortmund's fan commissary.'

I did not shake his hand. I stared at him.

'Quite a coincidence,' he said, helpfully.

'You are Aki Schmidt,' I said, open-mouthed.

'Yes, I am,' he replied, grinning.

'Oh, my God! I didn't recognise you. I am so sorry!'

'There's no reason to apologise,' he said. 'You're too young to have ever seen me play.'

'But I have just told you that I am a fan,' I protested. 'And as such I should know the handful of people who are real club legends. This is really, really embarrassing for me.'

'Embarrassing? Let me tell you a story.'

And then Aki Schmidt told me how, while he was in Sweden with West Germany for the 1958 World Cup, Dortmund's coach suddenly died from a heart attack and was replaced by the well-known Austrian Max Merkel. After the tournament, Schmidt had two weeks off before reporting back for duty.

'I went to Rote Erde and the only guy I saw was a man in a white suit,' Schmidt said. 'He looked ridiculous. A white suit in 1958! So I said, and maybe I sounded a bit rude: "Is the team already there?" And he replied: "Yes, they are in the dressing room." Then I asked him: "Is the coach there, this Austrian fella?" And he told me: "No, they are still waiting for him." So I went into the dressing room and said hello to the lads. Suddenly the door opened and there stood this guy in the white suit. He said: "Good morning, gentle-men, let's get to work." Then he looked me in the eye and added: "I think we'll do some conditioning today, so that Mr Schmidt will get to know me."'

Aki Schmidt laughed so hard he had tears in his eyes. 'That is what I call embarrassing – not recognising your own coach. Now please tell me more about this fan magazine.'

Aki Schmidt was perfect for the role of, as he put it, 'fan com-missary' (nobody had yet come up with the unwieldy 'supporter liaison officer'). He was enormously popular among BVB fans and possessed an engaging personality. He loved to travel with sup-porters to away games because it gave him the opportunity to entertain them with jokes and anecdotes.

Until the club asked him to work with the fans, the job had been done by Petra Stüker, who joined the club in the early 1980s. However, it all got a bit too much for her. Borussia had developed from a club for Borsigplatz boys to a club for the entire city to a club for the Ruhr area to a club for the western part of Germany. Now, under Hitzfeld, the support was growing exponentially yet again, as BVB became a club for the whole of Germany. The reason this could happen so quickly was that Borussia already had a large fan base outside the club's normal catchment area. And, in a way, Schmidt had been responsible for that.

Alfred 'Aki' Schmidt was the son of a Dortmund steel worker, but he didn't join Borussia until he was almost 21. He played for a local team, Berghofen, and there were many bigger clubs courting him. One was Cologne. Another was Schalke. Borussia only offered him a contract for the reserve team, which annoyed Schmidt, who was never one to suffer from self-doubt. In June 1956, Schmidt walked into Borussia's clubhouse and asked to see a board member. When he was told that everybody who had anything to say had gone to Berlin for the national championship final, Schmidt replied that, well, in that case he would have to sign a contract at Schalke. The secretary hastily put a call through to a Berlin hotel room and

Borussia's chairman Heinz Dolle took the next plane home to make sure another 'Alfredo' would wear black and yellow instead of royal blue.

It was one of Dolle's most inspired decisions. Schmidt became an overnight sensation. He missed only one league game in 1956–57 and scored a dozen goals as Borussia retained their Oberliga West title. In April 1957, a few weeks before the final rounds of the national championship were to begin, he even won his first cap for West Germany. Then he scored Borussia's crucial 2–1 winner in their opening group game against Offenbach. And then he was benched.

Shocked, Schmidt watched from the sidelines as Dortmund also beat Kaiserslautern and Hertha to book another berth in a final. His name was not on the team sheet for the title match against Hamburg in Hanover, either. The reason was both simple and perplexing. Borussia's coach, a former Bayern Munich player called Helmut Schneider, had got it into his head that he should make history by attempting to win back-to-back titles with the exact same XI. 'The day of the final was the worst day of my life,' Schmidt later recalled. 'If national coach Sepp Herberger hadn't given me a moral uplift, I guess I would have gone into the next season as a demoralised man.'

While it's hard to imagine the swashbuckling ladies' man Aki Schmidt in a state of demoralisation, one wonders what would have happened if Borussia had lost the final. Schneider must have had boundless faith in his team – and they repaid his trust. Almost 40,000 fans travelled from Dortmund to Hanover, two hours down the A2 motorway, so that half of the massive crowd supported BVB. Kelbassa scored twice and his buddy Niepieklo added his own brace for a final score of 4–1. A writer for the magazine *Sport-Illustrierte* paid the team the biggest compliment a German sports reporter was capable of in those pre-Bundesliga days: 'You'd think only professional teams would be able to put in a performance as perfect as Borussia's.' Hamburg's Jupp Posipal, who had won the

World Cup with West Germany three years earlier, told the press: 'We tried our very best, but wherever we turned our heads, we saw only yellow shirts.' In Dortmund, the fans prepared for another hero's welcome by painting the streets black and yellow.

Borussia were clearly on the verge of becoming one of the truly big clubs in the country. There weren't many of those. Due to the absence of a nationwide league, West German football was still regional football and most clubs had only local fanbases. The only exceptions to this rule were the two tradition-laden teams that had each managed to establish a dynasty at one point during the previous decades: Nuremberg and Schalke. (Kaiserslautern and Hamburg could also lay claim to having fans everywhere, though on a smaller scale, due to the massive national popularity of their respective star players: Fritz Walter and Uwe Seeler.) Two developments would change this. One was the slow gestation of the Bundesliga, a subject we'll come back to. The other was Germany's growing fascination with European football.

Whoever represented Germany under midweek floodlights, especially if they did so reputably, was bound to be popular. However, back then only national champions played in Europe (the Cup Winners' Cup wasn't introduced until 1960) and once Borussia were knocked out of the 1957–58 competition by AC Milan in the quarter-finals, they found it hard to return to this most glamorous of football's stages. As if the Oberliga West hadn't been difficult enough already, with rivals like Essen (national champions in 1954) or Schalke (in 1958), now there was another club going places – Cologne. Their visionary chairman Franz Kremer had grandiose plans for the team, dreaming of a German version of Real Madrid.

What sounds ludicrous today looked like a distinct possibility in the late 1950s and early 1960s. Cologne were the most professionally run club in the land and there are many people who believe they could have played the role that eventually fell to Bayern Munich if Kremer hadn't died suddenly from a heart attack in 1967. For many fans who saw Borussia play during those Oberliga days, the biggest rivals were not Schalke but posh, monied Cologne. 'They were always very stuck-up, arrogant,' Dieter Fiedler says, a BVB supporter born in 1944. Worst of all: they weren't even from the Ruhr area but from the Rhineland. 'And I know our players felt the same way about them,' Fiedler adds. 'Our "Hoppy" Kurrat, who played on all those teams in the 1960s, once told me: "When we played Cologne, we would arrive in our training tops while they walked around in suits and ties. But then, on the pitch, we always showed them."'

Not always, Hoppy, not always. Between 1958 and 1963, Cologne finished ahead of Dortmund in the Oberliga West every single year, despite the fact that Borussia had a strong side. This was proved in 1961, when BVB qualified for the later stages of the championship as runners-up in the Oberliga West and then squeezed past Frankfurt and Hamburg to reach the final against Nuremberg. This time, Aki Schmidt was in the starting XI, but Borussia were beaten rather unceremoniously, 3–0. The team's quality was underlined again two years later, in 1963. Again Dortmund finished the league season in second place behind Cologne and then brushed off Hamburg and 1860 Munich to reach the championship final for the fifth time in the club's history. It would also be the last time, because change was underway.

In the preceding years, a couple of things had happened that slowly altered the DFB's attitude towards a professional and nationwide league. One was the increasing number of Germans who had decided to play abroad and earn good money. Under the rules of the DFB, they were barred from playing for the national team. (Incidentally, that rule was the reason why the great Bernd, or Bert, Trautmann was never capped.) In April 1961, the country had been subjected to a mighty scare when Inter manager Helenio Herrera travelled to Hamburg to offer national treasure Uwe Seeler a contract and an annual salary of 155,000 marks (after taxes), or £13,000. Although Seeler's wages and bonuses at the time came to only 6,000 marks per year (before taxes), he declined the offer. But how many players could realistically be expected to be as loyal as Seeler?

There was also the problem of profitability. Under the Oberliga system, no fewer than seventy-four clubs across the country were technically playing at the highest level. Although they did not employ fully professional players, they had to pay semi-pro wages. According to the magazine *Der Spiegel*, 'a third of the clubs playing in one of the top divisions cannot survive'.

Finally, national coach Sepp Herberger had repeatedly pointed out that in the long run, semi-professional sides (including the national team) would not be able to compete with pros. This claim had often been refuted, not least by Herberger himself when he won the 1954 World Cup, or by club sides like Eintracht Frankfurt, who reached the 1960 European Cup final after disposing of fully professional Rangers 12–4 on aggregate in the semis.

But now the results appeared to be drying up. In February 1962, West German champions Nuremberg were hammered 6–0 away at Benfica in the European Cup. A few months later, the national team was knocked out of the World Cup in Chile by Yugoslavia as early as the quarter-finals. It meant that when 129 DFB representatives came together on 28 July 1962 in Dortmund, there was some hope they would at long last decide to set up a nationwide and professional football league in West Germany.

It was by no means a foregone conclusion, though. There were some club officials who honestly believed that football fans didn't want such a league. Why, they argued, would a Borussia Dortmund supporter want to watch teams from the far north or south when he could have a hot-blooded derby every weekend? Others were afraid that the clubs – who, as non-profit institutions, enjoyed considerable tax benefits – could lose their charitable status if they began to employ professional players.

At the end of a long afternoon, filled with speeches and debates, voting began. Meanwhile, just half a mile south of the hall where the DFB held the meeting, Borussia were playing a pre-season friendly against Bremerhaven, a team from the Oberliga Nord. As if trying to prove that competition was diluted because there were too many top-level sides in the country, Dortmund won the game 8–0. At almost exactly six o'clock in the evening, the stadium announcer informed the 5,000 people in attendance that a stunning number of DFB representatives, 103 in all, had just voted in favour of creating a federal league, or *Bundesliga*. The fans at Rote Erde stadium cheered loudly.

The historic ballot meant that the 1962–63 season would be the last played under the old system. As if on cue, the final on 29 June in Stuttgart was the first to pit two teams from the strongest league, the Oberliga West, against each other, with Dortmund meeting none other than their new rivals Cologne. Most observers considered BVB to be dark horses, but the team had given Cologne a very close run for the Oberliga West title, conceding first place only on account of a shock defeat in Wuppertal on the last day of the league season. Yet not even Borussia's biggest fans could have predicted that the last-ever championship final would amount to a walk in the park.

Local boy Dieter 'Hoppy' Kurrat, a midfielder who stood only 5 feet 4 inches and carried that peculiar nickname because he had a penchant for the television series *Hopalong Cassidy*, opened the scoring on nine minutes. Reinhold Wosab, who had joined Borussia at the beginning of the season, made it 2–0 with 57 minutes gone. Less than ten minutes later, Aki Schmidt, playing at inside-right, suddenly found himself one-on-one with the goalkeeper and coolly slotted home to decide the game. The next day, roughly 150,000 people followed the team's lorry around town (the reason why the number was smaller than in 1956 and 1957 was probably that the players came by train and didn't arrive in Dortmund before 6.20 p.m.). The festivities finished with a banquet at the Westfalenhalle, the famous multi-purpose venue in Dortmund. It meant the players celebrated the 1963 title right next door to the hall in which the DFB had decided to set up the Bundesliga eleven months earlier.

The new league would be intrinsically linked with Dortmund not just because it was voted for there. The first-ever Bundesliga goal – after 58 seconds on the first matchday, 24 August 1963 – was scored by a BVB striker, Friedhelm Konietzka, away at Werder Bremen. And the simple fact that Borussia were founder members of the professional league helped sharpen the club's profile, especially as some big clubs did not make the cut, either because they hadn't performed well enough during the previous twelve years or had failed to meet some other criteria. Bayern Munich, for instance, were left out in the cold because the DFB admitted 1860 Munich to the Bundesliga and didn't want two clubs from the same city. However, there were also those who said that neither 1860 nor Bayern deserved a place in the league because Offenbach had outperformed both clubs in the previous dozen years – and were still barred from the Bundesliga. The selection process was a messy affair and gave rise to many conspiracy theories. None of them had to do with Dortmund, though, as there was never any doubt that the reigning national champions, who also happened to be the most successful team in the history of Oberliga West, would grace the Bundesliga.

But it was not the first nationwide and professional league on German territory that was responsible for the most famous night in Borussia's history up until that point, a night that would serve to sort the wheat from the chaff in the stands for the next two or three generations of fans ('I was there and you weren't!'). A night that is still, after all these decades and even though nothing substantial was actually won, among the top three most memorable moments for Dortmund supporters.

In the second round of the European Cup, Borussia were drawn against Benfica, the team that had humiliated Nuremberg in February 1962. It's not an overstatement to say that Germans regarded Benfica with the same awe and mythical reverence they would reserve for Bob Paisley's Liverpool in the 1970s. The Portuguese side had just reached three European Cup finals in a row, winning the trophy in 1961 and 1962. They seemed like supermen and were often billed as the greatest team in the world.

Benfica certainly lived up to this reputation in the first leg in Lisbon, at least during the first half when they dominated the match. But Wosab scored what at the time seemed like a precious away goal and BVB lost only narrowly, 2–1. In fact, Benfica's winning goal was controversial, as Dortmund's goalkeeper – a 28-year-old local lad named Hans Tilkowski, who had spent a good deal of his career at neighbouring Herne before Borussia asked him to come home – may have had the ball under control when the legendary Eusébio knocked it in.

Eusébio missed the return leg on 4 December 1963 with an injury, but the whole of Dortmund was still itching to see the mighty Benfica. Although it was a very cold winter's day, Rote Erde was filled to the last seat hours before the 7.30 p.m. kick-off. Actually, it was filled way beyond the last seat. Wosab always said: 'The capacity was 40,000 – but nearly 60,000 people crammed into the ground. I was later told that some people peed themselves rather than go to the loo and lose their seat. Well, I reckon it was so cold that urine quickly froze anyway.'

Heinz Reinke, a fan who was seventeen at the time, said: 'It was the biggest game Dortmund has ever seen. Ever! When I got to the ground, two and a half hours before kick-off, there were already at least 10,000 people there. There wasn't much singing at the time, the fans usually just chanted "B–V–B". But I remember them singing a song that day. It was based on an old folk tune and went: "We'll carry Benfica out of the city's gate." That was before the game!'

It wasn't the only display of optimism. A group of fans gained fame that night because they carried a giant papier-mâché hammer with an inscription that read: 'And then we beat Benfica.' (In German, 'hit' and 'beat' are the same verb.) The hammer was built by a pub owner from Iserlohn, a town fifteen miles southeast of Dortmund, whose son told author Gregor Schnittker decades later: 'The thing was so large, they had to rent a bus to transport it to the game! I think it was my dad's idea. One of his customers then built the hammer and it turned out so big that it wouldn't fit in a car.'

It was around this time that fans on Liverpool's Kop began to sing popular songs of the day, 'She Loves You' by the Beatles and, of course, Gerry and the Pacemakers' rendition of the show tune 'You'll Never Walk Alone'. The people who supported BVB on that cold December night weren't a world removed from their English counterparts. Rattles were less popular than air horns or bugles and German fans didn't wear the traditional British rosettes. But they, too, had a penchant for banners and would soon be singing a lot more than their predecessors used to do. A particular favourite in Dortmund were two lines from the first club song, written in 1916 by Heinrich Unger, the club's original president, in the trenches on the French front: 'Yet there's one thing that shall remain: Borussia Dortmund will not go down!'

There was no need to sing these defiant, reassuring words on that night against Benfica, because Borussia – wearing their floodlight shirts from Manchester – played Europe's premier team off the park. In fact, watching the historic match again today, what first strikes you is that the sensational 5–0 scoreline actually flattered the visitors. BVB should have taken the lead long before Konietzka broke the deadlock after 33 minutes.

People were sitting on wooden benches that had been placed on the running track. After that first goal, they were still able to restrain themselves. Only a single supporter, dressed in a dark suit, ran onto the pitch and slung his arms around Konietzka's neck, the player giving him a nonplussed look. But after the third goal, the crowd could no longer be contained. Supporters invaded the pitch and embraced the men in the satin-like yellow shirts, while photographers ran onto the field of play to capture the players up-close. Within seconds of the final whistle, the field was dark with people, as the fans hoisted the players onto their shoulders and carried them around the pitch and then into the dressing room.

Despite the heroics of Eintracht Frankfurt in 1959–60, this mauling of Benfica was the most impressive display yet by a German club side and seemed to prove all those people right who said the country grudgingly had to allow professionalism in order to become competitive. However, it was also the first indication that Rote Erde stadium was not an ideal location for big European games.

In the next round, BVB knocked out Dukla Prague and were then drawn against Inter in the semi-final. Borussia's board seriously considered moving the match to the Niedersachsenstadion in Hanover, a modern and spacious ground that could hold 86,000. But the fans were vehemently opposed to this idea, so BVB took on Inter at another overcrowded Rote Erde, people sitting so close to the pitch their feet almost touched the sidelines. The teams drew 2–2, but Dortmund felt hard done by. With twenty minutes left, the Hungarian referee chalked off a BVB goal for offside that looked legit, and ten minutes later he denied the hosts a penalty. Worse was to come in the return leg at the San Siro. After twenty minutes, with the game still scoreless, Inter's Spanish superstar Luis Suárez patently kicked Hoppy Kurrat in the groin. Yet the Yugoslav referee Branko Tesanić allowed Suárez to stay on the pitch and Inter went on to win 2–0, quite deservedly but still controversially. In his seminal book *Inverting the Pyramid*, Jonathan Wilson says there were 'allegations that Herrera habitually rigged games' and cites this tie as an example: 'A Yugoslav tourist met Tesanić on holiday that summer and claimed the official had told him that his holiday had been paid for by Inter.'

No matter how you define these things, Borussia Dortmund were now one of the two or three biggest teams in the country and had heralded their arrival on the European stage. And things were getting better and better. In the summer of 1965, a dashing and fleet-footed forward by the name of Sigfried Held joined the club to strike up a telepathic partnership with the powerful Lother Emmerich, a miner's son born and bred in Dortmund. During the next season, Rangers legend Willie Waddell came to Dortmund on a scouting mission and raved about the duo in the pages of the *Scottish Daily Express*, where he had a column. The term he coined for Emmerich and Held was destined to survive the decades: the Terrible Twins.

In the same summer in which Held arrived, the club built a two-tiered wooden stand opposite the main stand, and one year later they added another stand in the south of the stadium. This structure was made of wood rather than concrete, too, but at least it increased the number of seats and thus the club's income.

This original South Stand was often used by the travelling support. Most BVB fans preferred to stand in the north-western curve of Rote Erde, as this part was close to the main entrance and lined by poplar trees. One of the boys who liked to climb into those trees to get a better view of the pitch was a bright teenager from a mining town just north of Dortmund. His name was Gerd Niebaum and he went to school in the city. One day, he would become famous as the architect of Borussia's second golden era. Today, though, most fans rather remember him as the man who almost killed the club.

Although Borussia were one of the most successful teams in the land, they were not known for good runs in the DFB-Pokal, the German FA Cup, contested since 1935. BVB had reached one final in their history (which they lost to Hamburg in 1963). Far more common were early and embarrassing exits, often at the regional level. That changed in 1965, when Borussia made another cup final and at last ended up on the winning side. The team played in white shirts, as their opponents, second-division Aachen, were one of the few clubs that also used black and yellow as their colours. Captain Aki Schmidt, still crucial to the team, opened the scoring and Emmerich added the second and final goal of the game before 20 minutes were up. It was a great success, but when you talk to Dortmund fans who were at the game, the first thing they mention is what a terrible match it was. BVB were nervous, afraid to be upset by the lower-division team, so they basically just knocked the ball about after taking that early two-goal lead. As a result, the match is now infamous for having produced the most boring 70 minutes in the history of cup finals in Germany. It was so tedious that contemporary reports point out that Borussia were booed after the game not just by the neutrals but by their own fans – and that the players hung their heads in shame when they heard the catcalls. This might very well be true. To this day it is one of the most fundamental differences between Schalke and Dortmund fans that the former do not use a figure of speech when they refer to their club as a religion and will often display not just the devotion but also the lack of discrimination common among believers. Dortmund supporters, by comparison, pride themselves on keeping a critical eye on their club and tend to be more rational and objective. When I started going to Bundesliga games, in the second half of the 1970s, it was still perfectly normal for Dortmund fans to applaud a nice move or a fine combination by the visiting side. That would have been unthinkable at Schalke, and elsewhere, even then.

After the final, the local newspaper *Westfälische Rundschau* said: 'The more insightful among the players will have realised that they need to play a lot better to survive even the first round in the Cup Winners' Cup. Let's hope the team can rise to the occasion in much the same way as they did in the 1963–64 European Cup.' These were prophetic words. Borussia's European season in 1965–66 would rank as the club's crowning achievement for more than three decades, as the Germans became the ultimate spoilsports in a competition that seemed to have British triumph written all over it, with two English sides, title-holders West Ham and Liverpool, joining Scottish Cup winners Celtic in the semi-final. The odd team out were the Germans from the Ruhr area.

The semi-final between Bill Shankly's Reds and Jock Stein's Hoops was not an amiable affair. According to *The Celtic Wiki*, the return leg at Anfield 'was played in monsoon conditions which turned the pitch, which had already been covered in snow and lashed by rain in the past week, into a mud bath'. When Bobby Lennox had a goal ruled out in the last minute that would have seen Celtic through, the Scottish fans began to riot, pelting the pitch with missiles and hurting many spectators: 'Cans and bottles are said to have been lined up together and went round the pitch perimeter three times.' One interesting aspect of this match is that it must have been the night when the Celtic fans picked up 'You'll Never Walk Alone' and made the anthem their own.

In early 1991, three contributors to the St. Pauli fanzine *Millerntor Roar* would trek across Great Britain to meet like-minded souls. They ventured as far north as Glasgow, where they struck up a friendship with the Celtic fans behind *Not the View* magazine. Later that year, the St. Pauli fans produced a season-review video. Inspired by their new Celtic friends, they used a punk version of 'You'll Never Walk Alone' by a band from Ipswich called the Adicts for the soundtrack. It struck a nerve with the club's supporters and they took up singing the song at games. Since the Adicts' version was hard to get hold of in those pre-internet days, the Hamburg band Rubbermaids recorded their own take on the tune. It came out in January 1994 and would be played before St. Pauli home games for years.

From St. Pauli, the song spread like wildfire through the league, as Germans considered it a football classic rather than a song specifically connected with one or two clubs. The Kaiserslautern version, sung with religious fervour, was particularly stirring, but Borussia's attempt at the tune was not far behind. Perhaps the song resonated strongly with BVB fans due to two fan parties held in Dortmund for Celtic supporters in 1987 and 1992. In any case, one can state with some certainty that Dortmund fans, who are now so famous for singing 'You'll Never Walk Alone', acquired the song via Glasgow rather than Liverpool.

Which is ironic, given that Borussia's support was treated to the original, meaning the Liverpool version, only two weeks after the Hoops, BVB having knocked out West Ham with surprising ease, winning 5–2 on aggregate, to book a date with the Reds at, of all places, the vast bowl that was Hampden Park in Glasgow. When UEFA asked Borussia if the club would prefer a non-British venue for the final, suggesting the Swiss city of Lausanne, BVB declined, probably on the assumption that the locals were certainly not going to support Liverpool. Yet what the locals did instead was stay away – only 41,000 saw the game, 90,000 below capacity.

It was the first European final for both clubs, yet Shankly never doubted the outcome. A few days earlier, his team had won the English league title, and he declared: 'Today we'll win this Cup Winners' Cup – and next year the European Cup.' It's not that he didn't know who he was up against. Liverpool scout Reuben Bennett had been to West Germany quite a few times to watch BVB. But perhaps Shankly underestimated how much Borussia had perfected their fairly modern counter-attacking game, which meant the team was rarely out of contention in a match, even if key players should happen to have an off day.

One of these players was right-winger Reinhard Libuda, known to all and sundry as 'Stan', because he did the Matthews turn to absolute perfection. Libuda was a phenomenal dribbler who loved nothing more than taking on defenders. 'We would be waiting in front of goal and not getting the ball, because Stan was doing his circus tricks on the wing,' Aki Schmidt told me when I asked him about his room-mate on away trips. 'Sometimes, he would literally wait until the defender was back on his feet, just so that he could dribble around him again.' One day, posters appeared in the Ruhr area advertising a touring evangelist. The tagline read: 'Nobody can go past God.' To which a fan famously added the words: 'Except Libuda.'

There were three problems with Libuda, though. The first was that he didn't really want to play for Borussia. He was a Schalke boy who had left his hometown club only because they were relegated. (With typical rotten Libuda luck, the league was expanded from sixteen to eighteen teams and Schalke stayed up nonetheless.) The second was that Libuda suffered from monumental shyness, which is precisely why he was told to room with Schmidt, the life and soul of every party. The third, and most pressing, problem was that Libuda was easily intimidated. The word in the Bundesliga was that he would vanish from the game if you roughed him up in the first minutes. And that's what happened at Hampden, against a Liverpool side feared for their physicality even in England.

Accounts vary about how many Dortmund fans were on hand for that final. A contemporary book puts the figure at 2,000. But a fan called Franz-Josef Schlüter, who as a 28-year-old made the journey together with seven friends, recalled: 'Most of the people were Liverpool fans, but I guess that about 5,000 *Borussen* were there. Several planes went from Düsseldorf to Prestwick Airport. That's pretty far outside of Glasgow, but we had special buses that took us to the stadium. When the teams came out we chanted "B–V–B" as loud as we could, but of course the English drowned us out with their "Li-ver-pool cha-cha-cha".' The Reds also sang 'You'll Never Walk Alone' (and 'When the Saints Go Marching In'), but it was a few years too early for German fans, who spoke little English at the time, to adopt a British song. (English had become a compulsory subject in all secondary schools only in 1964.)

Borussia took the lead on 62 minutes when they hit Liverpool on the break. Gordon Milne lost possession and Emmerich floated a beautifully timed pass into the path of Held, who volleyed home from the edge of the box. But only six minutes later, the two sides were even. As John Williams describes the moment in his Liverpool book *Red Men*: 'The Liverpool equaliser, scored by the struggling Roger Hunt, came from a cross after Peter Thompson had run the ball over the byline, undetected by the linesman or referee. But, unfazed by this setback, the Germans would not be denied.' That's because they had their own struggling forward, Libuda.

Deep into extra time, after 106 minutes, Aki Schmidt released Held with a tremendous long pass. With Held bearing down on goal, Tommy Lawrence raced off his line. He blocked the ball at the edge of the box and it bounced out to Libuda. There was a lot of space in front of the winger – forty yards between him and an open goal. Aki Schmidt figured that Libuda would now control the ball and move forward to get a better angle, but for once the man who loved to run with the ball at his feet tried a first-time lob. It came back off the inside of the post, hit the onrushing Ron Yeats and bounced into the back of the net.

Schmidt knew that Libuda's winning goal had made history. As the two men were lying in their beds a few hours later, staring at the ceiling and knowing sleep would not come for some while, Schmidt said: 'Can you imagine what will happen when we get home? We are the first German team that has won a European trophy. People will go nuts.'

Libuda replied: 'Rubbish.'

But Schmidt was right. The next day, more than 300,000 people delirious with joy filled the streets of central Dortmund. Again and again they chanted: 'Li-bu-da!' Yes, they were celebrating a Schalke boy, but most people in Dortmund felt this had been a triumph for football in the Ruhr. Five members of the team that had defeated Liverpool were born in Dortmund, another four had grown up less than twenty miles away from the city.

But of course it was also a triumph for the entire country. When the final whistle sounded in Glasgow, the radio commentator Kurt Brumme stated: 'German football is now established in Europe. It has earned the right to be mentioned in the same breath as Real Madrid, Benfica, Inter.' Two months later, three Borussia players – Hans Tilkowski, Sigfried Held, Lothar Emmerich – would be regulars as the national team came close to winning the game's biggest trophy. When West Germany met England at Wembley in the World Cup final, no club was represented by more players (on either side) than Borussia Dortmund, who had three players on the pitch and one non-playing squad member.

BVB were at the peak of popularity. You could find Dortmund fans everywhere, even in deepest Bavaria. In Vilshofen, a town close to the Austrian border, a young boy named Klaus Augenthaler, destined to become a Bayern Munich icon, grew up supporting the team from a distance. 'One of my best friends looked like Lothar Emmerich,' Augenthaler told me. 'And I was blond, like Sigi Held. So whenever we played, we pretended to be Emmerich and Held. I idolised Sigi Held. That's why I supported Dortmund.'

If you would have told young Augenthaler and his idols Emmerich and Held that within less than ten years Borussia Dortmund would be playing in the second division while recently promoted Bayern Munich would be dominating European football, all three would have certainly laughed their heads off. But it was no laughing matter. Even while Borussia were collecting silverware, there were forces at work, many of them beyond the club's control, which would soon bring BVB to their knees.

CHAPTER 5

At 8.15 p.m. on 28 June 1981, a Sunday, more than 15 million West Germans were seated in front of their television sets, eagerly awaiting the latest episode of *Tatort*, the long-running crime series. (The majority of East Germans could receive West German television, but of course we have no clue how many of them tuned in.) People knew that a new fictional investigator would make his debut that night. He was called Horst Schimanski and it was not an accident that his family name sounded Polish. Detective Chief Inspector Schimanski lived and worked in Ruhrort, a working-class district of Duisburg, thirty-five miles west of Dortmund.

The people watching were in for a major shock.

For three minutes and thirty seconds, not a word of dialogue was spoken. All you saw was a muscular but unkempt man with a moustache, obviously suffering from a hangover, in a messy flat. While the 1964 pop hit 'Leader of the Pack' by the Shangri-Las (which is about a ne'er-do-well everybody warns the girl singer about, though she knows he's really only 'sad') was coming from a cassette player, the man gulped down egg yolk from a glass, then he stuffed some empty beer bottles into plastic bags and left his flat. He stepped into an almost post-apocalyptic scenario. The skies were grey. On a dirty street in a rundown neighbourhood, a Salvation Army choir was singing a solemn hymn while a deranged man hurled pieces of furniture out of his second-floor window. Just as he audibly mumbled 'Fucking television ain't no fucking use anyway' and proceeded to dispose of his TV set, the moustachioed man spoke his first line.

'You idiot!' Schimanski cried. 'Cut that shit!'

Quite apart from the choice language, an uneducated (though deeply honest) brute like Schimanski was not exactly the kind of German policeman viewers were used to. The Nuremberg newspaper *Nürnberger Zeitung* called the episode 'an opprobrious insult to every decent and punctilious officer who serves the general public with dedication'. Even more jolting than the man himself was his world. Houses were decaying, storefronts boarded up, cars rusty. Schimanski's Ruhr area was a depressing, rotting place in the land that time forgot. Also, in contrast to other *Tatort* episodes, there were no class conflicts because there were no conflicting classes. In Schimanski's Duisburg, everybody was poor, beaten, disillusioned and fatalistic, even the police. The only difference was that the investigating officers had jobs, while everyone else was on the dole or a gangster.

But the strangest thing of all was this: Schimanski seemed to like the place.

Once people had got over the initial shock, they began to warm to the rough charm exuded by Schimanski and his locale. For the next ten years, the *Tatort* episodes set in Duisburg proved to be the most popular and Horst Schimanski, portrayed by the Berlin-born actor Götz George, became a symbol for the Ruhr area. One reason for this was that the people living there felt themselves accurately portrayed, if occasionally overdrawn for effect. Yes, the place wasn't pretty, the jobs were gone and there was little hope they would ever come back, but you stuck together and got on with life.

The decline of the Ruhr area had begun in the late 1950s, as more and more cheap hard coal was being imported from America. By 1959, a staggering 18 million tons of unsold coal were piling up around the mines in the Ruhr area, where the deposits are so deep underground that mining is complicated and expensive. In the first half of that year, 52,000 miners lost their jobs. In late August, 22,000 miners demonstrated in the Town Hall square in Dortmund, threatening strikes.

There was no turning back the clock, though, and by the mid-1960s it had become apparent that coal mining was a dying industry. In 1963 alone, more than a dozen mines closed, including the one in the part of Dortmund known as Dorstfeld, where Lothar Emmerich's father had spent his working life. And although various governments tried to save jobs by subsidising Ruhr-area coal, there were only very few mines left by the mid-1970s. Needless to say, the economic disasters that rocked the coalfields did not spare the football clubs. It's not a coincidence that Schalke won their last national championship to date in 1958, just as the initial coal crisis began.

Dortmund held out longer, partly because coal was not quite as important to the city as steel and beer. But a few years after the coal crisis, there were the first signs that a steel crisis was imminent. In early 1966, a few months before Borussia Dortmund won the Cup Winners' Cup, the big Ruhr-area steel companies decided to form what was effectively a cartel to ward off imported steel. But in the 1970s, it all imploded. Even the biggest and most tradition-laden businesses were fighting a fight they could not win. Hoesch, the company so closely linked with Borussia, felt forced to merge with a Dutch competitor in 1972. It only bought time. In 1991, a hostile takeover by the Essen-based Krupp company ended the history of Hoesch – and soon steel production in Dortmund – for good.

Of course the Ruhr area's economic hardships are not the only reason for the problems that beset Borussia in the second half of the 1960s. But in those days – long before television money, lucrative sponsorship deals or large Champions League bonuses – German clubs, who were not owned by rich entrepreneurs, felt the effects sharply when their community suffered, when fans lost jobs and income.

But even if that hadn't happened, chances are that Borussia would have run into trouble sooner or later. In the wake of the triumph against Liverpool, then-chairman Wilhelm Steegmann, deputy CEO at Hoesch, wistfully said: 'If we had a proper stadium, we could now get back on our feet financially for years to come.' Steegmann had seen the balance sheet for 1965. Although it had been a good year on the pitch, BVB had lost money again. Rote Erde was simply too small to generate the sort of gate money that was needed to fund what was now one of the best teams in Europe. The city, as the ground's owner, refused to invest heavily in, as municipal director Walter Kliemt put it, 'only one of many sports clubs in the city'.

Lastly, Steegmann and other members of the board seemed unable to come to grips with a rapidly changing game and the realities of professional football. Branko Zebec, a former Yugoslav international and now an up-and-coming coach, had already agreed terms with BVB when Steegmann suddenly tried to haggle his wages down. A young player named Jupp Heynckes from a little-known club called Borussia Mönchengladbach was eager to join BVB, but the board were reluctant to spend too much money on the team. While Bayern Munich were employing Germany's first full-time, salaried business manager (and would win their first Bundesliga title under Zebec), Borussia felt that the Dortmund way was to go with cheap, young local lads. This approach had been successful for two decades, so why fix something that was not broken?

But when Aki Schmidt finished his long, illustrious career in 1967, when Stan Libuda finally returned to Schalke in 1968 and when Lothar Emmerich was sold – pretty much against his will – to a Belgian club in 1969 to raise a badly needed 175,000 marks (then the equivalent of £18,300), there were no adequate replacements for them.

Gradually, the modern age pushed BVB, and the entire Ruhr region, to the margins. Rot-Weiss Essen were relegated from the Bundesliga in 1967. A season later, Dortmund and Schalke both finished in the bottom five. Football was still huge in the region and the Bundesliga would never feel like a proper league without four, sometimes five or even six teams from the area. But now they were by and large only there to make up the numbers, for the folklore and the atmosphere. Duisburg were Bundesliga mainstays, but between 1969 and 1982, when they suffered the drop, they finished in the top half of the table only three times. Bochum won promotion in 1971 and graced the top flight for twenty-two consecutive seasons, but their best result over those two decades was one eighth-place finish. Once-proud Schalke, like Dortmund crippled by perennial money problems, somehow hung in there and even managed to give Bayern a scare for one year (and one year only), but in 1981 they finally went down – four weeks before Horst Schimanski first appeared on television to lend a face and a voice to the hopeless and downtrodden but somehow likeable Ruhr prole.

For Schalke and Borussia, the most notable consequence of their fall from grace was that their rivalry, always bubbling under the surface, escalated into antagonism. With little else to play for, apart from avoiding relegation, their encounters became the most important matches of the season for both clubs. Things got so heated that in the early 1970s, the term 'Ruhr derby', which until then hadn't been in general use simply because Ruhr-area football consisted of nothing but derbies, began to be reserved for BVB vs Schalke.

When the two teams met on 6 September 1969, chaos reigned before the game had even begun. Rote Erde was sold out, but apart from the 40,000 fans who had tickets, there were perhaps as many as 10,000 inside the ground who had found another way to get in. Since they had nowhere else to go, they simply stood on the running track, blocking the view of the people in the stands. After a few tumultuous scenes and near-fisticuffs, stewards with German Shepherds restored a semblance of order by pushing people back from the sidelines and telling them to sit down. Still, the ground was so overcrowded that people literally sat on the back netting of the two goals. Schalke's and Borussia's coaches couldn't see the pitch from the dugout and took up positions on the running track as well.

Eight minutes before half-time, Schalke's Austrian striker Hans Pirkner fired the ball into the top corner from a tight angle. The Schalke fans behind the goal jumped up to celebrate – and got carried away. Within seconds, dozens of Schalke supporters were on the pitch, hugging their players. The stewards tried to drive them back. Unfortunately, their dogs were unmuzzled. Two Schalke players were severely injured. A dog bit Gerd Neuser's leg, another sank its teeth into Friedel Rausch's backside. Both men were initially able to continue, Rausch after having been given a tetanus shot. Eventually, though, Neuser's leg went numb and he hobbled off. The game finished 1–1. Schalke at first filed a protest but then agreed to let the result stand.

This derby is still one of the most famous games in Bundesliga history and came to be known as the *Hundebiss* – dog bite. Five days later, *Kicker* magazine reported: 'The *Hundebiss* of Dortmund is becoming more and more complicated! Investigations carried out by Borussia Dortmund have revealed that the dog Blitz, which bit defender Friedel Rausch's posterior and forward Neuser's leg, was not a member of the official canine squad. Blitz was used by his master, Wolfgang Musanke, to get into the Rote Erde ground for free. He had borrowed the dog from a friend for this purpose. Borussia Dortmund, who face a DFB penalty, will hold Musanke responsible should Rausch and Neuser sue for compensation.'

Looking at some of the photos taken at the match, it seems highly unlikely that it can have been one and the same dog that attacked both Schalke players, so this story sounds like an attempt by the club to pass the buck. In any case, the events of the day would lead to the introduction of fences in Germany (and the strict separation of home and away support). It also led to a rapid deterioration in relations between the clubs. When Dortmund's players walked onto the pitch for the next derby, in January 1970 and away from home, they were greeted by four young lions. Schalke's president had rented them from a local safari park to retaliate for the Dortmund dog bites. Borussia's centre-forward Werner Weist later said he realised the spectacle was supposed to be tongue-in-cheek but that he still felt 'uneasy'. The result was 1–1 again.

The last Ruhr derby for some time was played in the spring of 1972. The atmosphere was depressing, almost spooky. Borussia had suffered some very heavy defeats in the previous months. The team lost 5–1 at home against Werder Bremen and 6–0 away at Kaiserslautern. But the worst debacle had befallen the club in Munich, against Bayern. Gerd Müller had found the target four times in a shocking 11–1 rout. Now, in early March, BVB were mired in the relegation zone.

Schalke, meanwhile, topped the table. For the first, and only, time they were able to compete with Bayern and Mönchengladbach, having assembled a very good team around the Kremers twins, Erwin and Helmut, centre-forward Klaus Fischer and towering defender Rolf Rüssmann. However, a dark cloud hung over the Royal Blues. Nine months earlier, Kickers Offenbach's president, a man by the unlikely name of Horst-Gregorio Canellas, had disclosed that he had secretly taped phone conversations during the previous season which proved beyond any doubt that players on a number of teams were taking bribes to throw games. An investigation was underway, and the DFB had already banned more than a dozen footballers for life and demoted Arminia Bielefeld to amateur football. But there was a general sense that this was only the tip of the iceberg. In the week leading up to the derby, Canellas told the press: 'The worst perpetrator in this scandal is not Bielefeld but Schalke.' What's more, a Bielefeld official had stated in court that his club paid Schalke players 40,000 marks to lose against Arminia (which Schalke had done). A few weeks after the derby, a number of Schalke players would swear under oath and in court that they were innocent. When they were found guilty regardless, all were charged with and convicted of perjury.

Which is why Dortmund fans sometimes refer to their rivals as *FC Meineid*, Perjury FC.

As if all that wasn't bad enough, there was violence outside the ground. Ahead of the first derby of the season, at Schalke, almost thirty policemen had invaded the away end and searched a group of teenagers among the travelling Dortmund support. They found a loaded gas pistol, two coshes, a cow chain and what the police called 'half a dozen other impact weapons'. The superintendent in charge told the press: 'Unfortunately, we couldn't conduct a similar operation among the Schalke fans because the game began. I'm sure we would have found similar weapons there as well.' The rivalry was turning ugly.

At Rote Erde in March 1972, Schalke went ahead after 17 seconds, the fastest derby goal in history. Borussia lost 3–0. Three months later, BVB were relegated from the Bundesliga.

Of course the club hoped to bounce back immediately, not least because the second level of the league pyramid was split into regional sections at the time. Yes, this meant that you couldn't be promoted directly from one of the five divisions but had to survive a gruelling round-robin tournament after the end of the league season. But it also meant that Borussia would meet some lowly opposition in the western division, part-timers like Mülheim, Gütersloh or Erkenschwick. Thus optimism reigned during the first months and the fans followed the team in great numbers. The first away game was against Sportfreunde Siegen, a club with an average crowd that season of 8,200. But on that day, more than 24,000 filled the small stadium to cheer Borussia.

Gradually, though, reality sank in. Relegation was not an accident that would be quickly repaired. Borussia Dortmund, the toast of Europe only a few years before, would have to adapt to life in a lower league. On the last day of the season, a BVB team that no longer had any chance to qualify for the promotion tournament played at home against Preussen Münster, winning 9–0. The record books say that 3,000 people were at Rote Erde. This is unlikely, though. The match report in the local newspaper said: 'The game against a Preussen side coming apart at the seams was a conciliatory end to the season, attended by only 1,500 people.' It was Borussia's smallest crowd for a competitive game since the end of the war. The club had lost its Bundesliga status, it was still losing money and now it also seemed to be losing its support.

The next season wasn't much better from a footballing perspective, though Borussia's sixth-place finish meant the club at least qualified for the new Second Bundesliga, which was split into northern and southern divisions. And yet something happened that would have long-term repercussions. In February 1974, Borussia's match programme ran a competition. The five lucky winners would get to spend an evening with goalkeeper Horst Bertram. One of them was a bright 18-year-old boy from Holzwickede, a town eight miles east of Dortmund. His name was Peter Noisten and he was one of the few Dortmund fans left who followed their team everywhere. He even had to repeat a year at school because he spent more time with BVB than with his books.

Now, all these years later, he can laugh about it. 'God, what awful games we saw,' Noisten says. 'For more than ten years, I didn't miss a single game. Just the other day, an old friend said to me: "Peter, what have we done wrong? We travelled thousands of miles with Borussia to all these tiny shitholes. And now that there are all these highlights, we have families and we are too old to watch every game."' Noisten hesitates for a moment, then he adds in a more serious tone: 'On your way up, you make tons of friends. But on your way down, nobody wants to know you. At one point, our support had become pathetic. That's when we said: that's wrong, something has to happen here.'

When Noisten met Bertram, the goalkeeper, there were also some club officials present. Talk quickly turned to a few recent instances of crowd trouble that were giving Borussia a bad name. Noisten argued: 'These are young kids. You don't understand them, you don't reach out to them. You are not in touch with your support.' The club replied they didn't know who they should talk to because the fans weren't organised, they had no representatives.

At that point Bertram told Noisten: 'If you can get something off the ground, I'll help you in any way I can.'

'If I organise meetings,' Noisten shot back, 'will you come and talk to the fans?'

'Yes, of course.'

Three days later, Peter Noisten called the editors of the match programme to inform them that he had gathered thirty like-minded people and would form the 'BVB Fan-Club', or BFC, the first Borussia Dortmund supporters' club. Unbeknownst to Noisten, and Borussia, it was not in fact the first such club. In October 1968, fourteen women and eighteen men from Iserlohn had started a Borussia fan club which is still in existence. (This was not the group around the pub owner with the big papier-mâché hammer.) However, their club life consisted of little more than going to the games together and hanging out at their local. Which, to be honest, is basically what most supporters' clubs do to this day. The club Noisten envisioned, however, was something else entirely.

Less than four years later, in January 1978, the noted political magazine *Der Spiegel* devoted an article to the achievements of BFC. It said: 'At every home game, the fans push disabled spectators in wheelchairs to the edge of the pitch. They have collected 18,000 marks to open the first kindergarten in a football stadium, the so-called Fan Club Play Parlour under the South Stand. They came up with another 4,000 marks to arrange a bazaar for children's clothes. Above all, though, they made sure there was no fighting at the ground. They organised cheap trips for teenagers to away games, they rehearsed a BVB waltz and pressed it on vinyl, they put out their own magazine.'

This magazine first came out in March 1976, when the supporters' club had about 500 members (the number would eventually rise to 1,000). It very quickly grew into an astonishingly good, almost professional looking publication, in no small part thanks to one of Borussia's sponsors, the local Stifts brewery. The company helped the supporters' club because the head of marketing was a BVB fan himself – and smart. He realised that anything that tarnished the club's image would fall back upon his product, so he made sure the fans would sort things out among themselves. 'The brewery promised us a big party if there would be no fighting or rioting for one year,' Noisten recalls. There wasn't and Stifts kept its word. A quarter of a century later, the biggest and most influential Dortmund online fanzine – *Schwatzgelb.de* – would say: 'Borussia's reputation as having the best fans in the league can ultimately be traced back to this initiative.'

The most important thing which the fans did, though, was keeping Borussia afloat at a time when the newly elected president, Heinz Günther – director of one of the few remaining coal mines in Dortmund – openly mentioned the possibility of bankruptcy, having checked the books and found the club to be 1.3 million marks in the red (then £230,000). In fact, the only reason the members had elected Günther, who admitted to having no interest in football at all, was that they hoped his business acumen could avert the worst. 'Help us now,' Günther told the supporters' club, 'and we will reward you once we're healthy again.' Noisten made sure that everybody who joined the supporters' club also became a Borussia member and would pay fees accordingly. The fans also collected money for BVB in the streets, running around with collecting tins, asking people to help save the local football club.

Why did these young people decide to become involved in the running of their club? Why did they go to such lengths? Why did professional educators and nursery workers decide to spend their Saturdays in the kindergarten which BFC had opened in the bowels of the stadium so that fans with young children could watch the game, safe in the knowledge that their offspring were in good hands? For one, it fit the zeitgeist. West Germans had become politicised during the 1960s and there was a community spirit in the air, a general feeling that it was your duty to help shape your society.

But there was also the fact that German fans, while still patterning themselves after British supporters, didn't look at their clubs in quite the same way as a fan in England or Scotland would. A German club was not a commercial enterprise, it could not be bought or sold, it was not part of the entertainment industry. It had no owners. Or more precisely: it was the property of the community. The club was what you wanted it to be. At the time, this difference between Britain and Germany seemed almost negligible, but over the next two decades, it would grow into an important distinction.

It wasn't a group of fans, though, no matter how committed and inventive they were, that ultimately bailed Borussia Dortmund out. What turned the club's fortunes around was the opening of their new ground, the Westfalenstadion. The fact that Dortmund became a host city for the 1974 World Cup and received state funding (from the state of North Rhine-Westphalia and also the federal government) to build a new ground was a substantial stroke of luck. It also helped Noisten and his friends in their attempts to drum up support for Borussia and lure people to watch the team. In 1973–74, BVB finished sixth and the average attendance was 8,900. In 1974–75, the team finished sixth again – but this time 25,400 fans flocked to every game! Suddenly, Borussia Dortmund were drawing more fans in the second division than Bundesliga champions Mönchengladbach (and twelve other top-flight clubs).

The fans' enthusiasm and Günther's steely pragmatism would soon clash, but only after this combination had produced the desired result. In 1975–76, Dortmund's fourth year outside the top flight, the team got off to an excellent start in the northern division of the Second Bundesliga and was never far outside of first place, an automatic promotion spot, or second place, which meant promotion play-offs against the second-placed team from the southern tier. This was the chance the club had been waiting for – and for once Günther's ruthlessness stood him in good stead. In January, when the team began to slump, he sacked coach Otto Knefler and replaced him with Horst Buhtz, who guided Borussia to a second-place finish.

There was a problem, though. Buhtz had already signed a contract at Nuremberg for the next season. And, with no little irony, it was Nuremberg who finished second in the southern section of the second division and would meet Borussia in the play-offs. Although, or perhaps because, Günther didn't really understand football, he felt he had to act. On the day after the final league game, a 3–0 home win over Schwarz-Weiss Essen watched by a stunning crowd of 48,000 and followed by a celebratory pitch invasion – Günther relieved Buhtz of his duties. His successor, the man who would be in charge of BVB during the play-offs, was a fairly inexperienced coach, a former player who had hung up his boots only a few seasons earlier and was not yet 38 years old: Otto Rehhagel. Upon leaving the club after only five months, Buhtz said: 'Dortmund have everything a Bundesliga club needs. If they are run properly during the next years, this club has a brilliant future ahead of it.'

The team's right-back was Lothar Huber, then aged 24. He would play more than 370 games for Borussia and later work as the club's assistant coach and, finally, groundsman. Maybe none of that would have happened if Günther hadn't signed Rehhagel. 'There was no time to train, so we just talked,' Huber remembers. 'Everybody knows that Rehhagel likes to talk, he is an incredible motivator. He fired each and everyone up until we felt there was no way on earth we could lose these games.'

However, most observers considered Nuremberg, coached by Dortmund legend Hans Tilkowski, to be the favourites in the play-offs. But Rehhagel must have done something else besides just communicating. Because for the first leg, away from home, he taught his team the approach he would become famous for much later, when he turned Werder Bremen into a domestic superpower and Greece into champions of Europe: defend well, be patient, then hit them on the break. It worked brilliantly in Nuremberg, because while the hosts enjoyed the bulk of possession, Borussia created the much more promising scoring opportunities. The hosts had a man sent off for a professional foul and then, four minutes from time, BVB striker Egwin Wolf left three defenders in his wake and poked the ball past the goalkeeper to score his most important goal for the club since he had joined four years earlier.

But there was still a return leg to be played – and it turned into such a nailbiter that three people in the stands suffered heart attacks. The Westfalenstadion was sold out, of course, which earned the club 570,000 marks – the biggest single pay day in Borussia's history up until that point. The players in yellow shirts and black shorts twice took the lead, but when Nuremberg drew level for the second time with ten minutes left, it was all up for grabs and the visitors threw everything forward. In the final minute, Borussia started a counter-attack and right-back Huber trudged upfield on tired legs. He received the ball and scored the winning goal with his weaker left foot, right in front of an ecstatic South Stand.

'My teammates started talking to the referee, asking him how much time there was left,' Huber says. 'And then they all moved over to the left side of the pitch, towards the subs' benches. I was the right-back, so I was at the other end. When the final whistle came, they all ran into the tunnel and within seconds the pitch was full of people. I was the only player left on the field and the fans stripped me of everything except my underpants. They even got my boots and socks.'

Although it was not yet common, or easy, to buy replica shirts, many of the fans who invaded the pitch, for the second time in ten days, wore yellow long-sleeved shirts with a black trim that resembled the club's old kit. The front of the shirt sported the 'BVB 09' logo, which a designer called Eduard Birk had created in 1922. The back of the shirts read 'Fan-Club Borussia Dortmund'. Every member of the supporters' club had been given such a garment, so that the South Stand sometimes looked like an early attempt at a Yellow Wall.

As the youngsters stormed the pitch to celebrate their club's return to the limelight, the police turned a blind eye. In fact, the next day the *Westfälische Rundschau* newspaper reported : 'The policemen clapped their hands in time with the songs sung by the supporters. They, too, seemed to be looking forward to Bundesliga football in the coming season.'

When an almost-naked Huber got into the dressing room, the champagne was flowing freely. He plonked himself down on a bench next to Burkhard Segler, a long-limbed forward, and Horst Bertram, the goalkeeper who had inspired Noisten to form the supporters' club two years earlier. The three players started to sing:

Aber eins, aber eins
Das bleibt bestehen:
Borussia Dortmund wird nie untergehen!

They were the lines written by Heinrich Unger during the Great War: 'Yet there's one thing that shall remain – Borussia Dortmund will not go down!' The chant had been given a boost in popularity when the team that lifted the 1966 Cup Winners' Cup recorded it as a single. A newer club song, which dates from 1934, was on the A-side. At the end of the song, though, the players belted Unger's twelve words with gusto.

Now, ten years later, another record was put out to commemorate another great success, winning promotion. This one, however, was not written or recorded by players or even club members. In Cologne, surprisingly enough, a composer and producer saw an opportunity to cash in on the euphoria that surrounded Borussia. He sat down to write a song called 'Heja BVB'. ('Heja' is a Swedish expression, meaning 'let's go', which became well known in Germany during the 1958 World Cup.) The tune was recorded by a singer called Karl-Heinz Bandosz, who was born in Hamm, twenty miles northeast of Dortmund, yet had no real interest in either Borussia or football. In the new season, Bandosz was allowed to sing his song at the ground. When he heard thousands of people sing along to the simple and catchy chorus, he knew he had a local hit on his hands.

What Bandosz had no way of knowing, though, was that he had recorded a song that four decades later would still be played at the Westfalenstadion, or Signal Iduna Park. Actually, for the majority of fans, 'Heja BVB' is the true club anthem. You often meet people, usually from abroad, who wonder why Dortmund fans sing a Liverpool song, 'You'll Never Walk Alone', instead of an original tune before games. But they do. 'You'll Never Walk Alone' is sung just after the stadium announcer has read out the line-ups. But when the teams come out of the tunnel, just before the game begins, what is played over the tannoy is 'Heja BVB'. In 2001, at a time when the club resembled a ship lost at sea and was losing its identity, there was an attempt to bury 'Heja BVB' once and for all and replace it with a more contemporary tune. A howl of protest went up. The fans on the South Stand stubbornly sang 'Heja BVB' before kick-off until the club relented and reintroduced the song.

But 'Heja BVB' was not the only song the 1976 promotion spawned; there was also the matter of the 'BVB waltz', to which the article in *Der Spiegel* alluded. It was indeed a waltz, a popular German folk song by the name of *Schneewalzer*, snow waltz. It had been given a new text by one of Noisten's closest – and most extroverted – allies, a man called Peter Erdmann, a man whose family was Borussia royalty. His uncle Herbert Erdmann had scored both BVB goals in the 'Heat Battle of Stuttgart', the 1949 championship final. His father, Werner Erdmann, had also been a member of that team, though he missed the final, and went on to play many Oberliga games for Borussia.

The version of the snow waltz which Peter Erdmann recorded was called 'BVB Waltz' and reflected the boundless exhilaration that had gripped the city and the club's support in the wake of promotion: 'Yes, so now we're back/And the masses cry 'Hooray'/It's always Ha-ho-he/Yes, that's BVB/And when we've won the league/ We'll parade around Borsigplatz.'

They wouldn't win the league for another nineteen years, though this would have seemed hard to believe in those heady, wonderful months in 1976 and 1977. Rehhagel made a few fantastic signings, especially upfront. The highly prolific striker Erwin Kostedde, the son of an American soldier and Germany's first black international, joined from Hertha Berlin. The Dutch winger Willi Lippens, known as 'Ente', the duck, for his strange walk, came from Rot-Weiss Essen and became an instant hit among the fans. Finally, three months into the new season, Rehhagel secured the services of the 26-year-old offensive midfielder Manfred Burgsmüller. 'I was with Uerdingen in the second division at the time,' Burgsmüller said. 'Dortmund's offer was interesting because they had got off to a really good start in the Bundesliga.' Indeed, they had. In their first game back in the top flight, Borussia beat mighty Hamburg at their own ground, 4–3. By February 1977, the black-and-yellows were in sixth place, only two points behind a Bayern Munich team that had just lifted the European Cup for the third time in a row.

Borussia eventually finished eighth, a tremendous achievement for a newly promoted club. What's more, this side was entertaining and captured the imagination. Lippens was a lovable rogue, a showman who would ask a fan for his cap and then take a corner wearing the black-and-yellow headgear. Burgsmüller, who rarely tucked his shirt into his shorts, was impossibly cool, surging through midfield with a casual, elegant gait that countless kids tried to copy on the streets of Dortmund.

Pundits expected BVB to do even better in their second year – the UEFA Cup didn't seem beyond them. And some fans surely took Peter Erdmann's song to heart and dreamed of celebrating a title on Borsigplatz square. And why not? In November, goals from Huber and Lippens secured a home win over Hamburg and

Borussia were the sixth-best team in the country, a mere four points off the top. Everything seemed possible. Unfortunately, it was.

Why would an investigative, highly political magazine like *Der Spiegel* publish an article about the fans of a football club in early 1978? Because of mudslinging behind the scenes. The piece was headed 'The Last Waltz' (four months before Martin Scorsese's film of the same title about the last concert of the Canadian group The Band was released) and opened with these sentences: 'On the verge of bankruptcy, the football club Borussia Dortmund mobilised teenagers. They collected money and canvassed club members. Now, with the coffers full, the board have fired the supporters' spokesman.'

Some members of BFC, the supporters' club, had openly criticised president Günther and wanted to know why Borussia, after years of teetering on the edge of financial collapse, was suddenly spending money left, right and centre. In the summer of 1977, BVB had bought a defender called Werner Schneider for some 800,000 marks (then £200,000), which was an enormous sum for a German club at the time.

'So they revoked my Borussia membership,' Noisten recalls. 'They didn't even tell me. I was on holiday in Holland when I saw a newspaper that said: "Fan revolt in Dortmund! Head of the supporters thrown out of the club!" Then they took away our BFC magazine and told us we could no longer use the club's logo. I was even banned from the ground! But I still went. I stood on the North Stand, where the stewards didn't know me.'

It was the first but perhaps not the last time that the club would ask fans for help in a moment of crisis and then forget about them when the worst of the storm was weathered. Of course it was a coincidence, but it fit the picture that Borussia suddenly began to struggle on the pitch in the second half of the season. For no apparent reason, the team suddenly could not buy a win. In mid-March, there were nervous looks all around. BVB had sunk into eleventh place and the six-point lead over the relegation zone was treacherous, since Saarbrücken, in sixteenth place, had two games in hand. It was only a late surge, which included a sweet derby win at Schalke, that saved the season.

Or so it seemed.

Until the last day of the season.

When Borussia met their namesakes from Mönchengladbach.

CHAPTER 6

Dortmund's Westfalenstadion was a piece of good fortune in more senses than one. It was built for the 1974 World Cup, of course, and played a prominent role during that tournament. It was here that Johan Cruyff's fabled Dutch team thrilled the world with their Total Football. The Westfalenstadion witnessed Holland's 4–1 mauling of Bulgaria and Oranje's famous 2–0 win over Brazil.

However, when FIFA's organising committee had come together in Düsseldorf three years earlier, on 16 July 1971, to make the draw for the qualifying groups and then unveil the schedule for the finals in West Germany, the name Dortmund was nowhere to be found. The games of Group 3, the group into which Holland would eventually be drawn, were supposed to be staged in Hanover, Düsseldorf and Gelsenkirchen. And the final second-round game in Group A (which would turn out to be Holland against Brazil) was meant to take place in Cologne.

The reason was that Dortmund wasn't supposed to be a host city at all. The plan was to stage the tournament in ten cities: Berlin, Cologne, Düsseldorf, Frankfurt, Gelsenkirchen, Hamburg, Hanover, Munich, Nuremberg and Stuttgart. Naturally, Dortmund would have loved to be among the chosen few. But the plans for the new ground which the city had submitted to the DFB were considered to be, well, underwhelming.

As early as 1961, there had been ideas in Dortmund either to radically rebuild the Rote Erde ground or construct an entirely new stadium right next to it. The insurmountable hurdle was always money. A silver lining seemed to present itself when, in

1966, West Germany were awarded the 1974 World Cup, as public funds would certainly be made available. But it was impossible for the city to spend more than six million marks of its own money, which meant the ground either had to be very small or very cheap.

In May 1970, a council officer called Erich Rüttel had an idea. He was inspired by Autostade, a Canadian football stadium built near Montreal for the 1967 World's Fair. Autostade did not even remotely resemble what would become the Westfalenstadion, though. It was unpopular, not least because it stood next to an abattoir, and it looked downright bizarre: an oval shape formed by nineteen individual stands. The reason for this strange appearance was that Autostade had been constructed from prefabricated elements. You could literally dismantle the entire ground and put it up again elsewhere.

What, Rüttel wondered, if you almost exclusively used such prefab elements for the stadium in Dortmund? This idea was the first step towards the Westfalenstadion. The second step followed from the first: the best shape for a prefab ground was a rectangle, because opposite stands could be exactly identical. The third step followed from the second: a rectangular shape meant there could be no running track. Then again, why waste space and money on facilities you didn't need, anyway? After all, Rote Erde would be right next door and always available as a track-and-field stadium. Following this line of thought, you invariably arrived at the ground the Westfalenstadion became, with terraced North and South stands and the West and East stands as seated areas. Suddenly, the cost had come down to a manageable 33 million marks. Manageable, that is, as long as 80 per cent would be state funded.

But Rüttel's plans didn't go down very well with the DFB. The minimum capacity for a World Cup ground, the governing body said, was 61,000 (the size of the proposed stadium in Cologne). Dortmund's prefab ground, by comparison, would hold only 54,000. Worse, just 16,500 people would be seated. The

DFB also disliked the fact there was no running track. Finally, they complained that the four roofs were supposed to be supported by columns. (Well, at least there were roofs! Schalke's own World Cup ground, the Parkstadion, would soon become one of the most hated places in the land, as you were not only far from the action – due to the running track – but also largely unprotected from the elements as only the main stand was roofed.)

Then, in September 1971, *Kicker* magazine reported that some host cities were beginning to get cold feet and were considering backing down. Looking back, that sounds incomprehensible, but the big bribe scandal had just broken. The nation was in shock, football seemed like a dirty business and fans were staying away in droves. Sinking millions into building a football stadium suddenly looked risky. And so *Kicker* referred to Dortmund as 'sitting on the subs' bench', ready to come on for one of the other candidates. Only a few weeks later, the city was indeed asked to spring into action and replace Cologne, whose treasurer shied away from costs of 46 million marks. Almost immediately, on 4 October 1971, construction work on the Westfalenstadion began. (A few months later, Nuremberg withdrew as well. It was too late to find a stand-in and so the World Cup was staged in only nine cities.)

Construction went smoothly, or at least once thirty-four unexploded British bombs had been defused, and the stadium opened on 2 April 1974. The naming was a no-brainer, considering how close the ground was to the Westfalenhallen, which in turn lay adjacent to Westfalenpark, an inner-city park created for a horticulture show in 1959 that is roughly the size of Greenwich Park in London and dominated by one of Dortmund's few true landmarks, the television tower. Equally self-evident was the guest of honour for the opening. Schalke, then a division above Borussia, played a BVB team that was missing a few regulars. The Royal Blues won easily, 3–0.

But there was one surprising element on that opening day. The most vocal home fans gathered on the South Stand, where, it goes without saying, they can be found to this day. But why? If you have been to the Westfalenstadion, or Signal Iduna Park, you may have noticed that this is not an ideal solution. Only relatively narrow footpaths lead to the South Stand, because the terrace backs onto a large outdoor swimming pool. The North Stand, on the other hand, is the part of the ground you naturally gravitate towards when you come from the city centre and there is a good deal of open space in front of it.

When I was working on my (German-language) oral history of the club, I asked every single fan who was a member of the relevant generation the same question: 'When you moved from Rote Erde to the Westfalenstadion, why did you move from the north-west curve to the South Stand?' I have never seen so many people shrug their shoulders. The only plausible theory I heard came from a long-time supporter called Thomas Grüner: 'The Parkstadion opened eight months before our stadium did. The Schalke fans decided to stand in the North Curve. So we said: well, if the Blues choose the north, we will choose the south.'

What is certain is that the new stadium was an immediate hit and the envy of many. Cologne's playmaker Wolfgang Overath remarked that 'the only downside to the ground is that it's not in Cologne', while national coach Helmut Schön went as far as to say: 'Next to Estadio Azteca in Mexico City, this is the most beautiful stadium in the world.' The most typical statement came from Schalke's goalkeeper Norbert Nigbur (who, remember, had just moved into the spacious but somewhat cold Parkstadion). He said on opening night: 'I feel right at home here, because I like grounds where people are close to the goals. These are typically English conditions. I think Dortmund will profit from this ground.'

They did, and not only financially. Borussia would lose only one of their first forty-eight competitive games staged at the new ground! A major reason for this streak was the atmosphere, what Nigbur referred to as 'typically English conditions'. It would become one of the most regularly repeated lines about the West-falenstadion – that it was like an English ground and that the fans were like English fans, back then still the biggest compliment you could possibly pay a German football supporter. And it was true. When the Westfalenstadion opened, the German fans were still one or two years away from developing that most peculiar look which would set them apart from supporters in other countries: wearing sleeveless denim jackets covered by as many patches as possible. (German fans referred to such a jacket as a *Kutte*, habit. The fashion was adopted via the heavy metal subculture, which in turn had borrowed it from biker gangs.) There was also the fact that quite a few British Army of the Rhine soldiers who were sta-tioned in Dortmund began to go to the games. It wasn't unusual for a BVB fan in the 1970s and 1980s, especially during a lull in the game, to suddenly hear a chant on the South Stand that extolled the virtues of, say, Sheffield United.

Football-only grounds like the Westfalenstadion were rare in the upper echelons of the German game because the stadiums were almost without exception municipally owned. It took a lot of gall for a city treasurer to suggest spending large amounts of taxpayers' money on a facility that served only a single club, and a single sport, and could not be used by schools or athletics clubs. It was a slightly different matter in Dortmund, because even though the steel and beer industries were still in fairly robust health, everybody was aware of how important Borussia was to the city's image. (Although it was probably another stroke of luck that BVB were relegated as late as the summer of 1972, when construction was already well underway. Nobody knows if the council would have given the green light with Borussia in the second division.)

That is not to say, however, that the Westfalenstadion was totally unique. The Betzenberg stadium in Kaiserslautern was another football-only ground noted for its intimacy and great atmosphere. As was the Bökelberg in Mönchengladbach. Both grounds though were considerably smaller and offered less comfort. The Bökelberg held 34,500 people. Just 7,000 of them had a roof over their head and less than 3,000 had seats. That is why Gladbach often moved to the Rheinstadion in neighbouring Düsseldorf for really big games, such as the European Cup semi-final against Liverpool in late March 1978.

But when Gladbach moved another home game to Düsseldorf, only four weeks later, there was a different reason. The main stand at the Bökelberg was being demolished and completely rebuilt, so the team played their last game of the 1977–78 season in Düsseldorf – against Borussia Dortmund. Gladbach were in second place, level on points with FC Cologne but trailing their Rhineland rivals by ten goals. If Cologne won their own game, away at relegated St. Pauli, there was no realistic chance for Gladbach to catch them. But maybe they would drop a point? Dortmund's coach Otto Rehhagel told the press: 'The team is happy that we're the centre of attention again at the end of the season.' *Kicker* magazine said: 'The small Borussia from the Ruhr area is eager to put up a great fight against the big Borussia from the Left Bank of the Rhine.'

Only older BVB fans would have scoffed at being called the small Borussia. Gladbach dominated the domestic game during that decade (more so than Bayern) and had just won three Bundesliga titles in a row. On the previous weekend, they had scored half a dozen goals in barely half an hour to win 6–2 away at Hamburg. They were an excellent team and on a roll.

Still, what happened in Düsseldorf on 29 April 1978 is very hard to explain. After 27 seconds, Jupp Heynckes scored a looping header to put Gladbach ahead. The hosts, fielding only three defenders, went on a rampage. At half-time, it was 6–0 and although Cologne had gone in front at St. Pauli, they saw their lead eroded. In the second half, Dortmund somehow stemmed the tide for almost a quarter of an hour, but when Heynckes headed a cross into the net past a stranded goalkeeper, the levee broke for good. The final result was 12–0, the biggest win in Bundesliga history. Cologne, having scored five without reply at St. Pauli, lifted the title by the skin of their teeth, a mere three goals.

Just a few years after the big bribe scandal, the result looked highly suspicious, to say the least. But no evidence of foul play has ever been brought forth. 'It was never our intention to gift Gladbach the title,' Manfred Burgsmüller says. 'This is malicious gossip.' Lothar Huber told the magazine *11Freunde*: 'I'm still embarrassed by that game. I was playing sweeper and I had maybe three touches of the ball. After the sixth goal, it was the referee who had to take the ball out of the net, because we didn't want to do that for the Gladbach players. What I'm really sorry about is that everybody came down on Rehhagel after the game.' Dortmund's coach was accused of standing by and doing nothing while his team went down, although it has to be said that none of the subs was too eager to come on. He was also criticised for playing his number two goalkeeper, Peter Endrulat, who had only six Bundesliga games under his belt. Endrulat later said: 'At half-time, Rehhagel asked me if I wanted to come off. I should have said yes. But I thought there was no way I'd concede another six goals.'

Both Rehhagel and Burgsmüller lived in Essen at the time, so the coach gave his striker a lift home. The two men didn't say much, but suddenly Rehhagel spoke up. He said: 'I guess by this time tomorrow, you will have a new coach.' He was right. On Sunday, at 4.41 p.m., president Günther called Rehhagel on the telephone and relieved him of his duties. 'We had no choice after a debacle like this,' Günther told the papers. 'Such a disgrace calls for drastic measures.' The club also fined each player 2,000 marks. The president explained: 'The contracts say that 2,000 marks is the maximum fine for bringing the club into disrepute. And this is most certainly what has happened.' Another day later, on Monday, the entire team travelled to Frankfurt to be interrogated by the head of the DFB's supervisory committee, a lawyer who had investigated the 1971 bribe scandal. He reprimanded the players for 'passivity', but no further action was taken.

The Gladbach game dampened a good deal of the euphoria among the fans that had been building up in the four years since the opening of the Westfalenstadion. It was also the beginning of a slow decline that would lead to a dramatic game on Whit Monday 1986 that shapes the club to this day. That is not to say it was all doom and gloom, though. There were redeeming features and even moments of glory – but the simple fact that Borussia Dortmund employed eleven first-team coaches in the eight years between 1978 and 1986 speaks for itself. The more so since this list doesn't even include four interim coaches who stayed for only a couple of weeks or months!

With the benefit of hindsight, the club's decline may look logical, as it went hand in hand with unpleasant events in the stands. The hooligan-infested 1980s didn't bypass Borussia, quite the contrary. One of the most notorious German gangs came from Dortmund: the Borussenfront. It wasn't formed under that name until April 1982 but could trace its origins back to a loose coalition that started in 1978. Originally just a collection of thugs, it morphed into a right-wing group when a well-known local neo-Nazi joined the hooligans. From that point on, they not only fought other clubs' gangs but also whoever they considered to be an undesirable element, even if these people happened to be Dortmund fans.

The leader of the Borussenfront didn't have to search too hard to find people who felt left behind and were looking for scapegoats. While the Ruhr area was never really the dystopia in which DCI Horst Schimanski lived and worked (not even the most industrial part of Duisburg), the bleak picture painted by the fictional crime series often felt spot on emotionally. When the Borussenfront was formed, the unemployment rate in Dortmund was 11.8 per cent. A year earlier, it had been only 8 per cent. No city in the Ruhr area, the weekly *Die Zeit* reported in February 1982, was hit so hard, and so rapidly, by the most recent recession. The piece said: 'Walking through Union, the Hoesch steel works, you fear the worst. The place looks like a ghost building. Apart from the rolling train for heavy profile steel, nothing is moving any more. Many machines give the impression they have been deserted in a hurry.'

In June 1982, the Borussenfront attacked a pub on Borsigplatz square run by Peter Erdmann (the singer of the 'BVB Waltz') and his father Werner (the former Borussia player). Werner Erdmann died nine months later. He was only 56, and his family never doubted that his death was caused by the after-effects of injuries sustained on that day. Some years later, continuous harassment broke his son Peter's spirit. Once the club's most visible and pop-ular supporter, he left Dortmund and didn't return for almost a quarter of a century.

However, although football can often resemble Greek tragedy, it does not have the same stark inevitability. And so there were many moments on the road towards the brink of the abyss when BVB came close to taking the right exit, only to find the route blocked due to circumstances beyond the club's control. In March 1979, for instance, the members elected a brilliant successor to Heinz Gün-ther, putting their trust in a quick-witted lawyer by the name of Reinhard Rauball, who, at just 32 years of age, became the young-est club president in league history. Rauball landed a major coup when he signed Udo Lattek, one of the most decorated coaches in the world. In his first season, Lattek missed qualification for the UEFA Cup by a single point and guided Borussia to their best league position, sixth place, in almost ten years.

But during the next season, Lattek's teenage son was diagnosed with leukaemia. The situation must have put an inhuman strain on the coach and it's a minor miracle the season was fairly decent for the team. The 15-year-old boy died in mid-March 1981. Although Lattek was on Dortmund's bench for the next game, a mere three days later, he eventually asked the club to be released from his contract and left for Barcelona before the season was over. Lattek got a lot of bad press at the time, as he had pledged his future to Borussia only a few days earlier (even the usually reserved and sober *Kicker* magazine compared him to 'a seasoned hustler' who had disguised his hand well). In retrospect, though, it seems harsh to criticise a man whose life must have been in turmoil. Lattek himself always said the abrupt move was 'an escape'.

Rauball then made another excellent decision when he hired Branko Zebec, the man Borussia could have signed all those years ago. Zebec was a tactical genius, the man who had pioneered zonal marking in Germany while coaching Brunswick in the mid-1970s. He was not afraid to throw young players in at the deep end – it was Zebec who gave Michael Zorc his Bundesliga debut two months after the midfielder's nineteenth birthday – and his players loved him for the trust he placed in them. The fans loved him, too. 'Branko Zebec – *der beste Mann der Welt*' they chanted on the South Stand, crowning him the best man in the world.

On the penultimate day of the season, BVB fell behind 2–0 against Ruhr rivals Bochum at home. In the second half, the team attacked the goal in front of the South Stand and the atmosphere was so electric it made the hairs on your arms stand up even while you were singing. The supporters all but sucked the ball into the back of the net. Zebec's kids won 3–2 and were rewarded with a place in the UEFA Cup. Borussia Dortmund were back in Europe after sixteen years. And what did the board do? They sacked Zebec.

The bitter truth is that the club had little choice. Since at least 19 April 1980, long before they signed him, BVB had been aware that the Yugoslav was struggling with a demon. That was the day when Zebec, as Hamburg coach, travelled to Dortmund and was so drunk that he fell asleep on the bench during the game. But you always hope that such gifted men will find a way to overcome their addictions. (Zebec's problems began with a pancreas operation in 1970 that vastly reduced his alcohol tolerance.) However, ahead of a friendly against New York Cosmos in October 1981, Zebec was involved in a case of hit-and-run driving under the influence. Six months later, a court in Dortmund found him guilty. From that moment on, his position as coach was untenable.

Having to fire such a good coach was bad enough, but something much worse followed three months later, in July 1982. Rauball announced he would step down as president because he felt unable any longer to reconcile presiding over a professional football club with running his law office. It was only from that day on that the decline seems to have been really inevitable. Rauball's successors made a series of disastrous decisions and spent large amounts of money unwisely. It would later prompt one of Rauball's most quoted lines: 'It takes a long time to build up a Bundesliga club, but you can ruin it from one day to the next.'

This is only a slight exaggeration. A mere two years after Rauball had stepped down because he could no longer run a professional club in his spare time, Borussia were relegation candidates and so broke that the DFB's alarm bells went off. Perhaps the most bizarre aspect of this mess was that the team was led by the most gifted strategist Dortmund had seen since Max Michallek had hung up his boots all those decades ago. Marcel Raducanu, Romania's Footballer of the Year in 1980, had defected from his country following a game with the national team in Dortmund. After being suspended for one year by UEFA, he signed for BVB and began to pull the strings in midfield with an elegance and technical brilliance few fans had ever seen.

On 6 November 1982, Raducanu masterminded one of the most amazing games in league history. Borussia fell behind to Arminia Bielefeld after a quarter of an hour, but Burgsmüller soon tied the game and the teams went into the interval at 1–1. After the break, the roof fell in on Arminia. Right in front of the South Stand, the hosts scored ten goals without reply to win 11–1. To this day, no Bundesliga team has scored in double digits during 45 minutes of football. Burgsmüller became a member of an elite group on that day, joining six other players who managed to score five goals in one league match. (Since then, six more footballers have found admission to this particular club. Incidentally, only one player has scored six, Cologne's Dieter Müller. Burgsmüller could have drawn level with Müller, but when Bielefeld gave away a penalty in the final minute, he let Lothar Huber, the regular taker, step up and see his name on the scoreboard.)

A few months after this memorable game, Burgsmüller left the club to slowly wind down his career. Or at least that was the plan until Otto Rehhagel convinced him to play for Werder Bremen until he was almost 41. With 135 league goals for BVB, Burgsmüller was the club's all-time leading Bundesliga scorer when he took off the yellow shirt for good. The fact that he still holds this honorary title thirty-five years (and the goalscoring heroics of someone like Stéphane Chapuisat) later tells you how gaping the hole was which 'Manni' left. For the next three years, Borussia would constantly flirt with relegation.

And worse. In November 1984, less than three years after he had relinquished his position, Reinhard Rauball was begged to come back and save the club. When he was elected president for the second time, *Kicker* magazine called him 'the attending physician who's supposed to put the patient on the road to recovery'. Borussia had accumulated debts of 8.3 million marks (back then the equivalent of £3m), a stupendous sum for those times. Rauball eased the shock by demonstrating that the net sum Borussia were in the red – total debts minus the club's assets and outstanding claims – came to a more manageable 4.45 million marks. Still, for the second time in only ten years, going bust was a real possibility. And this time it wouldn't be enough for a president to ask fans like Peter Noisten (whom Rauball knew and rated highly) for help. This time, more rapid measures had to be taken. The city of Dortmund deferred rent for the Westfalenstadion – still a municipal building – and allowed Borussia to keep money earned through the stadium's advertising boards. The players agreed to forgo all bonus payments until the end of the season.

There was another threat, though, almost as bad as immediate bankruptcy. In Germany, clubs that want to play professional football need to apply for a licence. They have to open their books to the DFB and prove they are financially healthy. It's not rare for a debt-ridden club to be granted only a provisional licence, based on certain conditions, for instance that the club has to turn a profit on the transfer market. However, there have also been cases where licences were denied outright or later revoked, which means a club is automatically demoted to the amateur level. In May 1985, the DFB informed Borussia that the club's Bundesliga licence hinged on a solid, workable financial recovery plan that had to be presented within two weeks. Somehow, Rauball managed to come up with such a concept. Still, in late September 1985, he told the press: 'We have cut our net debts by one million. However, liabilities of 3.5 million marks are still way too much.'

This was the backdrop to the Pentecost drama of 1986, one of the two tales of resurrection without which you cannot understand modern-day Borussia Dortmund. The main reason Rauball had been able to draw up a realistic recovery plan was the Westfalenstadion. When BVB drew 1–1 with a strong Bremen team (featuring Burgsmüller) on a Monday evening in March 1986, the 41,000-strong crowd translated into earnings of more than 500,000 marks. If the club could draw such crowds on a regular basis and refrained from doing anything stupid, getting back into black figures sooner or later was not rocket science. However, this plan presupposed that Borussia were in the Bundesliga and playing Bremen or Bayern rather than minnows like Solingen or Salmrohr. In the spring of 1986, though, it looked more likely that the latter would be BVB's opponents the following season.

Despite an entirely unexpected 1–0 win away at Bayern Munich in early November, Borussia finished the season in sixteenth place, just a couple of goals behind Frankfurt in fifteenth. Five years earlier (and six years later), this would have resulted in automatic relegation to the second division. But between 1982 and 1991, the Bundesliga used a strange combination of promotion and relegation play-offs to allocate the last spot in the top flight: the third-placed team in the second division played the third-worst team from the Bundesliga over two legs (for which the away-goals rule was not used). The name of the club Dortmund were going to meet in those play-offs brought back unpleasant memories.

While clubs in Germany do not have owners, the country's football has a long tradition of old-fashioned patrons – rich men who sink money into a club because they feel some sort of emotional attachment to it. One famous such patron was Hans 'Jean' Löring, a businessman from Cologne who spent thirty-five years as the president of the city's smaller club, Fortuna. Löring's dream was to establish Fortuna Cologne in the Bundesliga, but apart from one season in the early 1970s, they were perennial mainstays of the second division, doomed to be overshadowed by FC Cologne. In 1983, Fortuna Cologne achieved their greatest success by reaching the cup final, losing to their bigger crosstown rivals. In the semi-finals of that competition, Fortuna stunned Borussia Dortmund, beating the highly favoured Bundesliga side 5–0.

Now, three years later, BVB faced Fortuna again, with nothing less than a berth in the Bundesliga at stake. The first leg was played in Cologne, though not at Fortuna's cosy ground, where Dortmund had been humiliated in 1983, but in FC Cologne's spacious stadium. Dortmund's team was actually quite good on paper, much better than Fortuna's, which is perhaps not too surprising, given that it was these players' wages and transfers that had caused BVB's precarious financial situation. Goalkeeper Eike Immel, for instance, was an international and about to travel to Mexico for the World Cup. But this fine collection of players had never managed to gel into a team. And the longer the game in Cologne lasted, the more lumbering and nervous the men in black and yellow became, while the hosts looked nimble and played with the freedom from care of the underdog.

Eight minutes into the second half, former FC Cologne player and West German international Hannes Löhr, working as a pundit for television, said: 'If Fortuna can manufacture a goal here, Dortmund will be up to their necks in trouble.' Thirty seconds later, Fortuna's playmaker Bernd Grabosch received the ball in a central position, a few steps outside the box. He elegantly shimmied past two defenders and then hit the top corner with a less elegant but very effective toe-poke from near the penalty spot. Twenty minutes later, the hosts won a corner that was flicked on towards the far post, where Fortuna's Karl Richter scored with a flying header while surrounded by three passive Dortmund defenders for a final score of 2–0.

Even though the game was another embarrassing disaster, the stadium repeatedly reverberated with 'Borussia!' chants. However, they sounded defiant rather than encouraging, let alone full of hope. I spoke to a few BVB supporters who were there that day. Without exception they told me that when they had travelled back home up the A1 motorway, they were convinced their club would go down. It was a scary thought. Star striker Jürgen Wegmann had already signed for Schalke to raise a much-needed 1.3 million marks in transfer money for BVB. Immel was on record as saying he would not even consider playing in the second division. Zorc and Raducanu had not yet signed new contracts and were likely to share Immel's sentiments.

Most moods improved over the next six days, though. After all, BVB were still the Bundesliga side in this duel and would be playing at home. Also, how probable was it that the team would underperform like this twice during one week? The second leg was scheduled for the early evening of 19 May 1986, which was Whit Monday, a public holiday in Germany. The weather was almost perfect: dry, sunny and very mild. Eight hours earlier, the West German national team had left for the World Cup; Immel was supposed to follow them two days later on his own.

In front of a capacity crowd that was in very good voice, Borussia looked like a different team, sharp and assertive. From the first whistle, they put Fortuna Cologne under enormous pressure. For twelve minutes. Then they conceded the opening goal from the away leg all over again. Once more, Grabosch collected the ball in his usual playmaking position. He rode a Zorc tackle with ease and then, through the legs of two defenders, buried a left-footed shot from the edge of the box. A nine-year-old Lars Ricken, standing barely twenty yards away, watched in horror as the ball hit the back of the net. Up in the South Stand, which rose behind this goal, a 26-year-old business administrator by the name of Hans-Joachim Watzke felt his world collapse. As he told a Hamburg newspaper decades later: 'I was scared to death. At this moment, we were clinically dead.'

At half-time, a regional television station reported that Borussia had been relegated to the second division. It remains unclear whether they thought the game was over or were merely expressing a strong probability. In any case, the question appeared academic, as the hosts seemed unable to translate their dominance into scoring opportunities. This time the pundit on television was a man born in Dortmund, the famous and much-travelled coach Dettmar Cramer. A few minutes into the second half, he mentioned that he was friends with Fortuna's benefactor Jean Löring. Then he said: 'But it would be a shame, really, if Dortmund – with this catchment area, this stadium, this enthusiastic crowd – go down.'

Four minutes later, BVB substitute Ingo Anderbrügge went down in the box and the referee pointed to the spot. The player had been pushed in the back, but was that enough to hit the floor? Zorc, a most reliable penalty taker, made it 1–1 with 36 minutes still left to play. When he was back in his own half, he clenched his fists and yelled something at his teammates you did not need to hear in order to understand. While the crowd ardently chanted '*Borussia Dortmund wird nie untergehen*', the players in yellow shirts pushed further and further up field, mounting attack after attack, while the visitors were visibly and rapidly tiring. On 68 minutes, a cross from the right found Raducanu near the penalty spot. The Romanian playmaker always maintained he stood 5 feet 10 inches, but surely only on a very warm day. In his entire career, he had never scored with a header. He did now. There was plenty of time left and Borussia needed only one more goal to force a third game, two goals to stay up.

But those goals just would not come. Fortuna put everyone behind the ball and stopped building from the rear entirely – they just hoofed the ball into the opposition half. Cross upon cross, corner upon corner sailed into Cologne's box, but there was always a leg, some other limb or goalkeeper Jacek Jarecki in the way. Five minutes from time, Wegmann volleyed the ball against the cross-bar, 30 seconds later Zorc missed the target by inches, then Jarecki brilliantly parried a flying header from Wegmann. That was the moment when the first people began to sit down on the South Stand, unable to watch any more. Some covered their heads with flags and began to sob silently.

With 32 seconds left in the season, Immel hurried to take a goal-kick and start the final attack of the game. The ball was still in motion when the goalkeeper knocked it to a teammate, but the referee turned a blind eye and didn't blow his whistle to have the goal-kick retaken. With nine seconds left on the clock, Anderbrügge sent in a low cross almost from the byline. Jarecki got both hands to the ball at the near post but palmed it awkwardly into the goalmouth. It almost went past Wegmann, who was a step ahead of the ball. But only almost. Wegmann stuck out his left leg, made contact with the ball and somehow nudged it goalwards. It gently rolled across the line with seven seconds left.

Immediately after Fortuna had kicked off, the referee ended the game. President Rauball ran onto the pitch to embrace the players. Most of the fans needed a few minutes to stomach what they had just seen, but then hundreds scaled the fences and invaded the pitch. Rauball was in the middle of a television interview when supporters lifted him onto their shoulders and triumphantly carried him away from the camera. Bewildering scenes took place – some fans even began to cut up the pitch to take home souvenirs. It was bewildering because Borussia had done nothing more than live to fight another day. But deep down inside, the players and the fans alike knew that there was no way they would now lose the deciding third game. And they didn't, winning 8–0 at a neutral venue, in Düsseldorf.

'I have never, ever heard a louder cheer than the one that greeted Wegmann's goal,' Lars Ricken says today. 'It was totally incredible. Just three years later, we won the cup. Imagine that! It wouldn't have been possible without this milestone, this unbelievable second game against Fortuna Cologne. And maybe none of what has happened since would have been possible without Wegmann's goal.' Indeed. Although BVB might have bounced back quickly, it's hard to imagine today's club without this scrappy, fluky goal scored by the Essen-born Jürgen Wegmann. The next time Borussia would come back from the brink of total disaster, the decision was not made on a football pitch. So it's probably not an exaggeration to say that what has come to be known as 'the Wegmann goal' was the most important goal in Borussia Dortmund's history.

And some people think it kick-started more than just the sporting renaissance. Reinhard Beck was then in his mid-twenties and just a normal fan. In the following decade he would first help set up the biggest BVB online fanzine and then orchestrate the formation of the club's fan division before joining Borussia as the club's head of human resources. He has seen many big games and has celebrated many trophies. Still, he says: 'This 1986 game was the most emotional experience I've ever had with Borussia. People who weren't there can't understand this, but I'm getting goose bumps right now, just from thinking back. When I close my eyes, I can still hear how people screamed after that third goal.' It may have been a primal scream. Michael Winkelkötter, who has hardly missed a game since the early 1970s, says: 'As far as I'm concerned, we have a South Stand since Wegmann's goal. It was the moment the stand woke up and came alive. Ever since, it has had a hammering pulse. The goal also created Borussia as a mass movement. When we went to Düsseldoerf for the third game, the whole motorway was black and yellow.

People began following the club in massive numbers. It's normal now, but it began in 1986. Just one year later, everybody went to Frankfurt.'

He is referring to the last game of the following season. Under the young coach Reinhard Saftig, who had taken over the team just three weeks before the first game against Fortuna Cologne, BVB had played a brilliant season and were close to securing a UEFA Cup spot. They needed a win away at Eintracht Frankfurt. There were 25,000 people on hand and conservative estimates put the number of BVB supporters at 15,000. The game was scoreless for an hour (Zorc had missed a penalty – a true rarity), then a striker called Norbert Dickel broke the deadlock and Borussia went on to win 4–0. Only a few years later, a dodgy knee would force Dickel to hang up his boots and become Borussia's iconic stadium announcer, but not before he got to score two even more important goals.

Borussia did well during that UEFA Cup campaign and would have reached the quarter-finals if it hadn't been for an inexplicable collapse in Bruges, where BVB blew a 3–0 lead from the first leg and went out after extra time. More momentous, though, was the very first round of the competition. Borussia were drawn against Celtic and although the Scottish club didn't have a particular reputation for violent fans, Dortmund officials were worried. Gerd Kolbe, the resident club historian, was the municipal press officer at the time. 'The head of police came to me,' he recalled. 'He said: "DFB and UEFA are totally against this, but what do you think about bringing the two sets of fans together before the game, on some central square, and having a party?" I was fascinated by the idea. Back then we had the Borussenfront in Dortmund, pretty dangerous terrain. The atmosphere could be explosive, especially when we were playing non-German clubs. I had always wondered what we could do about this.'

The plan was nothing short of radical. Violence at football matches had been a central problem of this decade, such a pressing matter that even the crime series starring DCI Horst Schimanski had devoted an episode to the hooligan issue in 1984. So far, it had been standard police tactics to separate the two fan groups; now the suggestion was to bring them together! But the party on 29 September 1987 was a success beyond anyone's wildest dreams, as the fans from Scotland and Germany bonded over drink and song. The only tense moment was based on a misunderstanding. 'The liaison officer of the British Army of the Rhine almost ruined the whole thing,' Kolbe recalls. 'He said: "Why don't you get the Gordon Highlanders marching band? They'll be wearing kilts and playing bagpipes." That sounded good. What he didn't tell me was that the Regiment had seen active service in Northern Ireland, fighting the Catholic Irish. As they climbed onto the stage, a Celtic fan came up to me and said: "Listen, get those guys off the stage in a hurry. Don't ask, just do it, man!"'

'Everything was brilliant, apart from that military band,' George Docherty, a Celtic fan from Edinburgh, agrees. 'There was a big interest in the game among Celtic supporters, because Murdo MacLeod had just moved from Celtic to Dortmund. I was twenty years old and it was the first time I was travelling to the continent with Celtic. I still vividly remember the fan party on the Old Market Square. I asked around among the Celtic fans, but nobody could remember any club ever having done anything like this for them.'

The unusual party not only resulted in good relations between the Hoops and Borussia (Docherty is now a member of the Edinburgh Borussen, a hundred-member strong Dortmund supporters' club founded in 2004), it also set a precedent, as many future European games in Dortmund would feature such a fan party. And the same month the party was staged, the Dortmund Fan Project came into being. Such initiatives were springing up all across West Germany in an effort to deal with the hooligan problem. The Fan Projects, still going today, are not directly linked to the clubs, but are financed through government funds as well as by the DFB and the League. The Fan Projects employ social workers who offer supporters, particularly juveniles, help and assistance. It is picture-book preventive social work, only directed at a specific group of adolescents.

And so the decade that had been tainted by fan violence and crowd trouble slowly but steadily began to look very different. At least in Dortmund, the dark age of the thug was over when BVB supporters and Celtic fans partied in the streets of Dortmund in 1987. Although, of course, the mother of all black-and-yellow parties was yet to come.

CHAPTER 7

On a cloudy but mild morning in December of 1988, television presenter Rob McCaffrey walked into the Manchester City club shop and asked store manageress Janice Monk: 'What type of bananas have you got?'

Without missing a beat, Monk replied: 'Oh, we've got small ones and large ones. We've even got a shirt and a hat to keep them warm.'

'So these go on the bananas?' McCaffrey wanted to know.

'On the bananas, yes.'

'How many have you sold of these?'

'Oh, hundreds and hundreds.'

'Where is it all going to end?' an incredulous McCaffrey asked.

'When we get to the cup final,' Monk said, laughing.

McCaffrey, then working for Granada TV, was in town to report on what Britain was referring to as 'the inflatable banana craze' that had gripped Maine Road. 'It's become fashionable to have bananas,' a young girl told him. 'You can't be seen without a banana.' When McCaffrey asked three City supporters why in heaven's name they were carrying plastic fruits to the game, he was told it went back to the Hungarian striker Imre Varadi, whose nickname was Banana.

As author Gary James found in researching his 1989 book *From Maine Men to Banana Citizens*, the craze actually started with a fan called Frank Newton, who collected toys and thus happened to possess a five-foot inflatable banana. On a whim, he carried it with him to the game between City and Plymouth Argyle in August

1987 and since the fans around him found this rather amusing, he continued to do so. Four months later, Varadi picked up his nickname due to a misheard chant. The City fans put two and two together – and the craze took off for good.

Club secretary Bernard Halford told McCaffrey: 'This is putting the fun side back into the game and taking away the thing about hooligans, Stanley knives and people being mugged. It's absolutely tremendous and the club is wholeheartedly behind it.' It did not stop at bananas, though. In March 1989, the BBC's Michael Peschardt reported: 'The craze has certainly spread. At Grimsby, it's haddock taking over the terracing. The food fad is gaining strength. At Bury Football Club, on Saturday, 3,000 inflatable black puddings will be going on sale for the first time.'

The craze also transcended borders and spread to the continent, where nobody picked up the fad more enthusiastically or famously than Borussia Dortmund's support. Doing something as silly as waving an inflatable banana on the terraces fitted the zeitgeist, as BVB fans were spearheading the movement to, as Halford said, put the fun side back into the game. And they had two big advantages over their Maine Road counterparts. One: yellow was Dortmund's colour. Two: unlike City, they would indeed get to the cup final.

It is unclear exactly at which point the inflatable toys appeared on the South Stand. When Dortmund won 3–2 away at Schalke, then in the second division, in December 1988 in the cup's round of 16, no bananas could be spotted among the sizeable travelling support. But when Borussia beat a VfB Stuttgart side starring Jürgen Klinsmann 2–0 in the semi-finals in early May 1989, the goals were greeted by celebratory banana-waving even in the North Stand. So the plastic fruits must have arrived at the Westfalenstadion at one point after the winter break, which ended in mid-February 1989. (When BVB drew 1–1 with Bayern Munich in April, there were lots of yellow balloons on the South Stand and also a few bananas.)

However, the Dortmund bananas would become synonymous with a particular game, the cup final in Berlin on 24 June. So synonymous, in fact, that many Germans have no idea the fad originated in Manchester but believe the craze began with Dortmund fans and on this particular day. Werner Wirsing, then the club's treasurer, recalled: 'The bananas were fashionable at the time. So I called Chiquita – but they wanted 70 marks per banana! I replied: "Listen, folks, I'm ready and willing to promote your product with our fans. We don't even want money from you for that. Just send us 1,000 inflatable bananas as soon as you can."' Chiquita quickly realised Wirsing was right, this was an incredible marketing opportunity. And so for most neutrals the most lasting image of the 1989 cup final was the sight of the away end (for some reason, Dortmund are nearly always allocated the away section when they reach the final in Berlin) as a sea of yellow inflatable bananas.

Dortmund had a team to match their support's exuberance, the nucleus of the side that Ottmar Hitzfeld would soon lead to dizzying heights. The skilful and fast midfielder Andreas Möller, then 21 years old, had joined Borussia from his hometown club Eintracht Frankfurt for 2.7 million marks. Young centre-back Thomas Helmer would soon win his first cap for West Germany. Partnering Dickel upfront was the veteran Frank Mill, who knew every trick in the book and some that weren't even in the book. (Mill was the third Essen-born striker within only a few years to write his name into the black-and-yellow history books, after Burgsmüller and Wegmann.) The Glaswegian Murdo MacLeod, meanwhile, had quickly grown into a firm fan favourite – the first, but not the last Scot BVB fans would warm to. He also spoke astonishingly good German, considering this was only his second season with the club. Finally, there was Michael Rummenigge, the younger brother of former Bayern star Karl-Heinz, a two-time Ballon d'Or winner.

His signing in the summer of 1988 from Bayern for 1.3 million marks had caused some unrest among the fans. In 1984, when

Rummenigge was only 20 and sported a preppy look, he had answered questions from Bayern fans via telephone and in front of a television camera. At one point, he fielded a call from a metalworker who complained that footballers were overpaid. Michael Rummenigge replied that there were 50,000 metalworkers in the country but only 500 footballers. Then he informed the caller in a condescending tone that he was not receiving top wages because he was not doing 'top work'. The incident cemented Rummenigge's image as an arrogant brat and when he was linked with BVB, many fans were annoyed.

But in August 1988, shortly after the beginning of the new season, the Sunday paper *Welt am Sonntag* said: 'A dandy, widely regarded as notoriously unlikeable, has moved to Dortmund. Michael Rummenigge, yesterday a fancy schmancy in Munich, today in the city of steel mills and blast furnaces? It just had to go wrong. Yet it didn't.' It didn't, because Rummenigge turned out to be a man who had learned from his mistakes. He knew he had to approach people on their own terms, not on his, and he made no qualms about the fact he had joined Dortmund precisely because he would be facing antagonism. He did it to grow up. As his BVB coach put it: 'His big brother had almost become a complex for him. He had to leave Bayern.'

This coach was no longer Reinhard Saftig but another recent arrival, the 40-year-old, Stuttgart-born Horst Köppel, who had some shared history with BVB. Köppel played on the great Gladbach team that crossed swords with Liverpool so often during the 1970s and would have started the 12–0 match had he not been injured. His first proper coaching job had been with Arminia Bielefeld. It was Köppel who sat on the bench when the team was hammered 11–1 in Dortmund.

Like the majority of successful Dortmund coaches, Köppel was first and foremost a fine man-manager. He did not adhere to the school that says coaches must rule with an iron fist; instead, he regularly asked his players for their opinion and then actually listened to them. The 1989 cup final was a good case in point. For the first time in more than twenty years, Borussia had the chance to win silverware. But there was a pressing problem. Köppel's best goalscorer, Norbert Dickel, had undergone a knee operation two days after the semi-final. He hadn't played a game in six weeks and couldn't even train with the team until two days before the final. During the night before the match, Köppel woke up at two o'clock in the morning and began pacing up and down in his room. Finally, he decided to take a risk and start Dickel, then he went back to sleep. But the next day, he had second thoughts. If Dickel was unable to perform, the press would tear Köppel apart. Eventually, the coach changed the line-up again: Dickel would start on the bench. That's when the three team representatives – Zorc, Helmer and goalkeeper Wolfgang 'Teddy' de Beer – pleaded with their coach to return to the original plan. Finally, even the club president raised his voice. The lawyer Gerd Niebaum, who had replaced Rauball three years previously, also felt the team needed Dickel so much that a gamble had to be made. At last, Köppel was convinced. Dickel was in the starting XI, suspect knee and all.

You could understand the coach's soul-searching, because there was next to no margin for error. In the final Borussia would be playing an excellent Werder Bremen team that had won the league in the previous season and finished seven points ahead of BVB in the one just past. It meant Köppel's Dortmund side went into the final as underdogs. That, however, had never stopped the great team of the 1960s, which had overcome the odds in 1963 when they beat FC Cologne, and in 1966 when they defeated Liverpool. Still, Köppel needed all the help he could get.

A lot of it came from the fans. The most popular chant during the last week of the league season on the South Stand had been 'Forty thousand are going to Berlin' – and they did. Dickel later remembered: 'When I stepped out of the tunnel, the sheer number of our fans and the atmosphere were overwhelming. I had to look somebody in the eye to regain my composure. I saw our president,

Gerd Niebaum, and thought he would give me strength. But then I realised he was struggling with his emotions in the same way that I was.'

In those pre-reunification days, getting to the cup final in West Berlin was not an easy matter or a pleasant journey. There were special motorways for westerners travelling through East Germany: *Transitstrecken*, or transit routes. They were heavily guarded by the East German police and the story was that you'd better not break down on one of those roads, because the police were always on the lookout for hard Western currency and would charge you a lot of money. However, these adverse conditions were exactly why the DFB had permanently moved the cup final to West Berlin in 1985. It was a gesture meant to underline that the city was part of West Germany. The final between Dortmund and Bremen would be the last for which football fans had to traverse a foreign, even hostile country, though nobody knew it at the time. In the summer of 1989, there were no indications that a peaceful revolution would bring down the Berlin Wall only five months later.

More help came courtesy of Frank Mill. In the build-up to the final, the striker wondered if there was some sort of good-luck charm that could be introduced. He hit upon hooped socks. BVB players had worn them until the summer of 1965, when the plain yellow socks that would be an integral part of the kit for more than two decades came into use. Mill suggested bringing back the traditional *Ringelsocken*, ringed socks, and Köppel agreed, as he tended to be superstitious, like most football people.

Dortmund needed the fans, and the hooped socks, because Werder, an experienced team that was used to playing big games, got off to a flying start against the players in yellow shirts, who were evidently feeling butterflies in their stomachs. Bremen's Karl-Heinz Riedle, a young striker from deepest Bavaria who would one day score a historic brace for Borussia, put the favourites ahead after a quarter of an hour and nobody knows along which lines this warm early evening in Berlin would have developed if

Borussia had not found a quick reply. And if Dickel's knee had not held up. But they did and it did. Six minutes after Bremen's goal, Mill raced down the left flank, briefly looked up to see where his striking partner was and then sent a low, outswinging cross towards the penalty spot, where Dickel tied the game with a fine first-time shot.

Borussia now became a lot more confident and adventurous. Mill was seemingly everywhere, as epitomised by the two moments that decided the game. Nine minutes into the second half, Helmer tried to clear a cross but mishit the ball. His only mistake of the game forced his own goalkeeper into a save and the rebound fell to Riedle, who nudged the ball towards an open net. A fraction of a second before it crossed the line, Mill was there to hoof it into touch. Four minutes later, Zorc volleyed a speculative cross into Werder's box. It was the sort of cross normally meant for Dickel, so Bremen's sweeper stayed close to the striker. But he was marking the wrong man. Mill rose into the air and headed the ball into the top corner.

Bremen, who were already playing with three strikers upfront, now had to become even more offence-minded. On 71 minutes, they were hit on the break. Mill saw his shot saved but regained possession. He spotted Dickel on the other flank and chipped the ball over to the man with the dodgy knee. Instead of trapping the ball, Dickel volleyed it into the far corner from twenty yards. Only three minutes later, substitute Michael Lusch finished off another counter-attack with Dortmund's fourth goal for a sensational 4–1 scoreline. To say that the ground, or at least the yellow part of it, was now a madhouse does not even begin to describe the atmosphere.

Kicker called the match 'a party in black and yellow' and when the team paraded the trophy around Dortmund one day later, cheered by more than 150,000 people, the magazine spoke of 'almost South European enthusiasm and an ecstasy that couldn't have been any stronger in Naples'. During the official victory banquet in Berlin, president Niebaum had addressed the squad and the club employees by saying: 'Our new team has breathed the spirit of the old Borussia. Our dream is one day winning another European title, as we did in 1966 when we beat Liverpool in Glasgow.'

Barely three years earlier, it would have been ridiculous for a BVB president to evoke the club's golden years and express even the faintest hope they could ever be coming back. But by June 1989, everything had changed. During the next weeks, the club sold 12,055 season tickets for the coming season. It may not have been much by Naples' standards, where Maradona's Napoli regularly sold 50,000 season tickets, but it was three times the league average. And the figure soon soared into regions hitherto unknown in Germany. In 1992, Borussia would sell 26,400 season tickets – at a time when the league average was 6,300 – and reach 45,500 before the 1990s were over.

At first glance, all this enthusiasm and nearly boundless optimism that suddenly carried the club seemed incongruous with the Ruhr area's economic situation. Once-majestic companies continued to crumble and people kept losing jobs. In Dortmund, the number of people employed by what was (not so) jokingly referred to as the Holy Trinity, namely the steel, coal and beer industries, had sunk dramatically during the 1980s – from 42,000 to 18,000 – and would be cut in half again during the 1990s. And yet something was stirring. The new catchphrase was 'structural change', meaning the gradual replacement of the Ruhr region's economic monocultures by encouraging diversification and by branching out into businesses not normally associated with the area.

Dortmund was more successful at it than most other cities in the Ruhr area. In the late 1960s, a Technical University had been set up less than three miles west of the Westfalenstadion, teaching chemistry, physics, electrical engineering and economics. In 1985, the *Technologiepark* was built right next to the university, a business park for technology companies. The financial sector also became more and more important. It's not an accident that the players who lifted the 1989 cup endorsed the local health insurance company Continentale on their shirts (or that the naming rights for the ground are today held by the financial services company Signal Iduna).

Clearly, changes were underway. Even Horst Schimanski's Ruhr area now looked less gritty and not quite as grim as it used to be. In an episode that premiered in early June 1991, the inspector went camping in the Duisburg hinterland, a strikingly rural territory where people bred horses and were sustained by their livestock. Needless to say, the harmless outing became a descent into a hate-filled, violent netherworld that gleefully toyed with elements of John Boorman's 1972 landmark shocker *Deliverance*. But for many viewers of the *Tatort* series it may have been the first time they realised that even the most desolate parts of the Ruhr area were just a short drive away from the woods and the farming areas that dominated this region before the Industrial Revolution took hold.

Barely seven months later, on 29 December 1991, the last regular *Tatort* episode starring Schimanski aired. In the very last scene, he flew a hang-glider above Duisburg, looking at the remaining steelworks from high above. Schimanski's last exclamation was similar to his first: 'Shit!' But now the word was spoken with glee. The final shot showed him flying towards the sunset above gently rolling hills and small lakes. It felt like the end of an era. But it was also the beginning of a new one. Because when the character that had so intensely chronicled the Ruhr area's stubborn defiance in the face of seemingly terminal decline left German screens, Borussia Dortmund – a team that had once been written off, together with the entire surrounding area – held down first place in the Bundesliga.

The man who had orchestrated this rise was not Horst Köppel, though. In his third season with the club, 1990–91, the team was expected to reach the UEFA Cup, although it had lost an important player – Andreas Möller, who returned to Frankfurt under somewhat controversial circumstances, souring his relationship with the fans. BVB then got off to the worst possible start, getting knocked out in the first round of the cup by a fourth-division team. (Such cup debacles were about to become a club speciality.) Although results improved, the team continued to struggle, especially at home. Many observers felt the crowd was partly to blame, as it expected non-stop attacking football from the players even when a more patient approach might be called for. Then, after the end of the winter break, Borussia just couldn't win any more. There was no logical explanation – it just happened. In April, following a 3–0 defeat at home against Frankfurt (in which Möller scored, of course), Köppel announced he would step down at the end of the season, one year before his contract was due to run out.

It was at this point that Borussia's business manager became a crucial figure in the club's future. His name was Michael Meier. At 41 years of age, he was relatively young, considering he'd already had some success with FC Cologne and Bayer Leverkusen. Even though those teams are both Rhineland clubs, Meier originally came from the northern edge of the Ruhr area, having grown up just eight miles outside Dortmund. He went to a Jesuit convent school and worked as an auditor until the football bug bit him and he jumped in at the deep end with Cologne. In 1989, he became Borussia's business manager and when Köppel announced his farewell, Meier suggested a successor hardly anyone had ever heard of.

'I first met Ottmar Hitzfeld in 1988,' Meier says. 'At that time, I was working for Bayer Leverkusen and we needed a new coach. Ottmar was having a lot of success in Switzerland at the time with Aarau, a small club, so he came to our attention. Not many people in Germany had heard his name and those who had thought he was Swiss. But when I talked to him, I came away mightily impressed. However, there was one other candidate: Rinus Michels. When we agreed terms with him, I told Ottmar: "I'm sorry, but if Leverkusen can get someone as experienced and famous as Rinus Michels, we just have to do it. But one day, I want to work with you."'

These were no empty words and Hitzfeld must have known it. Three years later, Meier convinced Borussia's board members to give a chance to somebody they didn't really know even though he had just won back-to-back titles in Switzerland with Grasshoppers. Then he dialled Hitzfeld's number. Meier picks up the story: 'Ottmar answered the phone and the first thing he said was: "I was expecting your call."'

It was understandable why only a few people were familiar with Hitzfeld's name, even though he held an unusual distinction: on 13 May 1977, he had scored six goals for VfB Stuttgart in the second division against Jahn Regensburg, which is today still the record for that level of the league pyramid. But he had spent the previous thirteen years in Switzerland, five as a player, eight as a coach. Which is why, once Hitzfeld had agreed to take over Borussia, Meier asked him how he felt about a 21-year-old Swiss striker called Stéphane Chapuisat.

It is often assumed that Hitzfeld brought Chapuisat with him from Switzerland, or at least alerted Borussia to the young man who had won his first cap the previous November. In fact, it was the former German international Felix Magath who signed him. Before he got into coaching, Magath worked as the business manager for Bayer Uerdingen. His coach there was Timo Konietzka, the ex-Dortmund player. Konietzka had spent a lot of time in Switzerland and knew the league well. Magath and Konietzka signed Chapuisat from Lausanne-Sport (after some wrangling with the club) for 2.2 million marks in November 1990. The young striker was supposed to make his debut after the end of the winter break, in February. But during one of his first appearances for his new German club, at an indoor tournament in Düsseldorf, Chapuisat suffered a serious knee injury that kept him out of action until mid-April, by which time Uerdingen were mired in the relegation zone – and Meier sensed there was a chance to get the player if Uerdingen went down.

Hitzfeld told Meier what he expected to hear, that Chapuisat could be a hit in Germany. The press got wind of it and the Swiss was linked with a move from Uerdingen to Borussia even before the two sides met in late May, for what was suddenly an important game for both clubs. Dortmund won 1–0 to move away from the drop zone for good, while for all practical purposes condemning the visitors to relegation. Although it was a scrappy, ugly match – Uerdingen wasted a penalty when it was still 0–0 and the winning goal came five minutes from time – and a disappointing season altogether, the fans were absolutely brilliant, doing the Mexican wave and celebrating their team. The outgoing Köppel called them 'fantastic' and president Niebaum said: 'Today it was the fans who put in all the hard work, while the team could only applaud.' He also promised to cut the ticket prices in half for the first game of the next season, as a thank you for the patience of the supporters.

Who knows, maybe the crowd was in such good spirits because they had read about the Chapuisat rumours and liked what they saw. At one point in the first half, the Swiss received the ball in an inside-left position and instead of bearing down on goal allowed himself to be forced towards the touchline by Dortmund's right-back Günter Kutowski. Chapuisat kept possession by putting his body between the ball and his opponent, seemingly waiting for a teammate to help him. In reality, though, he was waiting for a teammate of Kutowski's. At the exact moment when a second Dortmund player arrived at the scene to help Kutowski separate the Swiss from the ball, Chapuisat abruptly cut inside, using the split-second in which the two Dortmund players were unsure which of them should apply a tackle, to slip through them and run into the box with the ball at his feet. It was Chapuisat's signature move. Although Dortmund's fans would see it many times over the next eight years, the cheeky Houdini act never failed to delight them.

Hitzfeld and Chapuisat would become the club's biggest icons of the decade. One, the coach, respected for his fairness and humanity, the second gaffer, after Branko Zebec, to be christened the 'best man in the world' by the fans in song. The other, the player, revered for his modesty and for the fact that, for whatever reason, he shunned all offers from big European clubs to stay in Dortmund and become, at the point of his return to Switzerland, the Bundesliga's all-time leading foreign goalscorer. However, their joint start was rather inauspicious.

I reminded Hitzfeld of this more than twenty years later. In 2013, Sky Germany's concept for their live Champions League coverage was to invite a football writer onto the show who would discuss the events of the night with two celebrity pundits. When I was asked to take part on the day Dortmund played Shakhtar Donetsk, all they had to tell me, really, was that I would spend the evening in the company of Ruud Gullit and Ottmar Hitzfeld. I had written columns together with the Dutchman (during the 2006 World Cup) but, for some strange reason, never even spoken to the German. So I jumped at the chance to meet the man who was then, and still is, the most successful coach in Borussia Dortmund's history.

At the beginning of the show, we walked down a staircase, one after the other, to a theme song we had picked while the host of the show introduced us to the studio audience (and, of course, the one million people watching at home). While I was ambling down the steps, and the Fall were belting out 'Kicker Conspiracy', the presenter centred my entire introduction around the fact that I was born in Dortmund and would not be able to watch the team at the ground that night.

Later, when the games kicked off, we all retreated to a small, living-room-styled backstage area on the first floor to follow the matches on a few flat-screen TVs. Hitzfeld immediately made a beeline for me, offered his hand and said: 'So, you grew up as a Dortmund fan?' I explained that it was a family thing, that my older brother had been among the scattered few fans who followed the club home and away even back when they were in the regional second division. Hitzfeld was honestly, and movingly, delighted to meet someone from Dortmund. (After the end of the show, when we were all offered a glass of wine to celebrate and I politely asked for a beer instead, he burst into laughter and yelled: 'That's Dortmund for you! When I joined the club, the first thing Michael Meier told me was that I would now have to drink beer instead of wine!') We talked for a few minutes about the club and its fans and then I couldn't resist any longer.

'You know, there was a time when I went to the games wearing my scarf and maybe a hat, like everyone else,' I remarked. 'But I stopped doing this in August 1991. Ever since, I have not taken a scarf to a game.'

'Why's that?' he said, with a blink of an eye that had me suspect he knew where we were heading. 'What happened?'

'Well, we got this new coach nobody knew, some Swiss guy,' I began. 'One of his very first games was the derby against Schalke. We lost 5–2. I was so annoyed that I stopped wearing the club's colours in protest.'

Hitzfeld threw his arms into the air. 'But nobody had told me how important the derby is!' he cried in mock protest. 'I had lived in Switzerland for more than twenty years, I knew nothing about Dortmund. Nobody told me that this was the game you mustn't lose. Besides, I had my hands full winning the power struggle with Frank Mill.'

'Well,' I conceded, 'I guess you came very close to making up for it by winning two league titles and the Champions League. But only close.' Then we had a good laugh about it all and he asked me to call him 'Ottmar'.

But I hadn't been joking when I said I was annoyed. Everybody was by the end of August 1991, when Borussia were languishing in tenth place, having conceded the second-most goals in the league. Four days later, the team blew a 2–0 lead against second-division Hannover 96 in the cup and lost 3–2 at home. Hitzfeld had to do something. And he did. He announced he would bench the immensely popular goalkeeper Teddy de Beer and replace him with a Dortmund-born kid who had just turned twenty: Stefan Klos. Hitzfeld said: 'I have to play the people I trust.'

As would be so often the case during his coaching career, his trust was repaid. During the next eight months, Borussia lost only two more league games. When a goal by the young Danish striker Flemming Povlsen beat Karlsruhe in late November, the team found themselves level on points with Frankfurt and Stuttgart at the top of the heap. One week later, Borussia won sole possession of first place and would stay there for the next nine weeks of what was a mammoth season. For the first and only time, the Bundesliga had been expanded to twenty teams to accommodate two clubs – Rostock and Dresden – from a country that had ceased to exist, East Germany.

During the first half of 1992, Borussia mania reached a hitherto unknown scale in and around Dortmund. It was not just that the club had a real chance at their first-ever league title (and their first national championship since 1963); it was also that people were simply mad about the team. Hitzfeld's first side was unquestionably the most beloved BVB XI since the mid-1960s and would remain the most popular until Jürgen Klopp assembled his first gegenpressing machine twenty years later. The quietly prolific Chapuisat, who scored twenty goals, and the bubbling Povlsen were particular fan favourites; then there were local lads Zorc and Klos and people like the hard-working midfielder Knut Reinhardt, whose every touch of the ball was greeted with a drawn-out 'Knuuuut'.

It is hard to say how many fans followed this team to Duisburg on the last day of the season. It was a sell-out game, which means 30,175 were on hand. It is certainly not an exaggeration to say that two-thirds of them were there to support the visitors (while some 30,000 were watching the game on a giant screen in the centre of Dortmund), despite the fact BVB's chances were very slim. Borussia could only lift the league title if they won their game while both Frankfurt and Stuttgart dropped a point each. That seemed

TOP 15 january 1911: Borussia, still wearing the blue-and-white kit with the red sash, play their first-ever game on White Meadow. The man with the walking stick in the right half of the photo is Karl Hagedorn. His daughter Ilse shares some memories in this book.
MIDDLE 1913: Borussia's first black-and-yellow kit. The change came about when the members of Britannia Dortmund joined BVB and suggested Borussia should adopt their old colours.
ABOVE 1949: Although Borussia have lost their first final for the national championship, the players are given a hero's welcome in Dortmund. The fans carry them on their shoulders through a city visibly ravaged by the war. (Dortmund City Archive)

In the 1956–57 season, the 'Three Alfredos' — from left to right: Alfred Preissler, Alfred Kelbassa and Alfred Niepieklo — led Borussia to the second national championship in a row. Another Alfred (Schmidt) had to bide his time. (Gerd Kolbe)

Friedhelm Konietzka was known to all and sundry as 'Timo' due to his trademark crew cut that made him look like Soviet general Semyon Timoshenko. He was one of Borussia's most dangerous forwards in the first half of the 1960s and holds the distinction of being the man who scored the first-ever Bundesliga goal. (Alamy)

Lothar Emmerich (left) and Sigfried Held linked up for Borussia and the national team (both played in the 1966 World Cup final). They were so lethal that Willie Waddell christened them the 'Terrible Twins'. (Images Sporfoto)

In 1966, Borussia became the first German club to lift a European trophy when they won the Cup Winners' Cup final against Liverpool. The man holding the large trophy is captain Wolfgang Paul. Lothar Emmerich, on the far right, has been presented with a miniature version, as he was the competition's top scorer. (PA Images)

TOP 6 September 1969: The infamous 'Dog Bite' incident. Schalke's Friedel Rausch (centre) is being bitten in the backside, while either the same or, more probably, another dog has already sunk his teeth into the leg of Gerd Neuser (left). (PA Images/Sporfoto)

BELOW 1979: Borussia's young president Reinhard Rauball (left) has landed a major coup by signing Udo Lattek, one of the most successful coaches in the world. The glass of brandy on the table is Lattek's. (PA Images)

ABOVE 19 May 1986: Borussia come back from the dead against Fortuna Cologne and the fans invade the pitch, even though all BVB have really done is force a deciding third game in this dramatic promotion and relegation play-off. The player is Ingo Anderbrügge, who set up Jürgen Wegmann's immortal last-gasp goal. (Horst Müller Ltd/www.foto-horstmuller.de)

BELOW 24 June 1989: The bananas are in full bloom as Borussia win their first piece of silverware in 23 years. Some 40,000 fans followed the team to Berlin for the cup final and indulged in the inflatable-bananas craze which had reached Dortmund a few months earlier. (PA Images)

TOP 28 May 1997: Lars Ricken's lob from thirty yards stunned a favoured Juventus team in the Champions League final. (In 2009, when Borussia celebrated their centenary, the fans voted this strike the greatest goal of the club's first 100 years.) (PA Images)

ABOVE LEFT Matthias Sammer brandishes the Champions League trophy. His relationship with BVB fans was and is a complicated roller-coaster ride. Maybe all's well that ends well — in March 2018, he returned to the club in an advisory role. (Getty Images)

ABOVE RIGHT Paul Lambert, on the other hand, was loved immediately and unconditionally by the black-and-yellow army. His farewell in November 1997 was one of the last truly emotional and communal moments at the ground until Jürgen Klopp made emotional and communal moments the norm. (The spelling indicates the sign was made by a German.) (PA Images/Sporfoto)

ABOVE 12 May 2007: Polish striker Euzebiusz Smolarek climbs the fence in front of the South Stand to celebrate his goal that has just decided one of the most fondly remembered derbies. In an otherwise dismal year, Borussia beat Schalke 2−0 and prevented their most bitter rivals from winning the league. (AP Images)

ABOVE RIGHT 23 May 2008: Nobody knew it at the time, but the next golden era was about to begin, as a certain Jürgen Klopp was presented as the club's new coach. (And, no, there was no glass of brandy on the table.) (Getty Images)

RIGHT 19 December 2009: On a fiendishly cold day, the fans present a large tifo to celebrate 100 years of Borussia Dortmund. Everybody in that picture is mentioned in this book. (PA Images/Sporfoto)

TOP 9 April 2013: More famous, though, is this tifo — and the same goes for the game. Ahead of the Champions League match against Malaga, the fans expressed their yearning for the trophy. Then their team scored two goals in injury time to reach the semi-final. (PA Images/Sporfoto)

ABOVE LEFT 28 May 2017: Thomas Tuchel kisses the cup his team has won on the previous day. It was Borussia's first trophy in five years. In all likelihood, Tuchel knew it would also be his last a BVB coach. (Getty Images)

ABOVE RIGHT The Westfalenstadion, now officially named after a local insurance company. Franz Beckenbauer once likened the stadium to La Scala, the famous opera house in Milan, *The Times* voted it the best football ground in the world and many BVB fans simply refer to it as the 'Temple'. (Getty Images) highly unlikely when the games kicked off, but for 86 minutes, everything went Borussia's way. A Chapuisat goal was the difference between the two sides in Duisburg, while Frankfurt and Stuttgart were drawing their own matches. Then, with a mere four minutes left in the season, Stuttgart scored a winning goal at Leverkusen to claim the 1992 Bundesliga trophy on goal difference.

Hitzfeld and his players were devastated – until the fans invaded the pitch and began to parade them around the stadium on their shoulders, just as if the last few minutes had not happened. 'Even if we can't call ourselves champions,' Hitzfeld told the reporters, 'our fans can.' And Niebaum said: 'This is a historic day.' He cannot have known how right he was. Because as bizarre as it may sound, Dortmund's second-place finish was exactly what the club needed to become what almost the whole of the country had been waiting for – a proper rival for Bayern Munich.

As mentioned before, it is one of the strangest facets of German football that it has failed to produce the sort of oligarchy that characterises the game in Spain, Italy or England. There is no small group of big clubs that perennially finish there or thereabouts, there isn't even an equivalent of the Real/Barcelona or Inter/Juventus rivalry. There is only Bayern Munich. Of course this has to do with the peculiar lines along which the game in Germany developed and the fact that full professionalism was such a late-comer. Big clubs are usually big clubs for economic reasons. But for as long as there are no wages and no transfer fees, there is a level playing field and dominance may shift as generations come and go. In Germany, this changed in the early 1960s. For Bayern, the timing was perfect.

The Munich club had one of the strongest teams in the land until the Nazis came to power, viewing Bayern with suspicion on account of a strong Jewish influence. It took the club a long time to recover from the repercussions of this era, but by the early 1960s they had a wealth of young talent waiting in the wings. Some people consider it a blessing in disguise for Bayern that they were not admitted to the Bundesliga in 1963, as this gave the young team an extra two years to mature out of the spotlight and under comparatively little pressure. When the side finally won promotion in 1965, they found the German game pretty much there for the taking, as even the big tradition-laden clubs were struggling to come to grips with the intricacies of professional football. Bayern, meanwhile, had signed a full-time business manager as early as 1964, a shrewd man who doubled as Franz Beckenbauer's personal agent.

During the next ten years, Bayern built a dynasty thanks to their golden generation and have been able to maintain, and even expand, it to this day. It wasn't always plain sailing, though. Contrary to popular belief, Bayern were always in financial trouble until they sold Karl-Heinz Rummenigge to Internazionale in 1984, because all the money the club made went straight back into the squad. It wasn't until Uli Hoeness took control of financial matters that Bayern were on their way to becoming one of the richest clubs in the world.

Bayern were also lucky that their original Bundesliga rivals when the game turned professional happened to be Borussia Mönchengladbach. That's because it was always bound to be a mere matter of time until Gladbach fell by the wayside. The city was simply too small to sustain a truly big Bundesliga club indefinitely. (When Gladbach won their first league title, in 1970, the population was 151,000 – think Newport or Oxford.) When I asked midfielder Horst Wohlers, who won the 1979 UEFA Cup with the team, if the decline could have been prevented, he replied: 'It was an almost impossible task. It's a miracle that we dominated for as long as we did in the first place.'

Bayern's next rivals – Hamburg – had a lot more potential and did very well for six years, always finishing first or second under the iconic Austrian coach Ernst Happel. But when Happel's health began to deteriorate, the club lost its way and passed on the baton to Werder Bremen, another small-but-plucky club in the Gladbach vein. By the time Borussia Dortmund finished runners-up behind Stuttgart in 1992, it was an accepted fact of life for a football fan in Germany that Bayern's pre-eminence was overpowering, though occasionally and temporarily broken up by whoever put together a good season when the Munich giants happened to have one of their (back then still frequent) off-years. Such as 1991–92, in fact. It was truly a nightmare season for the biggest club in the country, as Bayern missed out on Europe for the first time in thirteen years.

This is an important detail, because 1992–93 was the first season of the Champions League – and the first year in which TV stations pumped previously unheard-of amounts of money into football. All sorts of new television deals were in place. Germany, for instance, used an unusual – and short-lived – system in the UEFA Cup under which all money went into a pool and was then distributed, round by round, among the Bundesliga clubs that were still in the competition. BVB knocked out Maltese club Floriana in the first round, then they eliminated their old friends Celtic and reached the quarter-finals by defeating Real Zaragoza.

When the dust settled, Hitzfeld's men looked around to find that they were the last Germans standing. From now on, all the money in the pool was there for Borussia's taking. And the team rose to the occasion, progressing past Roma and then Auxerre to reach their first European final since 1966. Even more importantly, the club pocketed a then-immense 25 million marks. (At the time, this equalled more than £10m and would have bought you two Paul Gascoignes, then the most expensive British player by a country mile.) Stuttgart, meanwhile, had bowed out in the first round of the Champions League to Leeds because coach Christoph Daum had fielded four foreign players at Elland Road. (In those pre-Bosman days, only three were allowed.) For the black-and-yellow nation, it was a sweet season indeed.

And it wasn't over yet. For the first leg of the UEFA Cup final, which was played in Dortmund, the club produced a match programme that would be unthinkable today. Above the welcoming words '*Herzlich willkommen, Juve! Ben venuti, Juve!*' was a photo of the South Stand spread across both the front and the back cover. The entire terrace was bathed in red, the glare emanating from at least sixty flares held up by fans. It was not only a breath-taking sight, in every sense of the word, it was also visible proof that German football supporters were beginning to move away from the classic English fan culture they had sought to emulate for three decades.

The modern use of pyrotechnics at football games in Germany can be traced back to the 1984–85 season. ('Modern' because old-fashioned firecrackers or fireworks go back a long way.) That year, many Kaiserslautern fans travelled to Italy on a regular basis. More precisely, they travelled to Verona to pay tribute to club icon Hans-Peter Briegel, who had just joined Hellas. The Germans were fascinated by the *tifosi* culture, especially by the use of what came to be known in Germany as 'Bengal lights'. The fans began to import flares from Italy or simply purchased locally available hand flares, those small torches used at sea for distress signals.

The general public first became aware of this new trend in early November 1991, when Kaiserslautern came within a whisker of eliminating Barcelona from the European Cup. Roughly one hundred flares were alight in the West Stand before kick-off, a spectacle that fuelled the fad even more, as people subsequently tried to emulate what was happening in Kaiserslautern. This city would remain the benchmark for pyrotechnics in German football, but the Westfalenstadion was not far behind. During the first half of the 1990s, a veritable terrace tourism began to develop: other clubs' fans travelled to intimate football-only grounds like Kaiserslautern, Offenbach and Dortmund just to take in the fantastic atmosphere that was such a hallmark of these years. The South Stand was often overcrowded, with the smell and heat of countless flares wafting through the air. What would be considered an unforgiveable safety hazard today just added to the excitement – to the feeling that something out of the ordinary was going to happen.

Not against Juventus, though. Borussia took an early lead in the first leg of the 1993 UEFA Cup final, but they just were no match for the Italian giants, who fielded stars such as Roberto Baggio and Gianluca Vialli alongside two Germans, Andreas Möller and Jürgen Kohler, and a sturdy but deft Brazilian defender called Julio César. Juve won the trophy 6–1 on aggregate. But as hinted earlier, more important for Dortmund's future was the financial windfall BVB would now invest in the squad.

Actually, the club began to invest while the momentous season was still underway. It underlined their new financial clout that BVB did not search for talent at home but began to bring back players who had been lured to Italy by the seemingly bottomless coffers of Serie A clubs. In January 1993, Borussia spent 8.5 million marks on midfielder Matthias Sammer, who had joined Inter only a few months earlier but could not cope with life south of the Alps. It was a record transfer for a German club, but it would soon be eclipsed – by Borussia themselves. A few months after the spectacular Sammer deal, Dortmund signed Karl-Heinz Riedle from Lazio for 9.5 million marks. And the black-and-yellow spending spree continued unabated: one year later, Andreas Möller returned to Dortmund accompanied by his Juve teammate Julio César for a combined 11.5 million marks. This was now a team that had obviously not been assembled to have a shot at Europe and maybe enjoy a good cup run. There were no two ways about it: Borussia Dortmund were throwing down the gauntlet to mighty Bayern Munich.

The fans could still identify with this expensive collection of star players, because Klos and Zorc were joined by another local hero, an 18-year-old kid called Lars Ricken. And, of course, because the city – and the entire region – had waited more than thirty years for a championship. This yearning for success, the hope that the Ruhr area could finally leave its mark on the footballing landscape again, was almost palpable. 'Before we brought Möller back, we tested the waters,' Michael Meier says. 'There was some controversy when he left, so we didn't know if the fans would accept him. But they told us: "Listen, if you can really get him – and all these other players – then by all means do it." And so we did.' (Meier's perennial favourite was the fan who told him: 'I suppose I'll be unemployed with or without Riedle. And in that case I'd rather be unemployed with him.')

Ironically, Möller and all these other players needed the help of their oldest rivals and their newest to finally deliver the big prize. With only three games left in the 1994–95 season, table-topping Werder Bremen lost against Schalke, which cut their lead over Borussia down to one point. Dortmund, who had been plagued by injuries all year, still weren't in control of their own destiny, but now there was a sliver of hope. Because on the last day, Bremen and their outgoing coach Otto Rehhagel would be playing away from home. At Bayern Munich, Rehhagel's new club.

On 17 June 1995, the city was on edge and it was almost as if the whole of the Ruhr area (well, apart from Schalke) held its breath. BVB's game against Hamburg was sold out, of course. Since the North Stand had been turned into an all-seater area in the wake of Hillsborough, the Taylor Report and new UEFA stipulations, the stadium held only 42,800. But the city had organised a public screening in the Town Hall square which could accommodate 50,000 people. Which is why stadium announcer Norbert Dickel told the crowd at the Westfalenstadion that the attendance figure was '92,800'!

Not all of them were watching the pitch. Or not after the eighth minute, when Möller cheekily curled a free-kick around the outside of the wall and into the back of the net. Now Bremen, with their inferior goal difference, needed the full set of points in Munich. Between the subs' benches and the South Stand, two club employees were perched in front of a small television set, in those pre-smartphone days the only way to follow events in Munich as they happened. At 3.44 p.m., the two men suddenly raised their arms and embraced each other. Instantly, the terrace burst into cheers. Never before, and never since, has a goal scored by Bayern Munich been received so enthusiastically in Dortmund.

The injury curse – between October 1994 and May 1995, Povlsen, Chapuisat and Riedle *all* tore their cruciate ligaments – meant that Hitzfeld had to start the biggest game of his career so far with two teenagers up front, Ricken and the Ghanaian Ibrahim Tanko, who was not yet eighteen. Yet the outcome at the Westfalenstadion was never in doubt. Shortly before the half-hour, Stefan Reuter, yet another Juventus alumnus, crossed from the right flank and Ricken scored with a header from near the penalty spot. From that moment on, the only question was whether Werder Bremen could come back in Munich. They could not. When Bayern made it 3–1 with only twelve minutes left on the clock, even the habitually cautious and guarded Hitzfeld knew this was the day when a 32-year-long wait would come to an end. Dozens of stewards began to line up around the field of play to prevent a pitch invasion, but they might as well have tried to push back the ocean. When the final whistle rang, wave after wave of fans scaled the fences and ran towards the players, who were hugging each other, many of them unable to hold back the tears.

At 5.21 p.m., Dortmund captain Michael Zorc was given the dish-like league trophy and proudly held it aloft for all to see. 'Ever since I was a small boy,' he told a reporter, 'I have dreamed of doing this. In 1992, I thought we would never come this close again, but I was wrong. This season was the crowning achievement of my career.' He paused for a moment. Then he added: 'For now.'

CHAPTER 8

'I made a mistake early in my time at Dortmund,' Michael Meier says. Meier became the club's business manager in December 1989, just a few weeks after his forty-first birthday. For reasons we will have to go into later, many Dortmund fans still bear a grudge against the man, but together with president Gerd Niebaum and coach Ottmar Hitzfeld, Meier was the driving force behind Dortmund's rise, so you could say he by and large built the modern club. One of his first tasks was to find a replacement for striker Norbert Dickel, who had sacrificed his knee for the 1989 cup triumph. (To this day, Dickel walks with a limp.) The player Meier targeted was a young Dane whom he had once signed for FC Cologne and who was now playing for Bobby Robson at PSV Eindhoven. Or rather not always playing, because the brilliant Brazilian Romário was Robson's number-one forward.

'We decided to sign Flemming Povlsen,' Meier says. 'But there was a problem. Back then, you could field three foreign players in European games, but only two in the Bundesliga. We already had Murdo MacLeod and a Russian defender called Sergei Gorlukovich. So I called them both into my office and explained the situation. Gorlukovich said: "Well, such is life." And MacLeod said: "I don't care. I'm playing anyway." But he wasn't. In the new season, he couldn't win a starting place. So he asked for a move and we let him leave. The fans were up in arms.'

Ironically, MacLeod made his last appearance in the yellow shirt in the first round of the UEFA Cup on 2 October 1990. The irony was that Borussia's opponents were Chemnitz FC from East

Germany – a country that ceased to exist six hours after the game kicked off. The travelling support (most sources say 2,200 BVB fans made the eastward journey, but the figure was probably closer to 3,000) had their passports checked on the way to the match, but when they returned home, there was no longer any border. Shortly afterwards, MacLeod joined Hibernian for a transfer fee of only 500,000 marks. BVB kept the sum low as a thank you to MacLeod, allowing him to pocket a decent signing-on bonus.

In early November, the club held a farewell party for MacLeod, attended by 200 people. The next day, he was guest of honour when Borussia played Universitatea Craiova from Romania in the UEFA Cup. He didn't watch the game from the VIP stands, though. MacLeod spent the first half on the South Stand, signing autographs and chatting with the fans who adored him so much. A reader's letter in *Kicker* magazine said: 'Murdo MacLeod leaves Borussia Dortmund – this can't be true! The one player who always, even in friendlies or against lower-division opponents, fought like a lion.'

Looking back, Meier says: 'My mistake was that we didn't inform the fans about those developments, we didn't involve them. They didn't know anything about my conversation with Gorlukovich and MacLeod. So the move came as a total surprise to them.' This was not the reason why Meier began to face up to the supporters on a regular basis – he had already begun to do so – but it reinforced his belief that the club's fans were more than just customers and that everybody would benefit from a constant exchange of opinions and ideas. In the first half of 1990, after only a few months on the job, Meier introduced a regular meeting with supporters, what came to be known as the *Fandelegiertentagung*, convention of fan delegates.

These meetings were organised by Petra Stüker, who had been working in the club's office for almost nine years. Stüker, then 33 years old, was asked to get in touch with the fan clubs and invite members to the meetings. She gradually began to do what

Supporter Liaison Officers do today, though it would be a few years until she was officially referred to as the club's *Fanbeauftragter*, fan representative.

Normally, Meier didn't face the fans on his own. For the meeting on 6 August 1990, for instance, he was accompanied by president Niebaum and three players, among them the immensely popular Flemming Povlsen. This meeting, one of the first, was attended by some fifty supporters. Soon, the number would grow into the hundreds and a rule was introduced that said fan clubs could not dispatch more than two members to the meetings, which would eventually be held every two months, all through the 1990s and well into the new century.

'I had a reputation as being quite domineering during these discussions,' Meier says, bringing up the subject before I have a chance to. 'But that's not true. I always came with an open mind and was willing to listen.' He is probably right. Meier didn't suffer fools gladly, but once he was sure you really had a point to make, you could be certain of his full attention. Volker Rehdanz, a prominent and opinionated supporter who would soon start the best-known BVB print fanzine (*Bude*, a slang word for goal) said: 'Meier could really dish it out at those meetings. But more often than not, he was just testing you out. He wanted to see whether you would knuckle under or stand up to him. If you did the latter, he respected you.'

All of which raises the question: why? Then as now, football clubs don't really like to involve fans, regardless of the lip service they routinely pay. So why did Meier go to such great lengths and spend draining evenings debating with supporters about transfers, away trips, replica shirts or the price of beer at the ground? (And make no mistake, those meetings could be long and gruelling. Often, Meier would come home so tired he hardly found the strength to greet his wife.) 'Back then, we had problems with some fans, we had the notorious Borussenfront,' Meier says. 'There was the fan project, but it had nothing to do with the club. So I felt that we, as

Borussia Dortmund, should start communicating with our fans. Originally, it was all about keeping the terraces clean. Clean from the Nazis, who were actively recruiting at the ground. And clean from the thugs. But eventually we debated about everything. And I learned a lot. When you run a football club, it's really helpful if you know what the people want and how they feel about the club.' Of course, what he doesn't say is that these conventions were also a good occasion to influence fan opinion and direct it towards the club's position. 'We talked about everything,' Meier says. 'Especially the stadium.'

In the wake of the Hillsborough disaster in 1989, most European countries gradually did away with standing areas, not least because UEFA decreed that from 1993 on, European matches had to be played in all-seater stadiums. In the summer of 1992, Borussia converted the terraced North Stand into a seated area, which reduced the ground's capacity from 54,000 to under 43,000. Walter Maahs, then BVB's managing director, told club historian Gerd Kolbe: 'Our idea was banal, really. We wanted to earn more money.' But even though you could charge supporters significantly more in seated areas, Borussia were reluctant to do the same with the iconic South Stand, the club's heart and soul. Rehdanz believes that the fan conventions played a major role. 'Many people don't realise that our discussions back then are the reason why the South Stand still exists as a terrace,' he says. 'We were trying to explain to Michael Meier that Borussia's most important marketing tool was this terrace.' When I asked Meier if it was true that the fans had talked the club into preserving the South Stand, he paused for an uncharacteristically long time. Then he said: 'That would be taking things too far. It was always our intention to keep the terrace. But it's true that we talked about what the ground should look like with the fans. For instance, they said they hated the idea of luxury boxes, so we didn't install any when we rebuilt the stadium.'

The issue of terracing was indeed one of those rare cases where the supporters stood side by side with many club officials. A pressure group called *BAFF* (an acronym that stood for 'Alliance of Active Football Fans') formed in August 1993 and organised a congress one year later that led to a high-profile demonstration in Frankfurt, where the DFB is based. In late November 1994, 396 supporters pleaded with the governing body not to go all-seater. (Each of the thirty-six professional clubs was represented by eleven fans, hence the symbolic number.) They said all-seater stadiums would hurt the atmosphere and destroy traditional fan culture while pricing many fans out of the game, all of which turned out to be rather prescient points. They also said that while the Hillsborough disaster had happened on a terrace, the terrace had not been the reason. This was another solid argument. In fact, the Taylor Report, the blueprint for UEFA's decision to go all-seater, explicitly stated that 'standing accommodation is not intrinsically unsafe' and then explained the primary reason for recommending all-seater grounds was that 'seating has distinct advantages in achieving crowd control'.

But as Meier indicated, the supporters weren't alone in their fight. The city governments, as the owners of most German grounds, protested loudly because they were unwilling to spend a lot of taxpayers' money on fixing something that, as far they were concerned, wasn't broken. And the majority of clubs backed their supporters. In April 1993, UEFA agreed to suspend the all-seater rule for European games for another five years, until 1998. Niebaum had lobbied loudly for this decision. When the news came, he said: 'From the very beginning, we have taken action against these plans, because they adversely affect people with low income.' He then thanked Egidius Braun, the president of the DFB, for fighting Dortmund's cause in UEFA's corridors of power. For all his later failings and mistakes, the fans must thank Niebaum for the fact they still have what is probably the most magnificent terrace in world football. He really believed that there had to be a large section with affordable tickets at a football ground and repeatedly called UEFA's rules 'ludicrous' and 'overshooting the mark'.

To understand why German football fans fought – and won! – this battle, one has to remember that going all-seater was never a rational decision, it was always about emotions. (Well, and profit, as ticket prices skyrocketed – especially in Britain – during the 1990s and beyond, but that is another story.) While there had been many terrible incidents involving British fans – the Bradford City fire and Heysel in 1985, then Hillsborough four years later – the worst stadium disaster in Germany happened in Hamburg on the last day of the season in 1979 and resulted in seventy injured spectators. It was grave, but it paled in comparison to the above-cited cases. And so the issue of ground safety could be looked at more objectively in Germany – the debate was never overshadowed by a tragedy, let alone a national trauma. When I travelled to Scotland in 2016 to report on the return of a standing area at Celtic Park, the fans in Glasgow told me that the very mention of the word 'terrace' triggered an irrational fear in Britain, which is why the fans hadn't dared to argue for a standing area by pointing out that their ground, once famous for its atmosphere, had become a morgue. Ironically, they had to sell the terracing by citing safety concerns. They argued that young fans would stand anyway and that it was only a question of time until someone would stumble over the seats and get hurt.

Another factor that informed the German fan protests against all-seater stadiums, one that has already been touched upon, was that the clubs were not businesses that existed to make money – they existed to serve their communities, their members. Even twenty years after the events described above, Dortmund chairman Hans-Joachim Watzke told me: 'The German fan wants to have the feeling that he is a part of the whole. In England, the fan is now basically a customer and can by and large live with that. But if you tell a German supporter that he is just a customer, he's going to kill you. He has to feel connected to the club.' Going all-seater, many supporters argued, would send out an unmistakable signal that fans were now regarded as customers, or worse: consumers. And so the fight for the terraces also became a symbolic fight for the role of the game in society.

Niebaum had not really won this fight when UEFA gave his club the green light for terracing under European floodlights in April 1993. For one, it was only a postponement that bought him a few years' time to come up with a solution for the problem. Second, UEFA imposed a condition: only 20 per cent of the stadium's total capacity would be allowed to stand. 'So we are allowed 9,000 tickets for the terrace,' Niebaum calculated. 'At least this means we will still have a fine atmosphere at the Westfalenstadion.' But it also meant that while his club was becoming bigger and bigger, the stadium was getting smaller and smaller: 42,800 for domestic games, just 36,000 in Europe. And it wasn't only Borussia that needed a more spacious stadium. Germany's bid to stage the 2006 World Cup was well underway and many people, Niebaum among them, felt that Dortmund should host games, just as it had done in 1974. However, the city was in no position to finance a proper modernisation of the Westfalenstadion.

Niebaum and Meier came up with an unconventional and daring solution. In the first months of 1995, BVB set up a company called 'Westfalenstadion Dortmund Ltd' together with insurance brokers Continentale, then the club's main sponsors, and a local real estate enterprise. On 1 April 1995, April Fool's Day, Westfalenstadion Ltd acquired the stadium from the city through a thirty-year leasehold deal for an annual rent of one million marks. It was the first time in Germany that a football club for all practical purposes bought a municipally owned stadium. The next step was equally revolutionary: for the first time, a German club rebuilt an entire stadium on a massive scale without asking for public funds. For 60 million marks, largely financed through a bank loan, Borussia began to add second tiers to both the Main and the East stands during the summer of 1995 in order to bring the attendance roughly back to what it had originally been – 55,000.

But even while construction was still in progress, it was obvious that this could only be half the work. 'I remember that we all wondered if the new, bigger stands would dwarf the South Stand,' Meier says. 'So we would sometimes walk to the terrace and just stand there, staring left and right, trying to imagine what it would look like once it was finished, envisioning the South Stand sandwiched between those two-tiered stands.' Meier chuckles at the recollection. 'I still remember standing there on an empty terrace for a really long time, just staring at the skies.'

These were heady times indeed, with Borussia making headlines not just in the sporting papers. In May 1995, the respected nationwide newspaper *Frankfurter Allgemeine Zeitung* reported that BVB had been the first German club to break the 50 million mark barrier in revenue, were zeroing in on 60 million and aiming at 100 million for the year 2000. The paper also repeated the catchphrase for this era, coined by Niebaum: Borussia's plan was to invest in '*Steine und Beine*', stones as well as legs. One month later, the business newspaper *Handelsblatt* marvelled: 'Ten years ago, Borussia were as good as bankrupt, now they are the football market leaders.'

And they were. In May 1996, Borussia celebrated a second straight Bundesliga title. It was a deserved triumph, as the best team won the league, and yet it came against the odds. Ahead of the season, Borussia had signed yet another Juventus player – centre-back Jürgen Kohler for four million marks. However, that was peanuts compared to how Bayern were running rampage in the transfer market. Among the top seven most expensive Bundesliga deals that summer, no less than four were made by Bayern: the Austrian Andreas Herzog, the Swiss Ciriaco Sforza and the two German internationals Thomas Strunz and Jürgen Klinsmann joined the Munich giants for a combined 23 million marks. Add to this the most spectacular managerial change in recent memory – Otto Rehhagel leaving his old flame Bremen and joining Werder's biggest rivals of recent years – and you can understand why Bayern's squad was labelled the Dream Team.

It was a desperate attempt at regaining control of a league that the club had dominated throughout the 1980s. By the summer of 1995, though, Bayern looked back on five seasons in which they had won the Bundesliga only once. After decades of financial frugality, marquee names were now added everywhere, even in the boardroom (Franz Beckenbauer and Karl-Heinz Rummenigge had been given official posts in late 1991) to turn things around. As if on cue, Bayern won the first seven games of the new season under Rehhagel, setting a Bundesliga record that still hasn't been bettered. But then they travelled to Dortmund and lost 3–1 – and the house of cards collapsed.

While Borussia seemed to be a sea of tranquillity – with Niebaum, Hitzfeld and Meier running the show with one voice – Bayern would soon acquire the nickname 'Hollywood FC', as the club kept the tabloids happy with a dizzying succession of scandals, backbiting and intrigues. In March 1996, a feud between Klinsmann and Lothar Matthäus got so out of hand that the latter challenged the former to a live debate on television. In April, following a 1–0 home defeat at the hands of Hansa Rostock, Rehhagel was fired and Beckenbauer took over on an interim basis with three games left and Dortmund leading Bayern by three points.

At first it looked as if this panic measure would actually work. Three days after Rehhagel's sacking, BVB suffered what was arguably the worst and most unexpected disintegration of the Hitzfeld era, losing 5–0 at Karlsruhe. Hitzfeld, always eager to protect his squad, said: 'We held a team talk after the game and found we had all made mistakes, coach and players.' When Meier was asked whether it wasn't time for Hitzfeld to reprimand his team more sharply, the business manager replied: 'Every coach has his own style, and Ottmar prefers the quiet method.' A few days later,

Bayern raced into a 2–0 lead away at old foes Werder Bremen and were suddenly level on points with Borussia. But the quiet method prevailed. Bremen came back to win 3–2 and Dortmund's 2–2 draw at 1860 Munich on the penultimate day of the season sealed the club's fifth national championship, the second of the Bundesliga era.

But if you looked very closely, you could see the first hairline cracks appearing. The title celebrations seemed to be fuelled by enormous relief rather than boundless joy. Only weeks after clinching the championship, Borussia's vice-president Ernst Breer called the coach on the phone. 'He made it clear that we had to win the league yet again,' Hitzfeld told his biographer a decade later. 'He said economic reasons would mercilessly dictate this aim.' Dortmund had entered a cycle in which an awful lot of money was coming in, while an awful lot of money was going out in a desperate effort to make sure an awful lot of money would continue to come in. Hitzfeld had always been one of those coaches who were acutely aware of his responsibility – he knew very well how many hopes and dreams rested on him. As early as January 1994, he had suffered a ruptured bowel, a life-threatening condition often caused by job-related stress. And if anything, the pressure had mounted since then.

Apart from the pressure to produce results, there were also the first signs that Niebaum, Hitzfeld and Meier were no longer forming the unified front they tried to present – and that the team was not a band of brothers but a fragile collection of egos held together by a common goal. In the summer of 1997, Borussia signed another of those marquee names, and another Juventus player, when the Portuguese Paulo Sousa joined for eight million marks. I found him very amiable and open when I talked to him a few months later, but there are also those who say that he could – and would – be a bit of a prima donna, running clockwise during training when everyone else was running counter-clockwise, just to prove he was his own man.

Knut Reinhardt, still a member of the team and still beloved by the fans, recently told writer Christoph Biermann: 'There was a class division in that squad.' One clique included the players who had seen action in Italy. They would sometimes speak Italian during training just to rile the foot soldiers. As if that didn't provide enough potential for unrest, a few months into the season a number of players, Matthias Sammer among them, wondered loudly about yet another injury-strewn campaign and publicly accused the team physio of incompetence, ultimately forcing him to step down. There were no two ways about it, Dortmund had become so intent on playing the game the Bayern Munich way, they were about to start their very own Hollywood FC in the Ruhr area. All of which makes it even more stunning that a little-known Glaswegian who had just turned 28 was thrown into this shark-infested pool . . . and immediately began to swim.

No matter how many times I asked Hitzfeld about his problems with the team and with the ever more demanding Niebaum, he always remained the total gentlemen and refused to speak ill of anyone. 'It was a very difficult year because we were always forced to improvise,' he said about 1996–97, adding with a smile: 'If key players are getting old, problems arise. For the coach.' (He was referring to club icon and captain Michael Zorc, whom he began to bench that season.) But he did say this: 'Our most important transfer that year was Paul Lambert.'

A few years ago, Lambert told the *Guardian* that what the newspaper called his 'whirlwind journey from gun for hire to Dortmund legend' seemed as incredible to him as it did to anyone else: 'I walked into the dressing room at the training ground and I've seen all the players. Jürgen Kohler, Steffen Freund, Andreas Möller, Stefan Reuter, Matthias Sammer. I remember thinking: "No. You're never going to do it." There was unbelievable self-doubt that I couldn't handle that company because when I saw the players . . . He'd won Serie A, someone had won the World Cup, someone had won the European Championship, the Bundesliga titles . . . and I'm coming from Motherwell on a free transfer. I was worth a bottle of Coke. Jesus!'

I can attest to the fact that Lambert never lost this humility, even after he had broken into the first team. In the spring of 1997, I talked to him after a training session. He told me how he had let his contract with Motherwell run out, safe in the knowledge that Rangers or Celtic would come calling. Only, they didn't. The man who eventually called was a Dutch agent who said he could get Lambert a trial with Borussia Dortmund, who were having severe injury problems and needed a cheap and reliable back-up man. While we were talking, I noticed that Lambert had a BVB shirt tucked under his arm.

'Oh, is that for your son?' I asked.

'No, it's for me,' he replied. 'It's a souvenir. I'm living my dream here, but I'm aware that it could be over any minute.'

Neither of us had any way of knowing it at that time, but his dream would not only continue for some time but become even more outlandish: a few months after we chatted, Lambert set up the crucial opening goal in the final for the biggest prize in European football and, perhaps even more importantly, marked a certain Zinedine Zidane out of the game.

The very reason why Lambert was there in the first place – that BVB were beset by injuries – is probably the main reason why the league campaign was almost an afterthought during that historic season for Borussia. For the first but not the last time (he used a similar approach as Bayern Munich coach in 2001), Hitzfeld decided to focus on Europe. A third consecutive Bundesliga title would have pleased the fans and may have saved his slowly but steadily deteriorating relationship with Niebaum, but there was no way his depleted squad could put in top-level performances every three days. Defensive rock Julio César suffered an injury in October 1996 and didn't make another appearance that season. Sousa, one of the most technically gifted players ever to wear the yellow shirt, was sidelined from August to February.

Sammer, the game's most offensive sweeper since Franz Beck-enbauer and so masterful he won the Ballon d'Or in December 1996, was beginning to be plagued by the knee problems that eventually cut his career painfully short. In fact, Sammer hardly played in the Champions League at all, where the Austrian Wolfgang Feiersinger replaced him so capably that Hitzfeld still says it was the most difficult coaching decision of his whole career to put Feiersinger in the stands for the final and go with Sammer.

Almost the only thing that went according to plan was the re-building of the stadium. In April 1996, the second tier of the Main Stand had been inaugurated and the East Stand followed suit in October. But even before the remodelled ground, which now held 55,000 for domestic games and could accommodate 48,500 in Europe, went into general use, business manager Michael Meier announced that the North and the South stands would be en-larged, too. 'There is such a demand for tickets that we have to do this,' he said. There was never any doubt that the South Stand would remain a standing area in its entirety, making it the biggest terrace in Europe. 'We're sending out a deliberate signal against the reduction of standing areas, because we think it's wrong,' Niebaum said.

The first European game played in front of the rebuilt Main and East stands was also the only European game Borussia would lose that season, a 2–1 defeat at the hands of Atlético Madrid in late October 1996. It was of little consequence, as Borussia dominated their group and had already won the game in Madrid, 1–0. It was a result which would become a black-and-yellow speciality that year. Because when BVB beat AJ Auxerre 3–1 at the Westfalenstadion in the quarter-finals, the away goal meant that the tie hung in the balance – until Lars Ricken found the net in the return leg on the hour with a deflected shot. Both the scorer and the manner in which he scored would also prove to be hallmarks of the campaign.

Ricken's goal set up a highly memorable semi-final between BVB and Manchester United. It was the clubs' first meeting since the 1964–65 Inter-Cities Fairs Cup, when United had thoroughly demolished their opponents, winning 10–1 on aggregate. It was also the first meeting between Ottmar Hitzfeld and Alex Ferguson, then still a few years away from a knighthood. The two men would become good friends and have stayed in touch throughout the decades, these days mainly in the form of letters. ('It is almost impossible to understand him, especially on the phone,' Hitzfeld says about Ferguson's Glaswegian accent. 'That makes writing a sensible alternative.')

For the first leg, Ferguson had to replace defender David May and goalkeeper Peter Schmeichel, who both suffered injuries during training. But that was nothing compared to Hitzfeld's headaches. Sammer, Kohler, Riedle, César, the German international René Schneider and Chapuisat were all unavailable, while Möller was not fully fit and Feiersinger could only take to the field after the team physio adjusted two blocked vertebrae a few hours before the game. Which is why the *International Herald Tribune* later said about the pre-match ritual: 'Before the curtain rose on one of European soccer's big nights, a well-dressed man with a portable microphone strode onto the playing field and rallied the Borussia Dortmund fans at the Westfalenstadion. One after another, he shrieked the first names of the Dortmund team. As one, the fans bellowed back the last names, their enthusiasm undimmed even though every other name was an understudy.'

Yet those understudies dominated the game and created quite a few chances in the first half. After the restart, though, it was a different matter altogether. Three minutes into the second half, Eric Cantona set up May's replacement Nicky Butt, who hit the left-hand post with a low drive from the edge of the box before Ole Gunnar Solskjær fluffed the rebound, perhaps owing to the disastrous pitch. (The new tiers on the Main and East stands meant not enough sunlight was reaching the grass and Dortmund still hadn't found a solution to the problem.) At the other end, Paul Scholes tried to clear a corner but headed the ball against his own crossbar.

Yet the biggest chance of the game was still to come. Midway through the second half, Ricken lost possession and Borussia were hit on the break. Cantona played a perfectly weighted pass into the path of David Beckham and United's young star put the ball past Stefan Klos. Before it could cross the line, though, one of those Dortmund unknowns, centre-back Martin Kree, hoofed the ball into touch. Fittingly, it was an equally obscure name that decided the match. With a quarter of an hour left, Sousa was trying to get to a loose ball in a central position, twenty-five yards in front of United's goal. When his teammate René Tretschok collected the ball instead, the Portuguese half-turned away and looked at the night sky, as if to say: 'He should have let me handle this, I'm the star and he is a nobody.' Moments later, he raised his arms in sudden celebration. Tretschok had struck from a distance and the ball took a nasty deflection to arc into the net.

'We underachieved,' Ferguson said after the final whistle. 'There were some very disappointing performances. I'm not sure it was a good game. I think Dortmund can play better, too. I don't think the pitch helped.' It was, indeed, a scrappy win. And things would get even scrappier two weeks later. Only seven minutes were on the clock at Old Trafford when Ricken ghosted into United's box. Möller, with his back to goal, must have somehow seen this from the corner of his eye, because when he collected a clearance, he turned and immediately played the ball into Ricken's feet. The youngster's left-footed shot struck Gary Neville's shin and took a deflection that wrong-footed Schmeichel for what would prove to be the only goal of the night – 1–0 away from home yet again.

The hosts now needed three goals – but, truth be told, they could have got them. For almost the entire remainder of the match, BVB were under enormous pressure and the game has entered the club's annals as one of the great defensive fights. The moment that epitomised the night came only nine minutes after Ricken's goal: Andy Cole struck from a tight angle, Klos went down very quickly and did well to get his right hand to the ball, which now rolled parallel to the goal-line. Kohler, who was guarding the far corner, tried to knock it away, but couldn't quite make contact and lost his balance in the process. The ball reached Cantona, three yards out. Klos was back on his feet but at the other post. Kohler was lying on the ground. Cantona nudged the ball towards an open net – but Kohler stuck out his left foot and blocked the shot with the studs of his boot.

When the game was over, the tired but happy men in yellow shirts (or rather neon yellow shirts, a garish shade introduced when Nike became Dortmund's supplier in 1990) walked over to the away stand to celebrate reaching their first European final since 1966 together with 3,400 travelling fans. Or slightly less than 3,400. A supporters' club from Witten, a town bordering on the southwestern edge of Dortmund, had been delayed in Calais due to a strike. Although they knew they wouldn't be able to get to Old Trafford in time, they still crossed the Channel when the ferries were at last running again and then boarded a coach to Manchester. The ground was almost empty when they arrived, but they saw that their team was warming down, trotting up and down the pitch, so they went into the away end anyway to cheer the side – and coach Hitzfeld, who had just become the first manager to beat Manchester United in a two-legged European tie at home and away, a feat he would duplicate four years later with Bayern.

Borussia had been unlucky all those years ago when they went out against the Busby Babes in the European Cup; now they were lucky to have eliminated Fergie's Fledglings in the Champions League. But was it really luck, back then or now? United's Class of 92 was still on a learning curve back in 1997, which the BVB players had clearly put behind them. It may sound like a cliché, or an excuse, but it's true – you have to learn how to be successful in Europe. In the previous seasons, Dortmund had often been denied by teams with a lot of experience on this stage: Ajax, Inter and especially Juventus. The Bianconeri had played no fewer than six games against Dortmund in the preceding four years. Borussia managed to win only one of those, but it had been the most recent one, in November 1995, that gave the fans a glimmer of hope. Maybe their team now had the experience and the nerves you needed to lift a European trophy. The problem was the team they would face in the final. Who else but Juve?

And not any old Juventus side. This was the Juve of Zinedine Zidane, Didier Deschamps, Alessandro Del Piero, Christian Vieri, Alen Bokšić and Ciro Ferrara. They, too, had beaten United 1–0 both home and away (though in the group stage) and were undefeated in that season's Champions League. They were so frighteningly talented that a Ruhr-area comedian who was known to be a big Dortmund fan was in awe after watching Juve's last training session before the final. The man walked over to Hitzfeld's assistant coach Michael Henke, looked him in the eye and simply said: 'How?' Without missing a beat, Henke replied: 'We'll lose nine out of ten games against them. But this is the one we're going to win.'

It is sometimes assumed that Dortmund had a slight advantage because the final on 28 May 1997 was staged in Germany, but that was not necessarily the case. The site of the game was Munich, which is not only slightly closer to Turin than to Dortmund but was also home to Borussia's biggest rivals at the time. Which is why BVB's main sponsor, the Continentale insurance company, took out full-page ads in the local papers on the day of the final to drum up support for Borussia. Still, it was safe to assume that many of the neutrals (including the Bayern officials) would be rooting for the Italians.

Dortmund's players certainly knew they had their work cut out for them. In an interview with the website *Spox* a few years ago, Henke recalled that Paul Lambert, who was on modest wages compared to some of the star players, used to ogle the expensive watches worn by his teammates with thinly veiled envy. 'Before the game,' Henke said, 'some of the players came up to Paul. They all said: "Listen, if we win this one, I give you my watch!"'

Another factor working against Borussia – apart from the class of the opposition and the site of the match – should have been the disturbances caused by a press report. On the day before the game, the nationwide *Süddeutsche Zeitung* newspaper from Munich said Dortmund were travelling 'in mourning clothes to the biggest game of the year' and described an atmosphere that could only be called poisoned. The piece argued that Hitzfeld would step down if he lifted the trophy, because the squad had disintegrated into 'cliques and sub-cliques' and the team was distancing itself from their coach, hinting the same was true of the president. The paper may have been based in Munich, but the article was written by a Dortmund-born journalist called Freddie Röckenhaus. He knew the club intimately (and would play a crucial role in its future a few years later), so not many observers doubted the validity of his insight. Yet it didn't seem likely that the prediction would come true. After all, Hitzfeld first had to lift the trophy. And there was another, admittedly unscientific, reason why this was highly improbable. One week before the Champions League final, Schalke sensationally won the UEFA Cup against Inter. How likely was it that two European trophies would be won by clubs from the Ruhr area in the same year?

Although United had been eliminated by Borussia, there was a Manchester angle to the final. For the first time since the air disaster in 1958, all eight surviving Busby Babes were back in Munich together, on an invitation from the city. What they saw was a very cautious and nervous Dortmund team and a Juve side that played with conviction and confidence. For 28 minutes and 20 seconds. Then Möller took a corner from the left, right in front of the 1860 Munich end, which was where the Dortmund supporters stood that night. Juve's goalkeeper Angelo Peruzzi couldn't quite get to the ball, but he got some help from Vladimir Jugović, who headed the ball out of the penalty area and over to the right flank – straight to the only Dortmund outfield player who had started all eleven Champions League games, none other than Paul Lambert. The Scot immediately sent an in-swinging cross back into the box, where Riedle chested the ball down and then guided it past Peruzzi with his left foot.

The striker later told the story of how he had dreamed the night before the final that he would score two goals – one with his left foot and the other with the sort of trademark header that had garnered him the nickname 'Air' Riedle. If this was more than an apocryphal story, it came true less than five minutes later. Again Möller sent in a corner from the left, though this time not so close to the goal that Peruzzi could dare to leave his line. Riedle barely had to jump to make contact with the ball, heading it so powerfully into the net from eight yards out that Angelo Di Livio, who was guarding the near post on corners, simply didn't have time to react.

Although no team had come back from two goals down in a European Cup (or Champions League) final since Benfica in 1962, the game was far from over as a contest. Boksić had a goal chalked off for handball even before the break. And during the interval, Juventus coach Marcello Lippi made an inspired change. As a matter of prudence, he had started his secret weapon on the bench but now brought him on for the second half: midfielder Del Piero, who had found the target twice in his last two games against Dortmund. Make that three out of three. On 65 minutes, Del Piero scored one of the finest goals in the history of the European Cup finals when he backheeled a Boksić cross across the line from a few yards out.

But Hitzfeld also had an ace – and a wonder goal – up his sleeve. Almost like a baseball coach who calls a right-handed batter from the bench after the other team has pulled a left-handed pitcher out of the bullpen, he brought on Borussia's own good-luck charm four minutes after Del Piero's goal. A good-luck charm who was itching to see action. 'It's not a nice feeling to be sitting on the bench during such a game,' Lars Ricken said years later. 'I had scored in the semis, against United. I had also scored the winning goal against Auxerre. When you do that, you expect to start the final. But man-management was Hitzfeld's great strength. On the evening before the match he explained why I would be on the bench and told me that I would play an important role regardless. I was only twenty and we had a team full of internationals. He said my chances of seeing action in the game were great, so I was fired up for the final even though I wasn't a starting player.' Ricken paused for a moment, then he added something which made you wonder if the squad was really as torn as the newspaper reports had one believe: 'My teammates also helped me. They gave me a boost. Back then, the golden goal rule was in use. Jürgen Kohler told me: "If somebody scores a golden goal, it will be you."'

As Ricken stood at the touchline, waiting for Chapuisat to leave the pitch, the German radio commentator Manfred Breuckmann told his listeners: 'And now Lars Ricken is about to come on, the man for the deciding goals. He'll make it 3–1.' After a fraction of a second, he added: 'Or so we hope.' While Ricken jogged into a central position deep in his own half, Sousa kept possession against two opponents near the touchline and then knocked the ball into the path of Möller. The ball was still travelling when Ricken began the run that made him a club legend. He was already at the halfway line when Möller reached the ball and played a first-time vertical pass that sliced through the frantically backtracking Juve defence. Ricken, running at full speed, knew that he would get to the ball before any opponent could, probably a good thirty yards in front of goal. Now, what was he doing to do?

'It sounds strange, but I had prepared myself exactly for this moment while sitting on the bench,' Ricken said. 'We had noticed that Peruzzi used to position himself far in front of his goal. At one point I turned towards Heiko Herrlich, who was sitting next to me, and said: "If I come on, the first thing I'm going to do is hit one at goal, no matter where I am." So that was at the back of my mind when I was brought on.' He added: 'It was a simple goal in theory, putting it into practice was the hard part. Eight or nine out of ten attempts would have probably not hit the back of the net. But this one did – and that's what it's all about in big games.'

In the Dortmund end, you could hear sharp intakes of breath all around as the ball left Ricken's right foot, after his first touch of the ball. The shot was not a simple chip but sailed goalwards in a swerving arc, uncannily like Libuda's lob back in 1966. For those among the 30,000-strong black-and-yellow army who were standing directly behind the goal at the other end, it looked for a moment as if the ball would go wide of the target. The first person after Ricken to know that it would not was Peruzzi. He watched with a pained, resigned expression as the ball flew over his head and then swung inside to land in the back of the net.

There were almost twenty minutes left to play, but the body language of the Juventus players told you that Ricken's miracle goal had beaten them. With a minute left on the clock, Hitzfeld brought on Zorc so that the captain could receive the trophy. It was a moving gesture, because the fact that Zorc had lost his place in the team was a major reason why it was thought that there was so much unrest in the squad. The switch also meant that three Dortmund-born players – Klos, Ricken and Zorc – were on the field of play and celebrated the greatest triumph in Borussia's history when the final whistle blew. Two hours later, Lambert left the dressing room to go to the club's official victory party. He sported three luxury watches on each wrist.

The next day, more than 300,000 fans cheered the team on the streets of Dortmund. As the squad's open-top bus crawled around the Borsigplatz square, a reporter asked Hitzfeld if he had imagined winning the Champions League on 1 July 1990, when he became Borussia's coach. 'No, of course not,' Hitzfeld replied. 'Coming as I did from Switzerland, I was happy to be recognised in Germany at all. I was hoping we could maybe someday get into Europe. Winning the league was sensational and to top this off with the Champions League trophy – nobody could have expected that.'

CHAPTER 9

During his long and stellar career, Gianluigi Buffon had many happy Champions League nights. But although things got off to a promising start, 5 November 1997 in Dortmund was not one of them. Then keeping goal for Parma, Buffon saved a Stéphane Chapuisat penalty in the first half and was lucky two minutes later when the Swiss striker scored with a backheel only to see the goal erroneously chalked off. Buffon's luck ran out after the break, though. First he allowed himself to be duped by Andreas Möller's old free-kick trick – bending the ball around the outside of the wall. Then Fabio Cannavaro gave away another penalty deep into the second half.

As Möller grabbed the ball and walked towards the penalty spot, a chant started up on the South Stand behind Buffon's goal. 'Pa-ul Lam-bert,' the fans demanded. 'Pa-ul Lam-bert!' But Möller was determined to take the spot-kick himself. And almost paid for it. He fired the ball down the middle and Buffon blocked the shot with his legs. The rebound came straight back at Möller, though. Dortmund's playmaker coolly rounded the keeper and slotted home. As Parma kicked off, the fans picked up the chant again: 'Pa-ul Lam-bert!'

They had wanted the Scot to take the penalty and were chanting his name because they knew this was his last game for Borussia. After barely fifteen months in Dortmund, Lambert was returning home, joining Celtic for five million marks, at the time the equivalent of £1.9m. The transfer had nothing to do with Lambert's performances – or with BVB's new coach. Technically, Ottmar

Hitzfeld had not stepped down in the wake of the Champions League triumph but moved up, vacating the bench in order to become the club's director of football. However, it was really only a busy sabbatical to recharge the batteries. (He would take over Bayern within a year.) Hitzfeld's successor was an Italian, Nevio Scala, the very man who had guided Parma to the heights of European football's premier competition. Scala rated Lambert just as much as Hitzfeld had done and regarded him as an automatic starter. So the move to Glasgow had nothing to do with the player himself. Rather, it was his wife Monica who never managed to settle in Germany and wanted to return home.

In retrospect, Lambert's emotional farewell marked the end of an era, more so than the end of Hitzfeld's reign. That's because it was no ordinary farewell but one of the last magical days on the original South Stand. With fifteen minutes left in the Parma game, the two central blocks, numbers 12 and 13, began to sing the old nineteenth-century folk song 'Goodnight, Ladies'. It was a melody well known in the Bundesliga because a German composer had borrowed the tune in the early 1970s and turned it into a carnival hit. Normally, the fans chanted a player's name and then followed it with '*du bist der beste Mann*', you're the best man. But now they came up with: 'Paul Lambert, you'll never walk alone!'

More and more people on the stand joined in, the low ceiling capturing the noise and all but hurling it out onto the pitch. For a good fifteen minutes, and while the game was still in progress, the South Stand kept up the song. And it started all over again when Lambert slowly circled the ground after the final whistle to pay tribute to the crowd, brandishing a banner that read: 'Thank you fans of Borussia!' The fans sang and sang, while Lambert just stood and stared at the mass of people, unable to do much more than just wave. As he later told the *Daily Record*: 'When I got back into the dressing room, the tears were pouring down my face.'

Such long, repetitive chants from Dortmund fans were one of the hallmarks of the 1990s and can be traced back to a cold

November day in 1993, when Borussia travelled to Copenhagen to play Brøndby IF in the UEFA Cup. Two months earlier, the Pet Shop Boys had released their version of the old Village People song 'Go West'. It was on heavy rotation in one of the city-centre pubs where the visiting Dortmund fans were drinking the afternoon away. At one point, fairly early in the day, some fans changed the lyrics of the chorus from 'Go West, life is peaceful there' to *'Olé, hier kommt der BVB'*, here comes BVB. Fanzine editor Volker Rehdanz said: 'The pub was in the pedestrian zone and nearly all the away fans passed by during the day. So they all got to hear the song and everybody was singing it on the way to the ground. There was a street vendor hawking Santa Claus hats. He quickly sold out his entire stock.'

It was a memorable night, not least because the Dortmund players wore a bizarre and seldom-used away kit: purple shirts and socks with white shorts. It was very cold and the pitch had to be cleared of snow, which is why white walls of the stuff surrounded the field. Borussia fell behind and not much was happening. So the fans started up their new song again shortly before half-time, just to keep warm and have some fun. They sang for more than half an hour straight, all through the interval and far into the second half. On the hour, they briefly paused to cheer Chapuisat's equaliser, then they picked up the song again. Nobody at home, watching the game on television, had ever heard anything like it before – a chant that went on for more than an hour. Add to this the sight of hundreds of Dortmund fans wearing Santa Claus hats in the away stand and you can understand why that night captured the imagination of the club's support.

A year earlier, in 1992, stadium announcer Norbert Dickel had begun to play music when the team scored at home, one of the customs Bundesliga clubs borrowed from ice hockey. (Announcing only the first name of a player to have, as the *International Herald Tribune* described it, 'the fans bellow back the last name' was another one.) Dickel originally used the famous up-tempo middle part of Jacques Offenbach's 'Infernal Galop', but he soon switched to 'Olé, hier kommt der BVB'. Between 1997 and 2000, other songs were used, but from 2001 the chant invented by the fans was the club's goal celebration music once again.

However, such magical nights as Lambert's farewell in 1997 would become rarer as the 1990s began to lean towards the new century. Expansion, in a very literal sense, played a role. A few months after the emotional Parma game, in April 1998, excavators, cranes and concrete mixers were positioned behind the North and South stands. After the last home game of that season, on 2 May, the Westfalenstadion started to change again. At a cost of 40 million marks, or eight Paul Lamberts, one hundred construction workers moved 1,600 tons of steel and 2,800 cubic metres of concrete to extend the two stands in just fifteen weeks, in the process bringing down the iconic floodlight pylons that had lured Dortmunders towards the stadium for a quarter of a century.

A second tier was added to the North Stand, but that was never an option for the South Stand, as the plan was to create one large, open terrace across which people could move freely. So the stand was simply lengthened. However, you could still clearly tell where the original stand ends and the new part begins, because the upper, more recent sector is equipped with 4,600 so-called rail seats – permanently installed seats which are locked into an upright position for domestic games and can be unlocked for European games. By comparison, the old, lower section still looks exactly like it did in the 1970s. On European nights, 6,500 transportable seats are brought in and fastened, destined to disappear without leaving a trace once the game is over.

Something glorious was gained in the spring of 1998: a ground for 69,500 people, at the time the third-largest in the country after the Olympic stadiums in Berlin and Munich, and one of the most awe-inspiring sights in world football – a terrace for more than 24,000 fans. But at the same time, something was irretrievably lost: atmosphere. This is not to say that the Westfalenstadion atmosphere was never again as outstanding as it used to be from the mid-1980s to the mid-1990s. But after 1998, it would never again come automatically and easy. From then on, the fans – and of course the team – had to put in an effort to create it.

Make no mistake, even at a club that is as universally famous for its support as Borussia Dortmund (and you could make a case that the support is more famous than the team itself), the hard core which powers the terrace, the men and women who go really nuts during a game, usually number in the hundreds rather than in the thousands. The intimate old South Stand had been so compact that it was not too hard for them to stimulate the others and generate atmosphere even when the terrace wasn't sold out. (Yes, there used to be days when that happened.) Now it was a lot more difficult, and not only because an additional 10,000 people filled the stand. There was also the problem of architecture, as the new, spacious and airy structure no longer captured the noise.

But it was also a different kind of expansion that served to sour the mood. You could say it was another cue taken from ice hockey, because this game underwent a seismic shift in 1993. Until that year, ice-hockey teams followed the traditional German club model, same as in football and every other sport. But severe financial problems led to a radical change. The German ice-hockey clubs hoped that following the example of the National Hockey League in North America would solve their woes. And so they became commercial enterprises and formed the closed-shop German Ice Hockey League, the first sports league in the history of the country in which limited companies rather than old-fashioned clubs competed.

Similar plans had often been raised in connection with football. Now the idea was gaining wider currency. In 1994, Franz Beckenbauer was elected Bayern's president and remarked it was 'absurd for an enterprise like Bayern Munich, with an annual turnover of 80 million marks, to be run by honorary, unsalaried officials'. A few months later, his vice-president Karl-Heinz Rummenigge said: 'We have to ask ourselves: is it up to date that a club like Bayern is still run like a *Verein*, an amateur association?' Soon, Dortmund's Gerd Niebaum joined the alliance for a restructuring of the game. In August 1996, he told the *Bild* tabloid: 'Whether we want to or not, we have to think about turning the clubs into corporations. When I look at our turnover, then this has nothing to do with the classic *Verein* anymore. We are wholesalers and retailers, selling things like club merchandise across Europe. There are two solutions. Either the entire club is converted into a company or a professional football company is made separate from the parent club. We have to do this to generate more equity capital. I have already had queries from people who want to own Borussia Dortmund shares.' He added that English clubs had long since made the change ('which allows a team like Newcastle to spend 35 million marks on a player like Alan Shearer') and that German teams would soon no longer be competitive in Europe if they didn't do the same.

During the DFB's annual general meeting in October 1998, the clubs were finally given the green light for such fundamental changes. Despite the fact that the vast majority of the 203 delegates present at the meeting represented the amateur game rather than the professional elite, they voted to implement the second solution Niebaum had spoken about: the clubs would remain public, essentially amateur and non-profit, but they were allowed to turn their professional football divisions into limited companies. Such companies could then trade shares on the stock market or sell them in some other way.

In order to prevent hostile takeovers or any similar scenario under which the parent clubs could lose control of their own companies, the so-called '50+1 rule' was introduced. It said that 50 per cent of a football PLC's shares plus one share had to remain in the possession of the parent club. (More precisely: 50 plus one per cent of the equity shares, meaning shares that come with a right to vote.) This detail necessitated a special rule that came to be known as 'Lex Leverkusen'. Since chemical giants Bayer Ltd had such long-standing ties to the club and were in fact the reason the club existed in the first place, the company was allowed to acquire 100 per cent of the shares. Another exception then had to be made for VfL Wolfsburg, a club founded for workers of the Volkswagen factory around which the entire city was built.

In the years leading up to the vote, quite a number of clubs had said they would go public as soon as they were allowed to. Bayern, for instance, had repeatedly declared they were going to float shares and then use the profit to build their own football-only ground. But by the autumn of 1998, most clubs had changed their minds. Many didn't like the fact that as a publicly traded company they would have to open their books and become more transparent. Willi Lemke, Werder Bremen's business manager, said: 'There are too many negative points. Big investors won't be happy about the fact that the majority of shares stay with the parent club. And small-time investors will have a very close look at the balance sheet before risking money. That leaves the fans. But why should a fan buy more than one share to put on his wall and say: "I'm a part-owner of Werder Bremen or Bayern Munich?"' Even Bayern were no longer interested. Uli Hoeness said: 'Why should we do it now? It's nice to still have that up your sleeve. As long as we are competitive with our sponsoring, merchandise and television money, we don't have to exhaust our resources.'

The only club to view things differently were Borussia. A few days after the DFB's rule change, business manager Michael Meier said BVB shares would be traded on the stock market by 1999 or 2000. Why this rush? In the light of later events, namely the fact that Borussia were broke and technically bankrupt only four years after going public had given the club a mammoth cash injection, one has to conclude there was simply no choice. As early as 1998, BVB must have been haemorrhaging money at a rate that made issuing shares look like an easy and clean cure for all ills.

But there was another factor. Thomas Tress, a statutory auditor who played a major role in saving the club from going under, recently told the broadcaster *Deutsche Welle*: 'Borussia Dortmund's stock market launch in 2000 predates the running of the club by Hans-Joachim Watzke and me. But we think it must have been highly attractive at the time to get all this money off the capital market in order to have sporting success.' In the late 1990s, it seemed as if the club could see only one way to compete with Bayern Munich – by outbidding them on the transfer market.

In fairness, perhaps it was indeed the only way. Borussia won the German Under-19 title for five years running between 1994 and 1998. But only three players from all those teams would ever make more than twenty appearances for the first team. One was Lars Ricken, who won the 1994 title, the other two were Ibrahim Tanko and the Russian Vladimir But. A while back, I chatted with Edwin Boekamp, Borussia's director of youth football. When I asked him why hardly any of those youngsters from the 1990s broke through, he replied: 'You have to say that they just didn't have the quality to play Bundesliga football. Our scouting was better than the other clubs' scouting, that's why we won all those titles. But when you look back at it realistically, the players we produced weren't good enough.'

He has a point. These were the dark ages of the German game. The country had missed the boat in terms of talent development and was still a few years away from waking up to the fact that drastic measures were called for. On the other hand, Bayern had already taken action. As early as 1995, Uli Hoeness asked his former player Björn Andersson to come up with a wholly new concept for the club's youth football – a concept that would soon produce the likes of Philipp Lahm and Bastian Schweinsteiger. BVB, meanwhile, didn't seem to be really interested in promoting home-grown talent. In fact, when new DFB rules stipulated a few years later that every professional club needed to have an academy, BVB procrastinated until they were threatened with having their licence revoked! Yes, the club that would one day become

synonymous with Jürgen Klopp's youth movement had to be co-
erced into nurturing talent.

So, in the absence of talented German kids, Borussia had to buy
established stars to keep pace with Bayern. German internationals such as Thomas Hässler, Jens Lehmann and Christian Wörns
joined the fold, while fiendishly expensive players were signed
from abroad: the Nigerian Viktor Ikpeba cost almost 15 million
marks in 1999, the Czechs Tomáš Rosický and Jan Koller came one
year later for a combined 46 million marks, followed by the Brazilian Marcio Amoroso, who was at the time of writing, seventeen
years later, still the third most expensive player Dortmund ever
bought, as his move was valued at 51 million marks (at the time,
this came to £18m).

With the benefit of hindsight one wonders why Borussia Dortmund, a humble Ruhr-area team for a local community of steel
and coal workers, not to mention a club with a long history of
financial problems, felt they were in a position to win a rat race
against the biggest, richest and most successful team in the land,
a team they had never challenged before, on or off the pitch. I
suppose the only explanation is that sudden fame and riches had
resulted in a condition not too rare among the *nouveau riche* – an
exaggerated opinion of oneself. Read: megalomania.

If you think this is too strong a term, consider the bizarre tale
of goool.de. In 2000, Borussia let the deal with suppliers Nike run
out, even though the American company reputedly offered BVB up
to six million marks for the coming season alone. Behind closed
doors, the movers and shakers in the boardroom – Niebaum, Meier
and, first and foremost, the head of the merchandising department, Willi Kühne – had concocted a grandiose plan.

In early May, *Borussia live* (a glossy, hundred-page nationwide
monthly launched in August 1996 to cater to the club's dramatically growing fan base outside the Ruhr area) headlined 'New look
– new luck' and revealed that Borussia's kit for the new season
would be supplied by . . . Borussia themselves. The idea was obvious:

cut out the middle man who rakes in considerable profits from the sale of replica shirts, in this case Nike. The reason nobody had tried this before was equally obvious: it takes a lot of time and money to establish your own sportswear company. Undaunted, Kühne told *Borussia live*: 'When you try to create a brand, you normally have to invest 20 million marks per year into advertising. Our advantage is that we are able to promote the brand ourselves – through the team. Thus we save ourselves the promotional costs.' The new company was christened goool.de, which must have sounded awfully hip in the days of the dot-com bubble. Now Borussia were not only taking on Bayern Munich but also Bayern's long-time sponsor and partner, sportswear behemoth Adidas.

Slowly but surely, this megalomania spread from the boardroom onto the stands, as epitomised by a condescending fan chant directed at most visiting clubs: 'If we want to, we can buy you up!' Add to this a general attitude best described as 'Here we are now, entertain us' and you can understand why many people looked around in the stands and wondered what had happened to the fans who used to refer to themselves (to the tune of 'The Wild Rover') as *'die besten im Land'*, which probably needs no translation.

Olaf Suplicki, a very prominent supporter and the driving force behind the creation of the club museum, which opened in 2008, told author Gregor Schnittker: 'When Hitzfeld was made the director of football and Nevio Scala came in as coach, people were alienated from the team. There was this move towards total arrogance. Suddenly, a lot of glory-hunting fans were at the ground. The mood changed. After winning the Intercontinental Cup, perhaps even earlier, we had a team nobody could identify with.'

He was alluding to Borussia's 2–0 triumph over Copa Libertadores winners Cruzeiro from Brazil on 2 December 1997 (a month after Paul Lambert had left) in Tokyo. Fittingly, the opening goal was scored by Michael Zorc, who would hang up his boots at the end of the season and replace the Munich-bound Hitzfeld as the club's director of football. BVB were now technically the best team in the world and even came close to defending their Champions League title. A Chapuisat goal gave Dortmund a sweet 1–0 aggregate win over Bayern Munich in the quarter-finals, setting up a most memorable semi-final against Real Madrid.

Two minutes before the first leg in Spain was supposed to kick off, one of the goals collapsed, because Madrid ultras had violently jerked at the metal fence to which it was fastened. In a breach of UEFA rules, Real didn't have a replacement goal at the stadium and a frantic search began. In a piece for *ESPN*, James Horncastle wrote: 'Initially told that Real would be given half an hour to fix the goal, Dortmund found out that the deadline had been extended to an hour and a half. UEFA delegates, it seemed, were reluctant to call the game off for fear it would lead to disorder.'

Kick-off was delayed for 76 minutes, after which, Niebaum later said, 'the players' focus was gone and all the preparation wasted'. Borussia lost 2–0 and immediately filed a protest that looked promising, not least because the replacement goal Real had finally found at their training ground turned out to be slightly bigger than the one still standing. 'I don't believe you can play a game with two goals of different sizes,' Dortmund coach Scala said. But three days after the game, Borussia withdrew their protest. 'Seeing who reaches a Champions League final should not be an armchair decision,' Meier stated. 'It should be decided on the field of play.' On the field of play, the return leg finished goalless and Borussia were eliminated.

In footballing terms, the following years turned into a roller-coaster ride that dovetailed with the lack of direction and identity that was beginning to engulf the club. Scala lasted only one year and was replaced by Michael Skibbe, the reserve-team coach who had guided the Under-19s to all those titles. He did reasonably well in his first year, but the roof fell in during his second. As late as October 1999, BVB were top of the table, two points ahead of Hitzfeld's Bayern, but then the team collapsed. By February, BVB had sunk to sixth and Skibbe was sacked. The new man in charge,

Dortmund-born Bernd Krauss, went eleven league games without a win. When he was given his marching orders in April, Dortmund's star-studded side sat in thirteenth place, only five points above the drop zone.

The players were not only losing games, they were also losing the support. When Jens Volke, later the club's chief SLO and today employed in the media department, looked back on this season a few years ago he said: 'The low point was the game against Ulm. When I left the ground that day I told myself: "I'll never be back. There are only idiots here." I was aghast when our opponents were being cheered.' He was referring to a game against newly promoted Ulm back in February 2000, when Dortmund were still within striking distance of the European slots. During the match, which finished 1–1, large sections of the ground booed the home side and rooted for the visitors. After the final whistle, even the South Stand celebrated the Ulm players with a Mexican wave. The atmosphere was so acerbic that *Der Spiegel* magazine likened the stadium to a 'powder keg' that could blow up any minute. Suplicki said about that night: 'I was just shaking my head, thinking this was no longer my club. Many people felt this way and that's why the ultras movement became really popular. Something had to happen.'

The first German ultras groups were formed in the late 1980s, but the scene didn't take hold until the second half of the following decade. The football boom of the 1990s, with its attendant effects, such as a rampant commercialisation and the reduction of old-style terraces, had killed the atmosphere – and thus damaged what ad copywriters had begun to call 'the matchday experience' – not only in Dortmund. A new form of support was needed, and this time people could not look towards Britain for inspiration. The Italian ultras movement was very attractive because it offered more than just passionate and colourful football support – it was a fully fledged youth movement. German ultras borrowed many elements from their role models south of the Alps, but neither violence nor politics formed an integral part. Of course there are violent and right-wing or left-wing ultras groups in Germany, but by and large they should not be confused with hooligans or the radically political ultras you can find in Italy or Spain.

'In Dortmund, numerous ultras groups were formed between 1997 and 2002,' explained Jan-Henrik 'Janni' Gruszecki, who was an early ultra and is now – among numerous other things – a filmmaker who produced a widely lauded documentary about the founding of the club. 'Some dissolved quickly or joined the Desperados, formed in 1999. We had seen a pyro show by the Desperados Empoli and we liked the name because it carried connotations of the Wild West. We felt that was fitting, because Dortmund is in the western part of the country.' Two years later, in 2001, Jens Volke and like-minded fans started The Unity. It was supposed to be an umbrella organisation for the various ultras groups, hence the name, but eventually became the biggest independent group in Dortmund. Although the Westfalenstadion's very first tifo, or choreography, organised by the fans dates back to December 1999 and the club's ninetieth birthday, it would soon be The Unity who produced most of the bigger tifos, mainly because they had the manpower and the organisational skills to pull them off.

At many German clubs, there is some simmering tension between ultras and regular supporters. Some of the latter consider the ultras' unremitting singing and banging of drums annoying and monotonous. They disapprove of the ultras' fascination with flares and other pyrotechnics. They dislike the power ultras can wield on a stand and distrust their cliquish, arrogant behaviour. In short, they fail to realise that they are dealing with a subculture for adolescent boys. (While every third football spectator in Germany is now female, girls account for less than 10 per cent of the ultras.)

In Dortmund, however, the relation between the ultras, especially The Unity, and the rest of the stadium is far less strained. Most normal BVB fans are aware that the terrace is so vast that some form of organised support is needed and that many songs wouldn't travel beyond the central blocks without the conducting abilities of the *capo* (the singer who leads the chants with a microphone or megaphone). Finally, although the ground has seen some awful games, and even desperate relegation fights, since the ultras came to prominence, there has never been a repeat of the scenes that took place during the Ulm game in early 2000.

The irony of those scenes, the booing of the players in yellow and the Mexican waves in honour of the opposition, was that the Ulm match wasn't even the worst that season. That was probably a 3–1 home defeat at the hands of Unterhaching in April after which the club had no choice but to fire yet another coach. Now what? The decision Niebaum, Meier and business manager Zorc came up with would produce the desired result, though it also made the club the butt of countless jokes. Because nineteen years after leaving Dortmund for Barcelona and seven years after retiring from the game, a 65-year-old Udo Lattek was presented as the new coach.

To be fair, it wasn't quite as zany as it sounds. The club had always had the highest hopes for Matthias Sammer, who hadn't been able to play since October 1997. The great midfield strategist was clearly top managerial material, as his former coach Ottmar Hitzfeld had repeatedly pointed out. But could he be thrown in at the deep end, with the club in the midst of an unexpected relegation fight? So the 32-year-old Sammer was presented as Lattek's 'adviser', as the press release put it, in the hope that the unlikely duo would get the job done and that the apprentice could take over from the ageing master in the summer. Knowing what the public would think (and say), Meier told the press: 'This is not an act of helplessness. On the contrary, we are acting because the situation demands that measures have to be taken. Our primary goal is staying up.'

And the duo did get the job done. It was not the last and certainly not the first time that Borussia became indebted to Sammer. He had been an outstanding player, one of the finest of his generation, and never gave anything less than all he had. Many Borussia fans immediately think back to a tumultuous game against Gladbach in November of 1994 when they hear his name. After half an hour, Sammer collided with his teammate Heiko Herrlich and suffered an eyebrow cut that was bleeding profusely. It was the sort of injury that prizefighters dread, because although not serious in nature it's almost impossible to stop the bleeding, so it impairs your vision – unless you close the wound with stainless-steel staples. So Sammer called the team physio and told him to do just that. At the sideline, with the match in progress. 'I felt good,' he later told the reporters. 'So I said there is no way I'm coming off.'

And although Sammer was first a defensive midfielder and then the sweeper, he scored many important goals. For instance, there can be little doubt that a crucial game en route to the first Bundesliga title in 1995 was a 2–1 home win over Karlsruhe in April. The match is famous for one of the most controversial decisions in league history. With the visitors nurturing a 1–0 lead and less than fifteen minutes left, Andreas Möller produced what Germans consider the mother of all dives. The word 'blatant' doesn't begin to describe it, as defender Dirk Schuster couldn't have made contact even if he'd wanted to. When Schuster later remarked 'a small car would have fitted between me and him,' he was barely exaggerating. The dive was so awful that Möller was suspended for two games and slapped with a fine. He remains the only German player to be retroactively punished for a dive.

Zorc levelled the score from the ensuing penalty, and that is what most people remember about that game. Just as spectacular, however, was Dortmund's late winner. On 86 minutes, Möller took a corner from the left and Karlsruhe's defender Michael Tarnat headed the cross out of the danger zone. It fell to earth in a central position, some twenty-five yards in front of goal. Sammer, who had been guarding the rear, ran towards the ball and fired a first-time volley into the roof of the net. With his weaker left foot, no less.

His managerial career was nearly as successful as his playing time. After assisting Lattek in steering Dortmund clear of the brink in 2000, he took over the side and became not only the youngest coach in history to win the Bundesliga when he led BVB to a dramatic come-from-behind championship in 2002 but should by all rights have followed this up with a European trophy. And yet he is not enshrined in the club's pantheon of true greats. Like Dickel, he gave his knee for the club (though, admittedly, not as knowingly as today's stadium announcer), but the vast majority of fans express their gratitude, if they do this at all, rather grudgingly. There are two reasons for this: the man and his era. More precisely, Sammer's personality and the team he led to success.

Sammer, the player, was always respected in Dortmund – but not loved. There was something unhealthy about his intensity, such as when he would race across half the pitch to berate a teammate for not tracking back, his face contorted with rage (Möller was a favourite victim). Also, as the excellent BVB online fanzine *Schwatzgelb.de* put it, 'Sammer never acted quite as unselfishly and in the best interests of the team as he liked to portray. This became obvious for the first time in 1996 when Sammer pioneered a new form of marketing by provoking the "boot war" between Nike and Adidas. Although Nike were BVB's team supplier, he insisted on wearing Adidas boots and started a trend that snowballed, leading to the situation that almost every player now has an individual supplier.'

However, Sammer's current unpopularity among Borussia's fans – in 2015, the television news channel *n-tv* called him 'the ultimate controversial figure in Dortmund' – stems from the years following his dismissal in 2004. He remained a stout Niebaum supporter and regularly voiced the opinion that Borussia's former president should be rehabilitated. It may be a position worthy of consideration, but it will win you no friends, neither among the club's support nor in the club's boardroom, where Niebaum is considered persona non grata. Worse – actually, much worse – Sammer then joined Bayern Munich in 2012 in a capacity best described as a cross between director of football and general mouthpiece. As such he was involved in the Mario Götze transfer a year later, which left an emotional scar on Dortmund. Sammer also made numerous statements that rubbed his former club the wrong way, until Jürgen Klopp had had enough and remarked during a press conference: 'If I was Matthias Sammer, I would thank God every morning when I set foot upon Bayern's training ground that somebody at the club hit upon the idea of hiring me. I don't think Bayern would have a single point less without Sammer.'

Finally, Sammer is less fondly remembered than any other coach in club history who gave Dortmund a trophy, because BVB fans don't quite know what to make of the team that lifted the 2002 league title. Yes, it included one of the most revered players ever to wear the yellow shirt: the Brazilian left-back Dede, a huge fan favourite who made almost 400 appearances for the club and is one of only eight Dortmund players ever to be given an official testimonial. But apart from those supporters who came of age during those years and marvelled at the skills of a young Tomáš Rosický (like, for instance, a 12-year-old local lad called Marco Reus), most fans shared the feelings of Olaf Suplicki, namely that the club had a team you couldn't easily identify with. And it was largely Sammer's team. As *Schwatzgelb.de* said about his reign: 'During the four years under Sammer, BVB invested what was then an absurd sum in new players: more than 70 million euros. Only Bayern spent about the same amount, but they got two league titles, a cup win, the Champions League and the Intercontinental Cup out of it.' (The euro replaced the mark in 2002 at a rate of one for two. In 2004, when Sammer left, 70 million euros equalled £47m.) Of course, when *Schwatzgelb.de* wrote that, in March of 2014, it had become a defining element of Dortmund's collective psyche that the reckless spending of the Niebaum–Meier–Sammer years had led to catastrophic consequences.

On the other hand, all that spending also resulted in five of the most thrilling weeks Dortmund have ever had. On 4 April 2002, BVB beat mighty Milan 4–0 at the Westfalenstadion in the semi-finals of the UEFA Cup, certainly one of the most perfect games by any Borussia team of any era. Amoroso scored a hat-trick that night and Milan were so helpless that their coach Carlo Ancelotti, normally one of the most benevolent men in the business, darted lethal looks at the press pack after the game. (Back then, everybody had to take a lift from the press room down to the mixed zone. When Ancelotti walked in, every conversation died and the journalists all stared at the floor, trying to avoid Ancelotti's steely gaze.)

A mere ten days later, Borussia were beaten 1–0 at Kaiserslautern and now trailed Bayer Leverkusen by five points – with only three games left in the league season. 'They say that everything is possible in football,' a deeply disappointed Sammer commented, 'but now we have to focus on defending second place.' Business manager Meier echoed this sentiment: 'So far, we have tried to attack the top. But now we must change gears – and look over our shoulders. Bayern Munich, Schalke and Hertha have gained a lot of ground on us.'

A week after that, Leverkusen wasted a penalty and were surprisingly beaten at home by Werder Bremen, but it didn't seem to make much of a difference. With one minute left, Dortmund were drawing their own home game against Cologne 1–1. Then BVB's Nigerian midfielder Sunday Oliseh crossed from the right and Heiko Herrlich flicked the ball on with a backheel. It rolled across the goalmouth towards the far post and three men made a dash for it. One was Cologne sub Jörg Reeb, the other two wore yellow shirts: Kohler and Amoroso. Reeb was in the best position to get to the ball first, but Kohler grabbed him by the arm and pulled him back. As the Cologne player lost his balance, Amoroso stumbled and barged into him from behind. Reeb fell to the ground, knocking down Kohler in the process. The referee blew his whistle and pointed to the spot. Amoroso, a lethal penalty taker, converted with authority to cut Leverkusen's lead down to two points.

The following week, Leverkusen lost 1–0 away at Nuremberg, who were knee-deep in the relegation fight, while Dortmund earned three points with a memorable performance at Hamburg, the team's favourite opponent during those years. Suddenly, wholly inexplicably, BVB were in first place with one game left. These were the weeks that garnered Leverkusen their 'Neverkusen' nickname, as the side would come up second-best in the Champions League and the domestic cup as well as the Bundesliga.

But that's not to say they didn't put up a fight. On the last day of the season, Bayer beat a strong Hertha side 2–1 thanks to a Michael Ballack brace. It meant Dortmund now had to win against Bremen to defend first place. Naturally, one is tempted to say, the team added some more drama by falling behind. A low Koller strike from twenty yards tied the match before the break, but the clock kept ticking away. With seventeen minutes left, Sammer brought on the Brazilian forward Ewerthon. A few moments later, Dede made a run into the box and Rosický chipped the ball into his path. Instead of controlling the ball, Dede volleyed it into the goalmouth, where both Koller and Bremen's goalkeeper failed to make contact. Just before the ball went into touch, a sliding Ewerthon guided it from a tight angle against the inside of the post and across the line – right in front of the South Stand. While most of the players in yellow ran towards Ewerthon to celebrate what proved to be a title-winning goal, Dede sprinted at full speed towards the subs' bench. Without breaking stride and with the natural exuberance that was a major reason why the fans loved him so much, he jumped into Sammer's arms.

The following day should have seen one of those massive city-centre parties that had become a Dortmund speciality over the previous thirteen years, ever since the 1989 cup win. However, the festivities were postponed, as Borussia had one more big game to play – the UEFA Cup final. At the time, only three teams had managed to win all three main UEFA club competitions: Juventus,

Ajax and Bayern. (Two English clubs have since joined this elite circle: Chelsea and Manchester United.) So although the Champions League had become Dortmund's bread-and-butter competition, adding the UEFA Cup to the trophy cabinet was a very attractive proposition. What's more, Sammer's team should have gone into the final as the clear-cut favourites. Although their opponents, Feyenoord from Rotterdam, fielded a fine team starring set-piece specialist Pierre van Hooijdonk, former Newcastle striker Jon Dahl Tomasson and a young Robin van Persie, Borussia had more quality and more experience. There was just one problem: the final was played in Rotterdam.

It was not unprecedented for a team to enjoy home field advantage at a European final. But Rotterdam was a disastrous choice. Just two years earlier, in February 1999, 500 Feyenoord thugs had left a trail of destruction in their wake after a friendly away at Leverkusen. Two months later, violence broke out during the club's title celebrations. The BBC reported: 'Police in Rotterdam have shot and injured three rioters as street fighting erupted among hooligans celebrating local club Feyenoord's fourteenth Dutch soccer league championship. A group of about 100 to 150 fans attacked riot police with bottles, stones and other makeshift weapons, smashed windows and looted stores.' Later that year, when Feyenoord were drawn in the same Champions League group as Borussia, BVB returned their entire allocation of away tickets after the club had talked to the Dutch police who said they could not guarantee the safety of Dortmund fans in Rotterdam. Meier said: 'We can't sell tickets to a game and then walk in mourning behind a coffin three days later.'

And yet, in the first week of September 2001, the European game's governing body announced that the UEFA Cup final would be staged in Rotterdam. It may have seemed a defensible decision at the time, as Feyenoord (as well as Dortmund) were Champions League starters. However, both clubs finished third in their respective groups and continued in the UEFA Cup. Even when the right-wing politician Pim Fortuyn, who lived in Rotterdam, was assassinated two days before the game and many observers argued the fixture should be postponed or moved, UEFA remained adamant.

For the 14,000 travelling Dortmund supporters it was one of the worst games they ever attended. And not because Borussia lost 3–2 or because club icon Jürgen Kohler was sent off for a professional foul in his last-ever professional game. A train carrying Dortmund fans to Rotterdam was shot at with a rifle, during the match the away stand was pelted with missiles and flares, and the general atmosphere was best summed up by a famous photo that showed a little boy in a Feyenoord shirt giving the Dortmund fans the finger, his chubby face smeared with red colour and contorted with hate. When I called a friend after the game who was travelling on a special coach organised by the fan project to hear if he was all right, he said: 'I'm OK. But everybody here is glad that we lost the game. Otherwise I don't think we would've got out of there alive.'

It was a terrible ending to a memorable season. Still, the future seemed bright. The next day, more than 100,000 fans cheered the new Bundesliga champions in Dortmund city centre, although it was a regular working day. The team then travelled to Borsigplatz square, where another 10,000 supporters were waiting. The fanzine *Schwatzgelb.de* said: 'Feyenoord may have won the UEFA Cup, but they must have looked with some envy towards Dortmund. Because Dortmund partied instead of rioting.' Then the magazine argued that 'the seeds planted by Sammer have taken root' and said all those expensive footballing soldiers of fortune had 'moved closer together' and become 'a tightly knit community'.

Little did anyone know that the Sword of Damocles was already hanging over their heads on a rapidly thinning thread. All because Germany had been awarded the World Cup.

CHAPTER 10

On 31 October 2000, Borussia Dortmund – or more precisely: Borussia Dortmund Ltd, the professional football company owned by Borussia Dortmund – went public and sold 13.5 million shares. The board had hoped to earn 300 million marks that day, but since the share price, originally set at 22 marks, quickly plummeted, the club didn't quite reach that goal. Still, Dortmund walked away with a cool 270 million marks, or £95m.

Many of the people who today run Borussia Dortmund rue the decision to go public – and the same can be said of the fans, who saw nothing wrong with the move at a time when the future seemed as rosy as the present. The fact that BVB are still the only German club that is listed on the stock exchange had dramatic, though entirely unforeseeable, consequences in the spring of 2017, but that is not the reason why the club would probably jump at the chance to delist if it were at all possible. (Basically, delisting means you buy up all your existing shares and then remove them from the stock exchange. However, Dortmund have issued so many shares over the years that the costs involved would be prohibitive, at least 575 million euros, or £515m.) Rather, there are simply too many complexities a publicly listed company has to keep track of. Maybe worst of all, there is the image problem – a glaring incongruity which BVB's detractors never fail to bring up: a club that stands for authenticity and traditional values, stubbornly defends terracing and always speaks out in favour of the '50+1 rule' is technically far more corporate than any other team in the land.

Still, going public gave Borussia more money in one fell swoop than any German club has ever had. As hinted in the previous chapter, though, a sizeable chunk must have gone directly into just keeping BVB afloat. Unbeknownst to the public at the time, Borussia had sold their new sportswear company goool.de for 20 million marks only four months after it was launched and were now leasing it back at an annual rate of 1.5 million marks. Such deals are not uncommon if you have a valuable asset and need a cash injection. But the club was becoming a bit too fond for its own good of those models that promised quick money.

Take for instance the most important decision made that year in terms of the future of the German game. In the summer of 2000, a few months before Dortmund went public, Germany was awarded the 2006 World Cup. Niebaum, by now not only the parent club's president but also the CEO of the newly formed PLC, desperately wanted the Westfalenstadion to host big games at that tournament, preferably a semi-final. It would be good for the club's image and an excellent advertisement for the city. The problem was that FIFA demanded a stadium with at least 60,000 seats for one of the tournament's five high-profile games (the opening match, the two semi-finals, the third-place play-off and the final). And so Borussia decided to develop the ground some more. Since the South Stand was sacrosanct, it stood to reason that the best way of gaining additional seats was to close the four corners. On 6 May 2002, two days after Sammer's team had won the league and two days prior to the ill-fated Rotterdam final, construction work began.

Once more, the club wanted to finance the project themselves. To raise the necessary money, some 40 million euros, Borussia entered into yet another sale-and-leaseback deal. For all practical purposes, the club sold the Westfalenstadion to a real-estate fund set up by the Frankfurt-based Commerzbank, the second-largest bank in the country. This fund – the name of which was Molsiris, a meaningless word that still strikes terror in black-and-yellow hearts – was financed by 5,780 individual shareholders, each of whom had invested a sum ranging from a modest 5,000 euros to as much as 100,000 euros with one aim only: turning a profit. Molsiris paid Borussia 75.4 million euros for the stadium. The club then used this money to finance the rebuilding and paid the fund an annual rent-cum-leasing-rate of 13 million euros. If everything had gone according to plan, Borussia would have bought the ground back by 2017 and owned a large, shiny stadium, while the Molsiris investors would have pocketed a hefty profit, between 8 and 12 per cent – per year. For everyone involved, it must have sounded like a good idea at the time.

It has become part of the fabric of modern Borussia Dortmund to condemn the high-flying plans, the risky financial deals and the stubborn belief in non-stop growth that propelled the club around the turn of the century. While it's undeniably true that a modicum of modesty and down-to-earthness will always stand a club like Borussia in much better stead than the megalomania of this era, it's also slightly unfair to view Niebaum and Meier as the devils incarnate. (If you think this is too strong a term, visit supporters' forums and search for the word 'Niemeier', a clipped form often used to describe the men who came to symbolise the era.) After all, they were responsible for the biggest triumph in Borussia's history and turned the club from a regional phenomenon into a national powerhouse. Also, as club icon Aki Schmidt used to remind people: 'When we won the Cup Winners' Cup in 1966, the board made the mistake of not bolstering the team, they didn't want to spend money. So after winning the Intercontinental Cup in 1997, the club didn't want to make the same mistake again and invested.' And who knows, perhaps it would have all worked out if it hadn't been for a couple of events beyond the control of 'Niemeier'.

One of those events was the so-called Kirch crisis, named after media mogul Leo Kirch, the German equivalent of Rupert Murdoch. Kirch, whom *Forbes* magazine listed among the top twenty richest people in the world as late as the summer of 2001, held the Bundesliga's broadcasting rights (and the European rights for the

World Cup). At the end of the day, it was his television money that financed players' wages and transfer deals. However, in 2001 alone, Kirch's subscription television channel Premiere, which televised the Bundesliga, lost 989 million euros. During the first half of 2002, shortly before reconstruction work on the Westfalenstadion began, Kirch went bust, robbing the clubs of money they had banked on.

Then there was this other unforeseen problem: football. Borussia had branched out into all these other markets – apart from the sportswear brand and the national magazine we have already mentioned, BVB also ran a travel agency and an internet company – in order to 'become less dependent on sporting success', as Niebaum and Meier used to say. Now they found out the hard way that a football club's core business is football.

On 24 May 2003, the last day of the season, Borussia played at home against Energie Cottbus, who were already relegated. The hosts needed a win to qualify directly for the Champions League. After 25 minutes, Rosický put Borussia ahead. Ten minutes later, Energie's goalkeeper parried a powerful Ewerthon shot and Rosický headed the rebound against the crossbar from four yards. Two minutes before the interval, Ewerthon volleyed a Koller cross against the underside of the crossbar from six yards. If either attempt had gone in, the club's recent history might have looked different. But after the restart, a dominant Borussia totally lost the plot, gifted Cottbus the equaliser on 74 minutes and dropped into third place, at a time when only the top two teams went directly to the Champions League.

Yet that most lucrative of competitions still beckoned, as Borussia met Club Brugge in the qualifiers and came away from Belgium with a 2–1 defeat that appeared acceptable due to the away goal. But the return leg finished 2–1 as well and the tie went to penalties. Amoroso, who had never missed from the spot for Dortmund in twelve attempts, placed his effort well, but Brugge's goalkeeper saved brilliantly to deny the Brazilian and Borussia. Three months later, in November 2003, the team were knocked out of the UEFA Cup as well and suddenly there was no more money to be made under midweek floodlights. Less than three weeks later, *Focus* magazine reported that the disastrous showing in Europe would cost the club 40 million euros. It said: 'A severe financial emergency threatens if BVB should fail to qualify for the Champions League again, which seems an almost impossible task for head coach Matthias Sammer, who has had to replace fourteen injured players.'

But it would take another week for the public to realise just how fragile the club's position had become. Three days before Christmas, Freddie Röckenhaus (the journalist who had predicted Hitzfeld would step down if he won the Champions League) and Thomas Hennecke, the BVB beat writer for *Kicker* magazine, simultaneously published material they had gathered over the preceding months, assisted by still-unnamed whistleblowers within the club. Röckenhaus's piece in the *Süddeutsche Zeitung* was headed 'Borussia Dortmund face financial crash', and the subheading read: 'Horrific debts and balance-sheet tricks: how BVB-president Niebaum has manoeuvred the tradition-laden club into a disastrous economic situation.'

Röckenhaus – and Hennecke, in *Kicker* – said the club had spent 200 million euros in just three years and needed even more money so badly that Meier was preparing a loan deal with a London-based investment company for perhaps as much as 100 million euros, pledging Borussia's gate money for the next twelve years as collateral. The article also left little doubt that the main reason for Jens Lehmann's move to Arsenal five months earlier had been Dortmund's desperate need for the transfer money.

The news came as a total shock to the club's fans. Yes, Bayern's Uli Hoeness had repeatedly said that Dortmund's financial dealings seemed fishy to him, but he was the enemy. The supporters didn't expect anything else from Hoeness but badmouthing of a dangerous rival. This was different, though. Reeling from the shock, most people did what most people do in such situations: they went into denial.

Even the other journalists covering the team seemed to side with Niebaum and Meier, who quickly challenged the implication of the articles (though, crucially, not the facts), threatened both men with legal action and went on the offensive, calling the accusation that the club was in the process of selling the family jewels 'utter nonsense'. At the time, I was working for a national newspaper, so I visited the Dortmund press stand only for big games (which were becoming increasingly rare), but I clearly remember Röckenhaus and Hennecke in one corner, the rest of the press pack in another, as if the duo carried a contagious disease.

Needless to say, the two men wouldn't have risked their reputation and their careers if they hadn't been sure that their material was watertight. This has given rise to the theory that their informer was none other than Hans-Joachim Watzke, back then the parent club's treasurer and not in a position to influence the business strategy of the PLC. In any case, Röckenhaus and Hennecke were vindicated two months later, in February 2004, when Borussia, as a company listed on the stock exchange, had to publish their bi-annual financial statements. The balance sheet revealed that BVB had lost almost 30 million euros in the first half of the season, even worse than Röckenhaus and Hennecke had predicted. Now all those years of institutional arrogance came back to haunt the club. When Eintracht Frankfurt, a team mired in the relegation fight, travelled to town in April, their support took great delight in turning BVB's infamous fan chant around. 'Next week,' the Frankfurt fans sang with fervour, 'we're going to buy you up.'

All through those momentous months, the *Fandelegiertentagungen*, the fan meetings business manager Meier had started in 1990, were still taking place – and they regularly turned into tumultuous affairs. For more than a decade, leading representatives of the club and leading representatives of the fans had been in regular contact and debated about everything under the sun. Now it was beginning to dawn on the supporters that the most important thing, the actual running of the club, had never been discussed. Niebaum and Meier assured the fans that everything was all right during those meetings; at one point they even brought Reinhard Rauball along, because the former president was held in such high esteem by the fans that his presence alone seemed to signal there was no need to worry. (At the time, Rauball was concentrating on his law firm and had no idea how grave the club's financial situation was.)

During those weeks, an idea germinated among well-known fans like Reinhard Beck, Jens Volke and Olaf Suplicki: maybe the club would be less inclined to make decisions with far-reaching effects over the heads of the fans if the fans were a part of the club? Not just as members, but as an actual division of the parent club, just like the handball or table tennis sections? There were some precedents, though not many. As early as 1993, thirty-six Hamburg members had started an official club division for supporters with the stated aim to 'actively participate in the club's social life and influence club policy in the best interests of the fans'. In late 2000, Eintracht Frankfurt followed suit and it was to those supporters that the Dortmund fans turned during 2004 in search of knowledge and inspiration.

While they were preparing the creation of a supporters' association as the club's fourth division, the shocking revelations kept piling up. In June, a newspaper reported that Borussia had sold the naming rights to the ground six months earlier for a paltry five million euros. The club did not deny the report but said they had reserved the right to renege on the deal. But this right had come at a price. As the local paper *Ruhr Nachrichten* explained: 'If BVB withdraws from the contract, the five million euros have to be paid back. In case the club is in no position to do so, surrendering the transfer value of players is being debated. The names of André Bergdølmo, Dede, Guy Demel, Niclas Jensen and Christian Wörns are bandied about. Which means these players have potentially been in pawn since January.' Later that year, Borussia secretly sold the transfer rights to three much more coveted players – Rosický, Ewerthon and World Cup finalist Christoph Metzelder – for a modest 15 million euros. No matter how vehemently Niebaum and Meier may have refuted this accusation earlier in the year, the family jewels had well and truly been flogged off. There was nothing left.

An even stranger deal – news of which would not reach the general public until many years later – proved beyond doubt just how desperate the men running the club had become in the second half of 2004. Sometime around late August, Niebaum and Meier asked the most unlikely of men for help: Bayern's Uli Hoeness. They needed two million euros quickly, they said, and only for a month or two. Hoeness had every reason and every right to laugh in their faces. Less than three years earlier, Dortmund had all but stolen defensive midfielder Sebastian Kehl from under his nose – the player had already pledged his future to Bayern Munich and received a sizeable signing-on bonus for it. Then he suddenly changed his mind, paid back the money and joined Dortmund in early 2002 (winning the league a few months later). In effect, BVB were now asking Hoeness to pay Kehl's wages. Amazingly, Bayern's business manager agreed.

Turns out, he wasn't really that unlikely a man to ask for help. After all, Bayern had a long history of coming to the aid of competitors. In 2014, the German business newspaper *Handelsblatt* calculated that 'Bayern Munich have financially bailed out fifteen clubs'. You could debate all day long why they regularly do this. A recent book, co-authored by Borussia's chief press officer Sascha Fligge, speculated: 'Some said Hoeness acted the way he did because deep down inside, despite his Bavarian swagger, he is a decent guy. Others say that Hoeness never does anything without an agenda. It's not hard to guess his agenda in this case: once they agreed to a loan, Bayern had something they could use as leverage against Niebaum/Meier.'

In any case, when the affair finally came to light – in early 2012, at a point when Dortmund had managed an unexpected turnaround and were a threat to Bayern again, what a strange coincidence! – it fascinated the British press. 'Imagine, if you like, Manchester United bailing out Leeds United with an emergency loan back in those days when the Yorkshire side found themselves in the spiral of financial hardship that threatened their entire existence,' Dennis Taylor wrote for the *Guardian*. 'Or another wealthy, powerful Premier League team sending a seven-figure cheque to Portsmouth or any of those other clubs who know what it is like to be bucket-collection skint. In England it never tends to happen. The rich get richer and the poor rattle their tins. In Germany, they appear to have a more generous streak.'

But while everybody talked about Bayern's role in all this, pause for a moment and put yourself in the position of Niebaum and Meier. It must have been painfully humiliating for them to come, cap in hand, to the very man they had hoped to drag from his throne only a few years earlier. Although the short-term loan of two million euros did not, as has been claimed on occasion, save or even really help BVB, no single arrangement – and there were plenty of absurd deals in those years – better illustrates how hopeless Dortmund's situation had become.

In September 2004, the club announced the preparation of a 'capital increase', which simply meant issuing new shares. These were not publicly traded, though, but sold to what the club called 'institutional investors'. Ten million new shares earned Borussia barely 25 million euros, as the share price had fallen from 11 euros to 2.50 euros. Despite this influx of money, the bubble burst for good one month later. In October 2004, Niebaum and Meier had to present the next biannual financial statement. They said the club had lost 67.7 million euros in the last six months and was now 118.8 million euros, or £82m, in the red. Nine days later, Niebaum announced he would step down as the parent club's president and could already present a successor – Reinhard Rauball, for whom saving the club was beginning to become second nature.

But the parent club wasn't the problem, the PLC was. In February 2005, another disturbing item came to light. As early as 2000, the club had sold the marketing rights to their logo and their name to a Cologne-based insurance company (as part of the deal under which goool.de was sold, too). 'For a long time, we didn't want to believe that our former heroes on the board had got us into this jam,' Jens Volke said. 'Figures were mentioned you could scarcely believe. Selling the logo was the final straw. In football, symbols are powerful. For fans, the badge is untouchable.' Ahead of the next home game, against Bochum, 1,500 fans marched from the centre of town to the ground behind a banner that said 'Not For Sale'. And during the home game after that, a 3–0 against Mainz on 26 February, the support began to sing the lines the first club president had penned in the trenches: 'Yet there's one thing that shall remain – Borussia Dortmund will not go down!'

Volke was right: symbols are powerful in football. Niebaum had ridden out many storms over the preceding fourteen months, but in the wake of the badge scandal, the pressure became too much. He resigned as the PLC's CEO and was replaced by Hans-Joachim Watzke on 15 February 2005. The fans loudly demanded Meier's head as well, but Rauball explained that Meier's knowledge of all those intricate deals was needed to put Borussia back on its feet. Which was never going to be easy. During a press conference two days later, an economic adviser by the name of Jochen Rölfs told reporters that there was a financial recovery plan. But he bluntly added: 'If any of the creditors reject this plan, then that's it. It's over.'

It took a while for this to register properly with the club's support. Football fans take their club for granted: it has always been there and will always be there. Of course clubs sometimes ran into financial problems, but under the German system they would have their licences revoked, be demoted to the amateur level, say the third or fourth division, and would sooner or later claw their way back – it had happened to some big teams, such as Hertha Berlin or 1860 Munich. But clubs had become companies since then. And companies could actually go out of business.

Now it was Watzke's job to avoid this nightmare scenario. He was the founder and owner of a healthy mid-size company that made protective clothing, for instance for firefighters. It fed 250 employees and boasted an annual turnover of 20 million euros. Put differently, he had business acumen, but he was way out of his league here. Then again, money is money and a balance sheet is a balance sheet. So Watzke found himself some experts in reviving the half-dead – Rölfs and the aforementioned Thomas Tress – and drew up the said financial recovery plan. The next step was getting the club's creditors to agree to it – and there were no fewer than seventy of them. The vast majority were organised in a creditor group. They listened to Watzke's explanations and ideas during a general meeting, then considered the ramifications. They were promised they would get their money, only not as soon as they had hoped. Basically, they were told that if they insisted on the contracts being honoured immediately, the club was finished and they might not get anything, so it was in their best interests to grant a deferral. Grudgingly, the creditor group voted to give Watzke the benefit of the doubt.

However, there were three major creditors left that were not part of that group, including a real-estate dealer (the man who had acquired the transfer rights to Rosický, Ewerthon and Metzelder) and a Cologne-based bank. They negotiated directly with Borussia and eventually gave the green light. The club was not yet saved, but at last it was breathing again. Provided Watzke could also convince the final creditor – the Molsiris investment fund, the nearly 5,800 men and women who technically owned the stadium and were leasing it back to the club.

Unlike the other sixty-nine creditors, these people had no relationship with Borussia at all – they had just put money into a fund. Many of them didn't care about football at all and couldn't care less whether BVB lived or died. Which is why Monday, 14 March 2005 felt like the day of a cup final for Watzke and his allies. The Molsiris investors were invited to meet Borussia's board in Düsseldorf, listen to the club's plans and then vote yes or no. Since not all of them would attend the meeting, the club had sent every investor a letter, explaining that 'BVB is currently in an existence-threatening financial situation' and would not be able 'to fulfil our payment obligations over the next two years'. The letter concluded: 'The future of the club is now in your hands.'

It was an unpleasant day, cold and windy. 'The club had asked the fans not to come to the airport in great numbers,' Jens Volke said, at the time the spokesman for The Unity. 'They didn't want the investors to feel that we were trying to put pressure on them. You never know what people do when they are afraid. But I just had to be there, so a few friends and I went to Düsseldorf anyway.' One of them told a reporter for *Der Spiegel* magazine that he was cautiously optimistic. Then he added: 'If all else fails, we'll start all over again in the seventh division or whatever. No matter what happens, we'll be loyal.'

Daniel Lörcher, the 19-year-old ultra who had had the idea for the 'Yellow Wall' tifo and was now hoping there would still be a club when the fans put it into practice, wanted to go as well but couldn't. It was his first day on a new job, so he was sitting in the offices of an insurance company in Dortmund, sixty miles east of Düsseldorf. Lörcher, who hailed from a small city near Stuttgart, where Jürgen Klopp was born, had moved to Dortmund all of seven days earlier to save himself all that constant travelling from Swabia to the Ruhr to watch football.

'I'm sorry, but we can't allow you to listen to the radio or anything like that,' the boss said when his new employee walked in. Daniel nodded his head.

'But I tell you what,' the man went on, '*I* will listen to the radio. And as soon as there is any news, I will inform you.'

'That is very kind of you, thank you,' the young Swabian replied. 'Well,' his boss said, 'I know how much this means to you.'

For some reason he couldn't explain himself, Daniel had mentioned in his job application that he wanted to live and work in Dortmund because Borussia was his life. Now he was not only dating a beautiful local girl and living in a nice flat in the city, he had also found a good job, which wasn't easy in a region that had western Germany's highest unemployment rate. But maybe it was all in vain. Maybe there would soon be no football to watch.

When the meeting began at nine o'clock in the morning, there were 444 fund shareholders present. Since these people represented more than 15 per cent of the fund's capital, they were legally in a position to make a binding decision. The longer the meeting lasted, the more worried the handful of fans who were waiting in front of the hall became. Hour upon hour crawled by without a result. Why was this taking so long? The investors knew the situation, so what were they debating about? One of the Molsiris shareholders reported from within the hall that 'the investors are squabbling'. At which point the fans began to discuss the finer points of forming a new club and starting at the bottom of the league pyramid. Would this even be possible? Surely you couldn't have tens of thousands of Dortmund fans travelling to some tiny amateur ground in a rural town?

Finally, after six hours and thirty minutes, the doors opened and the first investors walked out. Seeing the questioning glances, they nodded their heads. Two weeks before Easter, the overwhelming majority of the Molsiris shareholders, some 94 per cent, had voted to let the club live. When the news reached Hans Tilkowski, the goalkeeper of the legendary 1966 side, he said: 'There are no words to describe our joy. This decision was far more important than winning the Intercontinental Cup. We have avoided the drop. Now Borussia has to be about credibility and honesty again.'

Today, 14 March 2005 is generally regarded as Borussia's second day of foundation and is deeply ingrained in the club's collective psyche. Exactly ten years later, on 14 March 2015, more than 2,200 fans re-enacted the 'Not For Sale' march to commemorate the anniversary. Jan-Henrik Gruszecki, the filmmaker and fan activist, said: 'Easter comes early for us. We celebrate the club's resurrection and we are proud of how far we have come in those ten years.'

For the supporters, and also for the men who run the club, the events of 2005 are not only remembered as the story of how BVB came back from the brink, they are also seen as an obligation. An obligation to never forget what happened – and why. 'In a prospectus which was published for the shareholders, in 2000 or 2001,' Watzke told me some years later, 'I saw that Borussia Dortmund were "seeking to develop other business activities in order to become independent from sporting success". It was the greatest rubbish I've read in my entire life. If you stink on the pitch, it'll never work. Which is why our credo now is: it's only about football.' He added: 'There's a headline above everything that we do. That headline is: we want to have maximum sporting success, but we will never again go into debt for it.'

The fans changed as well in the wake of the near-bankruptcy. For decades, Dortmund had been a city dominated by a single sport and defined by a single team, but now the relationship between club and community became even more intense. A poster designed by Tobias Hüsing, a member of The Unity, that said 'We are Borussia' popped up all around town, in shops, pubs, gas stations and the windows of people's flats. The new sense of togetherness was epitomised by the 'Yellow Wall' choreography two months later, in May. Bruno Reckers, a well-known supporter who has followed Borussia next to everywhere since 1963, said: 'After 2005, there was this spirit of change among the supporters, a euphoric mood. We all moved closer together.'

The fans had been very passionate but largely passive onlookers for a number of years. Now they went back to trying to shape the club they followed. The *Fanabteilung*, the supporters' division, was set up in late 2004 and became an official section one year later, during the parent club's AGM in December 2005. Two years later, Jens Volke was presented as Borussia Dortmund's new Supporter Liaison Officer. He was bolstering a team that was growing rapidly. Aki Schmidt had been joined by another former club hero, Sigfried Held, to fulfil the primarily representative duties, while Petra Stüker and a social worker called Sebastian Walleit were doing the hard work, maintaining very close contact with the fans. The Ruhr area magazine *RevierSport* explained that Volke was one of the people who had started the popular *Schwatzgelb.de* fanzine and said: 'Signing Volke means Borussia are getting one of the constructively critical supporters on board.' In 2013, Daniel Lörcher would follow Volke's example and leave The Unity to become a club employee.

Yes, it had all turned out well. Though not for everyone. Michael Meier was reluctant to talk about the last years of his long and largely successful tenure at Borussia Dortmund. He felt he has been made the scapegoat and complained that people only think in black and white. In May 2017, he told *RevierSport*: 'We wanted to achieve big things – and we did. But all the triumphs we celebrated have been forgotten and you are being reduced to one single thing. But I can't change this. If you're not the one who's holding the microphone, there is no resonance to what you say.'

In the first years after stepping down, Gerd Niebaum still gave the occasional interview. In 2010, he told the website *Spox*: 'We wouldn't have got into these problems if we hadn't rebuilt the ground all by ourselves. I have often asked myself if this was the right thing to do, expanding the stadium without public funds. But you also have to see that the rebuilding and the financial crisis have ultimately been shouldered. Yes, it took a lot of effort from a lot of people and the fans had to suffer, which I regret. But the club did come through. It has the stadium, which some people consider the best in Europe, and now also has a competitive team again.' He added: 'I always tried to give my best for the club.'

One year later, in 2011, Niebaum lost the right to work as a notary because of personal financial difficulties. (Notaries are not allowed to go into debt, as they could become susceptible to bribes.) In 2015, he stood trial for general fraud, embezzlement, credit fraud and the falsification of documents. The public prosecutor explained Niebaum had lost money in property deals, was more than 17 million euros in the red and had been driven to acts of desperation. Borussia's former president was found guilty and sentenced to 20 months on probation. He has all but vanished from the public eye.

Four years after the events described in this chapter, Borussia Dortmund celebrated their centenary. On 19 December 2009, exactly one hundred years after the club's foundation, BVB met SC Freiburg at what was now officially called Signal Iduna Park, after the naming rights had been sold to raise much-needed money. Before kick-off on what was a fiendishly cold Saturday afternoon, the ultras on the South Stand presented a spectacular choreography, a vast image that depicted many club greats. There was founding father Franz Jacobi, who defied the Catholic Church to start the club. There was August Lenz, the club's first international. There were Adi Preissler, Aki Schmidt and Lars Ricken. The club, meanwhile, printed a series of posters for the year-long festivities, most of which made some kind of reference to 'the best fans in the world'. At the bottom of the posters, it always said: '*Danke für 100 Jahre echte Liebe*', thank-you for 100 years of real love.

The expression eventually morphed into what may now be German football's most famous corporate slogan: *Echte Liebe*. (Bayern's motto *Mia san mia*, We are who we are, is not a club invention and had been used to describe the Bavarian mentality long before the Munich giants adopted it as their official rallying cry.) It was not the first time BVB attempted to come up with a motto. When the club went public in 2000, it used the slogan 'Tradition, passion and success'. But *Echte Liebe* struck a nerve – and stuck.

As these things go, it is smart, subtle and succinct. Yet it is not an expression you should use too freely these days, because that would mark you out as either a foreigner or as a recent – and even slightly gullible – convert to the black-and-yellow cause. In and around Dortmund, virtually nobody uses the term *Echte Liebe*, unless they are being sarcastic, since it reeks of marketing slang. However, the idea of formulating an identity, even a corporate one, harks back to the days when the club's future was in doubt. 'We sat down and first had a look at the status quo,' Watzke recalled when I talked to him, Michael Zorc and the club's director of marketing, Carsten Cramer, for the *FourFourTwo* cover story in 2013. 'Then we asked ourselves: what is it people expect in this part of the country, the working-class Ruhr area? The answer was that they expect an honest effort and that you give your all. So that informed our new philosophy. We defined the brand as: real and intense. The football should be intense, while we should be real.'

However, it's difficult to be intense and real when you are broke, and when not only the banks and various creditors are on your back but also the DFB. Borussia still hadn't built the youth academy which the game's governing body had been demanding from all Bundesliga clubs for quite some time. So although money was more than tight, BVB finally rented the site of the former Napier Barracks, which the British Army of the Rhine had left in 1995, from the city's municipal works division, with an option to buy it once the financial situation had changed, and began construction on a centre of excellence for the youth teams combined with a modern training centre for the first team. Just a few weeks earlier, on 6 August 2005, a midfielder of Turkish origin who was born thirty miles south of Dortmund and had joined the club as a twelve-year-old gave his first-team debut in a league game against Wolfsburg. At 16 years and 335 days of age, Nuri Sahin became the youngest player in history to make an appearance in the Bundesliga. Borussia Dortmund's youth movement had begun.

The first time I sat down with Jürgen Klopp for an in-depth inter-view, in 2011, I asked him if he had followed the events of March 2005. Was he aware what a close shave it had been for the club? At the time, Klopp was busy keeping newly promoted Mainz in the Bundesliga against all odds, so his mind might have been elsewhere.

'Of course I followed the coverage,' he said. 'After all, the papers were full of it. But I didn't realise the extent to which Borussia were in trouble. Watching from a distance, I thought it was one of those cases where a big club has run into money problems and will somehow solve them.' He paused. Then a smile crept across his face. 'The first time it occurred to me that Borussia Dortmund might not be that well-off was when I received the first offer from them,' he said. 'It was worse than what Mainz was willing to pay me in the second division!' Klopp broke into his trademark roaring laughter and slapped his thigh. 'I said, well, I guess this must be an error.' Giving the club's veteran press officer a wink, he added: 'But we sorted that out.'

Needless to say, even after the Molsiris investors agreed to wait two years for their profit, money continued to be tight in Dort-mund. All you had to do was look at the changing face of the team. In May 2005, Borussia sold Tomáš Rosický to Arsenal. Although the Czech, at 25 years of age, should have been about to enter his prime, BVB technically lost money on the deal. They had signed the player for 12.8 million euros from Sparta Prague and were now, five years later, selling him for close to 10 million euros.

What's more, due to the controversial deal under which the club had pledged some players' values on the transfer market, the move netted Borussia a mere 4.5 million euros. Only a couple of years earlier, this would have been petty cash for Borussia, not even worth a mention. Now it was a lot of money, not least because the club were also relieved of Rosický's considerable wages. That was the reason why Watzke told the press the meagre profit meant 'the club can become active again'.

The Rosický transfer epitomised Borussia's need for money in more ways than one. The team Rosický really wanted to join was Atlético Madrid and Dortmund had already reached an agreement with the Spanish club. But since Borussia demanded a bank guarantee, which Atlético could not or would not provide, the Czech was gently pushed towards London.

While the cost-intensive stars went out, home-grown kids came in. Young players like Florian Kringe, David Odonkor or Uwe Hünemeier had to somehow carry the team through the next years, which promised to be lean. Odonkor had his one moment of glory at the 2006 World Cup, when he used his stunning pace to deliver the cross that led to Germany's winning goal against Poland. (That cross earned him an ill-fated move to Real Betis in Spain – and gave Borussia a heaven-sent windfall of more than 6 million euros.) Hünemeier would help Brighton & Hove Albion to an unexpected promotion to the Premier League more than a decade later. However, with a few exceptions, most notably Sahin, these players were never going to be more than average Bundesliga players, or even slightly below average, because they had been schooled before the country radically remodelled its youth set-up, annually pumping 70 million euros into what was called the Talent Promotion Programme.

Not to put too fine a point on it, these were the years when it was time to leave a sinking ship. But some stayed. An international like Sebastian Kehl, for instance, could have easily found a new club, but while he must have looked around, I suppose he did it half-heartedly. 'I felt at home here,' he told me a few years later, when all had turned out well. 'Over time, the club has become close to my heart and it has given me a lot. Emotion, honesty – they live that here. When the club had problems, I felt an obligation to give something back.'

Although Kehl grew up a three-hour drive away from Dortmund, he truly came to like the place and could relate to the mentality of the people. And the feeling was mutual. When BVB were beaten at home by Hamburg in late 2004, angry fans blocked the team coach's exit and even a club icon like Reinhard Rauball could not reason with them. It was only when Kehl, accompanied by his good friend Metzelder, faced the supporters to discuss the team's performance that the blockade was finally lifted. 'You know, I'm happy that I was rewarded for it,' he told me, meaning his loyalty. 'In sports, there are always ups and downs, but I guess what I've experienced here over a short period of time is pretty unusual. That's why it's awesome to have this success now. It makes me proud.'

But it took a few years for Dortmund to find success again. Money, or the lack of it, wasn't the only reason: there were also a few misguided boardroom decisions. In late 2006, Watzke and Zorc sacked the Dutch coach Bert van Marwijk (the man who had guided Feyenoord to their UEFA Cup triumph against Borussia). That despite the fact van Marwijk had coped admirably with the misfortune of having taken over a big club just prior to its worst crisis ever. The coach had finished seventh in his first two seasons and the team was in ninth place when he was given his marching orders. While this may sound like the very definition of mid-table mediocrity, the popular van Marwijk had done a good job given the circumstances.

To be fair to the club's decision makers, all of this became obvious only after the Dutchman had left and Ottmar Hitzfeld politely declined to take over his former team again ('I was honoured by the offer and did seriously consider it, but at the end of the day it just wasn't right'). Because under the next two coaches, Jürgen Röber and Thomas Doll, the team went into tailspin. Dortmund even flirted with relegation when the team found itself in seventeenth place in late March 2007, just a few months after van Marwijk had been fired and with only seven games left in the season.

A year later, the situation was less dramatic but in its own special way more depressing. Although Dortmund were on a good cup run, their first in ages, the football was sterile and stale and the team ageing. In April 2008, only 61,400 came out to see a terrible home defeat at the hands of Hannover 96. For almost any other club in any other country, this would have been a healthy attendance, but it was almost 20,000 under capacity and nearly unheard of in Dortmund. Only a few months before Klopp arrived, the team was lifeless and lacking passion. In the press stand, and not only there, people pointed at Doll and said: 'He's playing this ground empty.'

A few days later, the coach cracked under the pressure and delivered an on-camera rant that was in equal parts entertaining and embarrassing. Many professional observers had argued in print that young players like Mats Hummels, barely nineteen and just loaned out from Bayern, should get more playing time ahead of veterans whose footballing days were numbered, such as the 35-year-old Christian Wörns and 34-year-old Robert Kovac. 'What's going on here is a total disgrace,' Doll all but spat out. 'There's no respect towards my players. A Wörns and a Kovac won't be here next season, I hear, but they and eight others as well are supposed to pull the chestnuts out of the fire for us. I'm laughing my ass off!' It reads better in print. The original made you wonder if Doll was losing it. And whether his position was still tenable.

Yet those drab, grey years immediately following Borussia's near-bankruptcy also produced one of the most magical, emotional games in club lore. It's the sort of game supporters still reminisce misty-eyed about and remember more fondly than even the 4–1 against Real Madrid. Although, bizarrely, nothing tangible at all was at stake. At least not for Borussia.

First, the background. When Doll was signed, in March of 2007, Dortmund fans still feared the drop ... and something worse. While their club was mired in the relegation zone, Schalke were topping the table. They had a really good chance to win their first ever league title, and their first national championship since 1958, because Bayern were having one of their customary off-years. (This used to happen with regularity, until Dortmund's renaissance under Klopp prompted the Munich giants to remodel themselves into a merciless winning machine.) A Dortmund relegation coupled with a Schalke triumph constituted the worst-case scenario for the black-and-yellow army, but even when a modest resurgence during April dispelled Borussia's most pressing relegation woes, there was still a dreadful spectre that just wouldn't go away. On the penultimate day of the season, 12 May 2007, Dortmund were to host Schalke. Since the visitors were leading Stuttgart by one point, a derby win could hand them the Bundesliga title in Dortmund, at the ground of their oldest and greatest rivals.

Eight days before the game, the Schalke ultras published an open letter, inviting all travelling fans to walk together towards the Westfalenstadion. 'We all realise this is not a derby like any other,' the letter read. 'It is something very special. It will be a uniquely explosive derby, as we can cement our title hopes in Dortmund together with 30,000 Schalke fans.' This figure was no pipe dream. Under Bundesliga regulations, 10 per cent of a stadium's capacity has to be made available to the away team, which in Dortmund entails more than 8,000 tickets. But Schalke fans are extremely resourceful when it comes to procuring tickets for the derby. Some even used to buy Dortmund season tickets, back in the days when these were still easily available, just to see this one game. In the weeks and months leading up to the 2007 derby, more and more tickets from neutrals and even disgruntled Dortmund fans found their way to Gelsenkirchen until the online fanzine *Schwatzgelb.de* urged all BVB supporters who did not want to attend the match to destroy their tickets and then post the shreds to Schalke. But why would a Dortmund fan in possession of a ticket choose to not attend this game? Well, there were many who dreaded a Schalke triumph so much that it made them physically sick and they preferred to stay away. Some even left town for the day. You could not blame them. BVB had won only one of the previous eighteen derbies!

An often-heard complaint says that professional players are merely mercenaries who don't understand the fans and don't share their passion. Maybe this is true. But there are exceptions. Borussia's team that season should have been no match for an excellent Schalke side, but I would sometimes meet Sebastian Kehl and his pal Christoph Metzelder in private during those weeks and it was almost palpable how focused and fired up for the match they were. 'We know how much this means to the fans,' Metzelder told me. 'I cannot promise you that we will win this game, but I promise we'll give everything we've got.'

On the day of the derby, there was a buzz around the entire city and you could sense that something was in the air. Dortmund fans hadn't had this feeling of tense but happy anticipation in a long time and they fed on it, so that the atmosphere at the ground was electric. The 30,000 Schalke fans made a lot of noise, but when Borussia created a chance after only 30 seconds, the home support drowned them out. With a minute left in the first half, Metzelder proved true to his word. He intercepted a pass a few yards into his own half, dashed down the right wing and then whipped in a cross. It was his seventh, and last, season in Dortmund, but nobody had ever seen the centre-back do anything even remotely like this before. What's more, the cross was so precise that Swiss striker Alex Frei was able to knock the ball in from ten yards to beat Schalke's talented goalkeeper Manuel Neuer.

A quarter of an hour from time, the stadium suddenly erupted, although nothing had happened on the pitch. A truly ear-splitting cheer greeted Stuttgart's go-ahead goal away at Bochum, because it meant Schalke had dropped into second place. On 85 minutes, Metzelder, whose imminent move to Real Madrid must have led him to believe he had morphed into some kind of silky-skilled midfield maestro, carried the ball through Schalke's half and tried a shot at goal. It was blocked and fell to Dortmund's Polish attacker Euzebiusz Smolarek. 'Ebi' was popular with the fans, although he missed way too many chances. Not now, though. He volleyed home from inside the box and right in front of the South Stand. Then he climbed the fence and saluted the frenzied mass in front of him.

'After the second goal I almost died from joy,' Reinhard Beck said, today the club's personnel manager. 'It was the most emotional derby ever and the most important in our history. It was really fitting that they had stolen our banner before.' He is referring to the large iconic banner that hung under the roof of the South Stand: *Gelbe Wand – Südtribüne Dortmund*. In November 2006, Schalke fans had broken into the stadium and stolen the banner. (Some hardcore supporters think the loss of the banner means that – under an unwritten ultras codex – Dortmund fans have lost the right to use the term 'yellow wall'.) Although it would be some years until the Schalke fans finally admitted to the deed by brandishing the stolen banner during a derby, there was little doubt who had committed the theft. Borussia's fans took revenge in style.

During Schalke's last game, they chartered a plane that flew over Gelsenkirchen carrying a banner which said: *Ein Leben lang – keine Schale in der Hand*. In this life, Schalke will not get their hands on the league trophy. No wonder that *Schadenfreude* is a German word.

But neither this legendary game nor reaching the cup final a year later thanks to the luck of the draw (in the quarter-finals and the semis, Dortmund met second-division teams at home) could save Doll's job. That tells you a lot about how listless the football had become. Yet who knows what might have happened if Doll had actually won the cup. His side was overmatched against a strong Bayern Munich team, but a late Mladen Petrić equaliser took the game to extra time, in which Oliver Kahn made a brilliant save from a Kringe piledriver before Bayern's Italian marksman Luca Toni put the game away with his second goal.

In a way Dortmund were lucky to lose the final, otherwise Jürgen Klopp might never have signed for Borussia. More luck was to follow. Two weeks after the cup final, second-division Mainz suffered a shock defeat at the hands of Aachen. Klopp had pledged his future to Mainz – provided the team could immediately bounce back to the Bundesliga, having been relegated the previous summer. But now it was unlikely they could win promotion, meaning Klopp was on the market. Yet Dortmund needed a third lucky break to get their man.

Borussia were not the only club interested in Klopp. Bayern's Uli Hoeness had given him a call as early as December 2007 but was unable to convince the other members of the board to hand over the biggest job in the land to a man who had never won anything. (Irony of ironies, the post eventually went to Jürgen Klinsmann, who hadn't even coached a club side before.) Bayer Leverkusen were also in the race, but the overwhelming favourites to sign Klopp were Hamburg, whose chairman Bernd Hoffmann was utterly convinced of his qualities and mesmerised by his character. The local newspaper *Hamburger Abendblatt* would later report that Klopp's wages had already been negotiated and that his wife had begun house hunting in Hamburg.

So why did the deal eventually fall through? Well, because of Klopp's beard. Hamburg's director of football Dietmar Beiersdorfer was less sure about Klopp. He had three other men on his shortlist: former player Bruno Labbadia, the Dutchman Fred Rutten and former Spurs coach Christian Gross. So five Hamburg scouts were sent out to monitor the four candidates and prepare dossiers on them. The scouts kept the coaches under surveillance for three weeks and then gave their verdict. According to their intricate points system, Rutten was the best man for the job. Klopp finished last, because the scouts found fault with his 'appearance', saying he was unshaven and wearing torn blue jeans. They also disliked his 'manner of expression'. At the time, Klopp was working as a pundit for television and the scouts noted with dismay that he would refer to Lukas Podolski as 'Poldi' or Bastian Schweinsteiger as 'Schweini'.

Hamburg's powerful board of directors overruled the chairman, crossed Klopp's name off the list – and then went out and signed someone who hadn't even been scouted, the veteran Martin Jol. 'I don't know if we would have reached the Champions League final if we had signed Klopp back then,' Hoffmann says ruefully, 'but it's highly likely that the club would be in a better shape today.' During the seven years Klopp spent in Dortmund, Hamburg had no fewer than thirteen different coaches.

When I asked Watzke why the club decided to sign Klopp, he replied: 'The reason was this Mainz team. They weren't Real Madrid, but they were unpleasant opponents. They had a plan, they had an enormous will and they always seemed to have more players on the pitch than you did. We felt that the man who had created this team spirit and this mentality could also do it for us.' When I asked Klopp why he had joined Dortmund, he replied: 'I came to Dortmund, because football is of such central importance here. I'm not stupid. I know there are things that are more important than football. But it's what I do and what I love, so I found it very attractive that football takes centre stage here and that people live the game so intensely.' He added: 'This is the most emotional football region in Germany. And even though there are some people twenty miles from here, in Schalke, who will vehemently deny it, I would say Borussia are the most emotional club.'

During his very first press conference, Klopp said he couldn't promise titles but would promise what he termed 'full-throttle football'. Then he said: 'If games become boring, they lose their right to exist.' It was almost as if he had read a manual on how to win black-and-yellow hearts. The hackneyed phrase that working-class people want to see their players work hard has never been totally true in Dortmund, a club with a long history of admiration for elegant, skilful players, from Max Michallek and a much-loved Hungarian called Zoltan Varga, back when BVB were in the second division, to heroes such as Marcel Raducanu and Paulo Sousa. And the reason workhorses in the vein of Murdo MacLeod and Paul Lambert were so popular has less to do with their grafting than their passion for the game, for the team, for the club. When you play for Borussia, you must love what you do. And from the get-go, Klopp oozed that he was loving every minute of it.

Yet there was some opposition. Klopp had been so entertaining on television that some fans, among them leading ultras like Daniel Lörcher, initially dismissed him as a poseur who merely talked a good game. He quickly dispelled those doubts by meeting all major fan pressure groups during the off-season to explain who he was and what he wanted. Still, he – and the club – needed one last lucky break in order to allow them to step into the future. It came at exactly 4.50 p.m. on 13 September 2008. That was the moment when Schalke striker Kevin Kuranyi rose to head a Rafinha cross into an open goal from close range. Miraculously, he missed the target. The goal would have made it 4–0 for Schalke in Dortmund, in what was only the fourth league game for Klopp as BVB coach. People in Dortmund had already become enamoured of his exuberance and fervour, but losing a derby 4–0 at home would have been no laughing matter. A few minutes after Kuranyi's miss, Neven Subotić pulled one back for the hosts. Three minutes later, Frei made it 3–2. And in the closing moments, Borussia were awarded a dubious penalty for handball, which Frei converted to salvage a point that was very sweet indeed.

Borussia did a lot of things right in those first seasons under Klopp, on and off the pitch. In barely three years, the board had managed to reduce the club's debts dramatically. What's more, a favourable deal with Morgan Stanley, the American investment bank, allowed the club to reacquire the stadium by paying off the Molsiris shareholders. Morgan Stanley's loan rates were much lower than the original ones, which gave the club leeway on the transfer market.

BVB still couldn't buy any player who cost more than five million euros, but they didn't really need to. Even when the club signed Poland's best goalscorer in 2010, a certain Robert Lewandowski, the transfer fee was only 4.5 million euros. That same summer, Shinji Kagawa joined for 350,000 euros, or £294,000. Bringing back local boy Kevin Großkreutz from second-division Ahlen was another inspired move. He had been let go at the Under-16 level, because he didn't seem to be much of a prospect. And in a way, he wasn't. But he was BVB through and through. Großkreutz was friends with many ultras, he would do anything for the club and play anywhere the coach asked him to as long as he could don the yellow shirt.

And this shirt was indeed yellow. The club had also done away with all the fancy away kits and atrocities such as purple socks or white shorts. As early as 2000, when the ill-fated company goool. de was formed and the deal with Nike came to an end, Borussia ditched the Americans' neon yellow and decided to stick to a more regular shade of that colour from then on. (Under the RAL colour standard, the ID number is 1023.) Now the club went a step further and decided to play in black and yellow only. It sounds trivial, but the traditionalists among the fans – and most German supporters are traditionalists – appreciated the fact that BVB were no longer issuing second or even third kits in non-club colours just to appear fashionable or trendy and separate supporters from their money.

All of which strengthened the ties between the team and the people in the stands. 'Having young players extends your credit limit,' Watzke told me. 'But not with banks, as in the old days. With supporters! In 2009, the average age of the squad was 22. If these players make mistakes, the fans will forgive them.' And he was right: the fans were patient. Dortmund were very unlucky to miss out on Europe in Klopp's first season (a stoppage-time goal from an offside position for Hamburg in Frankfurt denied BVB), but the second began ominously – with only one win from six games.

Following a disastrous 5–1 drubbing at the hands of Bayern Munich in Dortmund, Klopp decided it was time to leave the city. Literally. He and the squad holed up for two days in a hotel right next to an 800-year-old monastery, sixty miles northeast of Dortmund. It was a good place to take vows, and that's what the players did. During various team meetings, the squad came up with what they called the Pledge. They promised each other 'unconditional effort', 'passionate obsession' and 'determination regardless of the score'. Then they added four mottos: 'Help everyone', 'Allow yourself to be helped', 'Everyone shoulders responsibility', 'Everyone devotes his quality entirely to the best of the team'. Then they put all that in writing and signed it. To this day, Borussia's players see the Pledge each morning when they report for training, because the words and the signatures now adorn the entrance to the first team's building in the training centre. Every new player takes the vow when he signs for Borussia.

Another promise was made during the days near the monastery. Klopp said to me: 'We told the boys they would be getting an extra three days off over the festive season if they – as a team – covered more than seventy-three miles in each of the ten games until the winter break.' In most of the matches, the team exceeded this mark by a considerable margin, but they didn't manage to reach it in every single game. Yet the coach granted them their extra holidays regardless. 'I did that because the extra effort the team put in immediately translated into more liveliness on the pitch,' Klopp said. 'We were instantly more assertive, we created superiority in numbers – all the things you associate with additional effort.'

All that running earned Borussia Dortmund a fine fifth-place finish and the long-awaited return to the European stage. However, it was not yet quite the thrilling gung-ho game that would become Klopp's trademark: the radical gegenpressing BVB would become famous for between 2010 and 2014. Klopp had first used this term in a national publication in June 2008, after he had just taken over at Dortmund. Back then he told *Kicker* magazine: 'Every player will be judged by how much he is willing to chase lost balls or initiate gegenpressing. The perfect moment to win possession is shortly after losing it.' So the style had been on his mind all along, but he and the team had to work on it to take it to another level.

Klopp is often reduced to his man-management or his motivational skills, maybe because most of the drills during training are run by his trusted assistant, his former Mainz teammate Željko Buvač. However, Klopp football in its purest form requires not just supreme fitness and maximum effort but also excellent organisation. And, of course, the right players. Klopp players.

When Zlatan Ibrahimović ran into Klopp at the Ballon d'Or gala in January 2014, he asked in jest: 'When will you bring me to Dortmund?' Klopp protested: 'I would have to sell the whole team.' Whereupon the Swedish superstar said: 'No, I come for free!' Most football fans watched this humorous conversation that underlined how hip Dortmund had become with great delight and it went viral. For Dortmund supporters, though, the exchange was funny on another, second level. Because they knew Ibrahimović would struggle to get a game in Dortmund, even if he indeed came for free. He would never, to use Klopp's words, be 'willing to chase lost balls or initiate gegenpressing'.

In 2008, when Klopp arrived in Dortmund, I used to write columns with (as opposed to ghosting them for) the great Croatian striker Mladen Petrić, the man whose winning goal at Wembley had kept England out of Euro 2008. One week into Klopp's first season, Petrić was sold to Hamburg for a transfer fee and a player called Mohamed Zidan. He called me later that evening, pouring out his heart, telling me how much he would have loved to play for Klopp. However, I guess he knew deep down inside that although Zidan was the lesser player, he was the better Klopp player – a tireless and aggressive runner.

And so it took a while until Klopp had all the players he wanted, which is why it wasn't until the summer of 2010 that German fans finally began to grasp what gegenpressing could be all about if it was applied regularly instead of sparingly. The opening salvo had nothing to do with Klopp, though. It was fired during the World Cup in South Africa, where a fantastic German team dished out maulings to England and Argentina because their counter-attacking game was so overpowering. In the semi-final against Spain, though, the fans watching at home were in for a frustrating and confusing ninety minutes. Whenever a German player won the ball and looked up to play one of those lethal, slicing passes that had given the English such headaches, he saw only red shirts bearing down on him in a hurry. It seemed, to use Watzke's words about Klopp's Mainz team, as if Spain had more players on the field than Germany. When even Philipp Lahm, the smartest and most reliable player of his generation, began to give away possession, you knew Germany had no idea how to combat Spain's game plan. Most people had never seen gegenpressing taken to such extremes.

Four weeks after this game, Manchester City travelled to Dortmund for a pre-season friendly. Before the match, stadium announcer Norbert Dickel interviewed Mike Summerbee, who spoke about his memories of a friendly in 1967, when City beat Borussia 4–0 at Maine Road; he could even remember the names of a few Dortmund players. Times had thoroughly changed, though. City, awash with Abu Dhabi money, had made so many signings that the subs' bench was too small for their squad. ('I wouldn't be surprised if they present five new players an hour before kick-off,' Klopp had quipped on the day before the game.) But the young and cheap Dortmund team beat this expensive collection of superstars with astonishing ease. Kagawa and a rosy-cheeked Mario Götze ran rings round their opponents as BVB won 3–1, despite wasting a penalty. It was the shape of things to come.

If they had played league football in Henry David Thoreau's time, he might have remarked that the mass of fans lead lives of quiet desperation and go to the grave with the song still in them, because most supporters have to content themselves with the little things. It's rare to have success. It's even rarer to see exciting football on a regular basis. In the modern era it has also become unusual to root for a group of players you truly love (instead of respect or admire). Finally, it doesn't happen very often that the face of your club, the coach, seems to be the kind of guy you'd like to have a beer with. Many fans will be more than happy if they can cross off just one of those four points during their life as a supporter. Two would be a dream. Three, miraculous. All four, pretty much impossible. And yet BVB fans found themselves presented with that grand slam in the years that were to follow the City game.

Klopp was loved in Dortmund like no Borussia coach before, not even Ottmar Hitzfeld. Over the years, other teams' fans, who initially regarded him as a breath of fresh air and a welcome change, would tire of Klopp's antics, his intensity and emotionality, even his jokes. Not so in Dortmund. The reason is probably that most people knew the man only from television, while fans in Dortmund all had their very own personal Klopp story to tell, about the day they met him on the streets or in a café. And they invariably found out that the persona he presented on the screen was not a persona at all. He really was like that – intense and emotional. They found out he was mentally and physically incapable of putting up a facade, which is a weakness Ruhr area people welcome. And he was a natural in front of cameras and microphones. Klopp's throwaway line 'We all have a bit of a crush on this club' was better than everything any marketing man had ever come up with. For an obvious reason: he really meant it.

And his team was loved in Dortmund like no team since the side that came within four minutes of winning the league in 1992. It was even hard to identify the fan favourites because there were so many of them. Dede, sidelined by injury, was in his last year with the club in 2010–11, and his status may best be gauged by the fact that Götze scored a wonder goal against Hannover 96 in April and then celebrated by revealing he was wearing Dede's shirt under his own. Needless to say, Großkreutz was another hero and Sahin was considered a local boy. Skipper Kehl and goalkeeper Roman Weidenfeller were loved because they hadn't jumped ship but stuck it out during the crisis years. The most popular player, with Kagawa a close second, was the Pole Jakub Błaszczykowski, who had joined the club in 2007, even before Klopp.

But there was also Neven Subotić, who lived in a modest flat not far from the ground, in the part of the city populated by students and hipsters. There is some scarcely believable footage on YouTube that shows him celebrating the utterly unexpected league title of 2011 with the fans, literally on the streets. Two hours after clinching the championship with two games left, Subotić had been driving home from the stadium when he found the street blocked by partying supporters. He stopped his car right in the middle of a major thoroughfare, climbed onto the roof and began jumping around, bare-chested. Within seconds, he was surrounded by hundreds of supporters, some of whom scaled the car as well and began to pogo on the car boot. Dominik, the fan who preserved the scenes for posterity, told a reporter: 'I suppose his Serbian temperament got the better of him. But he is just a very likeable bloke. He is close to the people and likes to party.' Later, the fans marked the place where Subotić parked his car with a special sign. All these years later, it is still there to commemorate the day Borussia Dortmund became the best team in the league, just six seasons after almost going out of business.

And that was really the icing on the cake – that the highly popular coach and his likeable players delivered exciting football that was also successful. There were moments during Klopp's first title-winning season when most fans just stared at the pitch in disbelief and wondered how those kids who hadn't cost a penny could be so much better than everyone else. They beat Bayern home and away and should have done the same with rivals Schalke (otherworldly goalkeeping from Neuer resulted in a goalless draw in Dortmund). In hindsight, Borussia didn't have the better players, they just had the players with the better plan. And, of course, the good dose of luck you always need. Crucially, there were never any major injury worries, an important aspect because Borussia didn't have the money to add depth to the squad.

Soon, though, the money would come pouring in, if only by German standards. The club's annual turnover jumped from 110 million euros in 2009–10 to 150 million during the title-winning season a year later and then sky-rocketed to 215 million in 2011–12, when Borussia proved they were no fluke but here to stay. With four games left in the season, a cheeky Lewandowski backheel beat Bayern 1–0 at the Westfalenstadion. With four minutes left, Bayern winger Arjen Robben wasted a penalty. Adding insult to injury, the Dutchman then also missed the target from three yards in the dying seconds. The win gave Klopp's team a six-point lead in the league and for all intents and purposes sealed back-to-back championships, just like 1956/1957 and 1995/1996. The 1–0 was also BVB's fourth win on the trot against the Munich giants – and the fifth was not far away.

On 12 May 2012, the two new rivals met at Berlin's Olympic Stadium for the cup final. For the first time in the club's history, Borussia had the chance to join the small group of German clubs who had won the league and cup double, as apart from Bayern only Schalke (1937), Cologne (1978) and Bremen (2004) had pulled off this feat before. Two men in particular rose to the occasion that evening: stadium announcer Norbert Dickel and match programme editor Boris Rupert. That's because their side job is commentating on the games for Borussia's internet radio. Dortmund pioneered this form of coverage in Germany as early as April 1999. President Niebaum was on holiday in the USA and wanted to follow the game between BVB and Bayern from across the Atlantic Ocean. So he asked his marketing people to make the game available through the club's website. An astonishing 15,000

people from fifty-three different countries followed this first internet broadcast of a football match in Germany. Needless to say,
the server quickly collapsed.

Now, more than a dozen years later, as many as 200,000 fans from
all across the world listened to BVB's internet radio coverage. Many
of them certainly had other means of following the match at their
disposal, but they chose this one because of Dickel's and Rupert's
unapologetically partisan comments. In fact, Rupert became the
first-ever reporter to be suspended by the DFB when his emotions
got the better of him during a match between Leverkusen and BVB
in August 2011. A controversial refereeing decision prompted him
to call the man in black an 'asshole'. (Seconds earlier, Dickel had
deemed him 'blind', but was only fined, not suspended.)

The 2012 cup final provided both men with plenty of occasions
to go well and truly batshit. Barely three minutes into the game,
'Kuba' Błaszczykowski squared the ball for Kagawa, who knocked
it into an open net. 'How wicked is that?' Dickel hollered, while his
partner made unidentifiable noises. Robben tied the game midway
through the first half, but shortly before the interval, Kuba turned
Jérôme Boateng in the box and the Bayern defender clumsily
brought him down. 'Do it for us, Mats, do it for us!' Dickel pleaded
as Hummels stepped up to take the ensuing penalty against the
club that had schooled him (and where his father was still working
as the youth coordinator). Neuer guessed the right corner and got
his fingertips to the ball, but the shot was too well placed. Instead
of running down the clock to regroup during the break, Bayern
angrily went looking for another equaliser. Robben's crossfield
pass was intercepted and the counter-attack was lethal. Kagawa
found Lewandowski with a great through-ball and the Pole made
it 3–1. 'He nutmegged Neuer,' Rupert informed his listeners while
Dickel was giggling uncontrollably in the background.

In the second half, Lewandowski added two more goals to
become only the third player to score a hat-trick in a German cup
final – and not against any old team but the biggest and best club

in the country. When Großkreutz nutmegged Schweinsteiger to set up Lewandowski for the 4–1, Dickel hysterically stammered: 'Bugger me, this is sensational!' Ribéry pulled one back for Bayern, but nine minutes from time Neuer gifted Dortmund the fifth goal and Rupert wasted little time in reminding his black-and-yellow audience that Bayern's goalkeeper was 'a lad from Gelsenkirchen'.

While the fans went crazy in the stands, ecstatic about having just witnessed their club's first-ever league and cup double, Watzke paused for a moment. 'After that 5–2,' he later said, 'I looked into the faces of the Bayern representatives in the VIP stand. They were empty, disconsolate. At that very moment, I realised the empire would strike back now and try to hurt our team in a sustained manner.'

While it's undeniably true that Dortmund's youth, strength and stability gave Bayern a mighty scare and led them to redouble their efforts in order to retain their status, one also has to look at the bigger picture. It wasn't only Klopp's Borussia that gave them a headache. As strange as this may sound, by 2012 Bayern were in serious danger of acquiring a nasty, contagious habit – losing. The Munich giants had lifted only two of the six most recent Bundesliga titles. They had lost two Champions League finals in three years, one of them at home, after taking the lead with only seven minutes left and against an inferior Chelsea team. And now they had also lost a domestic cup final, football's equivalent of a cold day in hell (Bayern had suffered only two defeats in their previous seventeen final appearances).

Something had to change and it did. Seven weeks after the cup final, Bayern fired their Dortmund-born director of football Christian Nerlinger and replaced him with a former Dortmund player: Matthias Sammer. In the following month, the club signed Athletic Bilbao's defensive midfielder Javier Martínez for 40 million euros (£32m), 10 million more than Bayern had ever spent on a player. Then they shelled out another 18 million euros for defender Dante and striker Mario Mandzukić. As the reader may recall from the first chapter of this book, it was Mandzukić who scored Bayern's first goal in the 2013 Champions League final against Dortmund, a close game in which Martínez probably made the difference, because he was clearly his team's best outfield player.

Although Bayern won that final, they didn't stand a chance with regard to the popularity contest. As the *Daily Mail* put it: 'What's not to like about Borussia Dortmund? Led by a charismatic, though endearingly "geeky" manager with a university degree, proponents of thrilling, fast-paced, incisive football with some of Europe's most talented youngsters, and roared on weekly by one of the most formidable stands in world football. They are a "football hipster's" dream. Now they've gone mainstream with a place in the Champions League final, having left the likes of Real Madrid, Manchester City, Malaga and Ajax trailing in their wake.'

In other words, Franz Jacobi's ragtag group of rebellious Borsig-platz boys had become the coolest club in the world.

CHAPTER 12

Six months after the 2013 Champions League final, the *Guardian* journalist David Hytner tried to explain why Borussia Dortmund had become, as he put it, 'everyone's second team'. He listed five points: the matchday experience, the cheap prices, Klopp's 'high-octane playing style', the club's business model – and what he termed 'traditional values'.

This is an aspect non-Germans often bring up when asked to explain their fascination with Borussia. They don't always borrow Hytner's expression. Some say the club feels 'authentic', others remark that it still seems to be a 'real club', not a corporation milking the leisure market.

You could shoot many holes into this argument, as there is plenty of ammunition lying around, starting with the fact that BVB are a publicly listed company. Hytner admits as much, saying that his concept of traditional values 'is a wishy-washy notion and Dortmund's detractors accuse them of being holier-than-thou'. And yet there is still an awful lot of truth to the notion. Compared to many of their competitors on the international stage, BVB are an anomaly, a club owned by members (remember, the plc is the parent club's property) trying to hold their own against multinational megacorps.

That isn't all, though. There are quite a few other clubs among the European elite which are owned by their supporters rather than by rich businessmen or conglomerates, most notably Bayern, Barcelona and Real Madrid. However, there are two major differences between Dortmund and those teams. The first is that

Borussia are still essentially a community-driven club rather than a global brand. The second is the support. It is in the nature of such things that the fans often complain about not being heard or even being ignored, and BVB supporters regularly carp about that, but I am not aware of any club of this size that employs so many SLOs and is so concerned about what the people in the stands, as opposed to those sitting in front of a television set, want and need.

Yet maintaining this position is a daily struggle. On the one hand, Borussia are actively interested in proving the German philosopher Theodor Adorno wrong. He said: 'There is no true life within a false life.' In other words, Dortmund believe there is a way to compete at the top without betraying the core elements of the club's identity, which BVB themselves define as 'rebelliousness, loyalty and down-to-earthness'. But to do this, the club needs to have a certain amount of success. After all, anybody can be rebellious, loyal and down-to-earth in midtable mediocrity. You only prove a point when you reach the top and still refuse to sell out.

In the summer of 2014, I sat down with Hans-Joachim Watzke for a long interview, parts of which appeared in *11Freunde* magazine, the biggest German football monthly. Although a new season was about to begin, we talked only fleetingly about football itself. The more pressing subjects were money and a growing number of unhappy fans – or, more precisely, fans who were worried about their club's expanding commercial interests and BVB's internationalisation. Dortmund had just become the first German club with an office in East Asia, having opened one in Singapore. Carsten Cramer, the director of marketing, explained the decision by saying: 'Our main focus is still on German-speaking territories and neighbouring countries.' (This was a nod towards Poland, where Borussia had become massively popular due to the central roles played by Lewandowski, Piszczek and Błaszczykowski.) He added: 'But it is our duty to reach out into the world. We have to use the momentum our success in Europe has given us.'

A large part of Borussia's support was sceptical about this

direction. In contrast to the 1990s, the club's enormous success on the pitch had not led to complacency and smugness in the stands. Dortmund fans were still critical and active as regards fan matters. In 2010, a league-wide supporter initiative called 'Kein Zwanni für 'nen Steher' (which roughly translates as: not twenty euros for a standing-area ticket) criticised the Bundesliga clubs' tendency to overcharge the supporters on the terraces. The initiative's two main spokesmen were BVB fans (Daniel Lörcher and Marc Quambusch).

The lively, bustling Jan-Henrik Gruszecki, meanwhile, was the most prominent face of a spectacular campaign called '12:12'. At almost every ground in the upper echelons of the German game, not just the top flight, both sets of fans kept quiet for the first twelve minutes and twelve seconds during games in December 2012. This unusual display of solidarity among rival fans was a protest against safety measures proposed by the league that included cutting down on the number of tickets for away fans. Supporters across the league considered the plans unfair and excessive and a rush job. The demonstrations were ultimately successful and the regulations scrapped.

The anti-commercial, anti-sanitisation stance common among BVB fans would later lead to some unpleasant scenes and an unheard-of penalty. When RB Leipzig travelled to Dortmund in February 2017, some of their fans were attacked outside the ground while a great number of anti-RB banners, not all of them very tasteful, covered large parts of the South Stand. The DFB ordered the terrace to be closed for the next home game as a penalty. The club criticised 'a collective punishment against 25,000 spectators, of which the overwhelming majority cannot be blamed or accused', but accepted the decision because 'refusal of the penalty or parts of it by BVB could be misinterpreted as the club's lack of insight into the gross misconduct of parts of the fans. This impression would be fatal!'

The reason for all that antipathy was that RB Leipzig are

financed and controlled by Austrian energy-drink giants Red Bull, a scenario that should have been prevented by the '50+1 rule'. However, Red Bull broke the spirit, if not the letter, of the rule by simply forming their own club and somehow got away with it. In the eyes of many people, it proved that German football, Europe's last bastion of 'traditional values', was becoming more and more corporate and mercantile.

When I asked Watzke about those and similar concerns with regard to Borussia in 2014, he replied: 'We cannot model ourselves on St. Pauli. Because that would mean being moderately successful. Moderate success is no longer an option for Borussia Dortmund. We now have more than nine million fans. They would not be happy if we lower the tickets prices, remove all advertising boards from the ground, go back to calling the stadium Westfalenstadion, promote UNICEF on our shirts – and finish fourteenth.'

The great irony is that BVB of course didn't do any of that – but still found themselves stone last seven months after this conversation, as late as February 2015. Needless to say, though, Watzke was right. To stay with the analogy used by the *Daily Mail* of the hipster who has gone mainstream, in the wake of their 2012–13 Champions League campaign, Klopp's Borussia became football's equivalent of Kurt Cobain's Nirvana: a cult band beloved by the underground that had suddenly and unexpectedly broken through, capturing the imagination of millions of people and inspiring kids in every corner of the globe. Now the trick was to ride this wave of popularity – without losing your mind over it.

Another trick was holding on to players who had been catapulted into the limelight. Nuri Sahin had jumped at the chance to join Real Madrid as early as 2011, Kagawa left one year later for Manchester United, Götze joined Bayern in the summer of 2013. (Amazingly, all three would be wearing the yellow shirt again within a few seasons, but that's another story.) None of these transfers was avoidable. Both Sahin and Götze had release clauses in their contracts, while Kagawa was in the last year of his contract, so the sale to Man United was the only chance to get money for him. What's more, Borussia had already signed İlkay Gündoğan from Nuremberg, for a modest 4.5 million euros. The Gelsenkirchen-born (!) midfielder of Turkish origin could more than capably replace Sahin as a deep-lying playmaker or fill Kagawa's role in the hole behind the striker.

Things were different, though, when Lewandowski asked to be released from his contract to sign with Bayern in June 2013. Thanks to all that Champions League money, Dortmund did not need Bayern's millions. But they needed the player. In only three years, Klopp had taken the side from fifth place in the Bundesliga to the Champions League final, and there just had not been any time, or funds, to add real depth to the squad. Borussia's chief scout, the 40-year-old Sven Mislintat, had already targeted a lightning-fast forward called Pierre-Emerick Aubameyang at Saint-Étienne, but nobody knew if the deal would happen, as some other clubs, among them Newcastle United, were also interested in the Gabonese international. What's more, Aubameyang seemed to be an out-and-out winger so there was nobody who could take up Lewandowski's role at centre-forward. BVB put their foot down – the Pole had to stay in Dortmund for one more year. His agent Cezary Kucharski called the club's position 'inhuman' and reminded the fans that Lewandowski's 'heart and mind are elsewhere', yet Borussia were adamant.

It seemed a recipe for disaster, but instead of pouting and complaining, Lewandowski, always a model pro, got down to business and went on to lift the Bundesliga's Golden Boot for the first time, becoming only the third Dortmund player to win this honour. (The others were Lothar Emmerich and Marcio Amoroso.) Apart from a brief blip around Christmas, Borussia were never in danger of missing out on the Champions League, eventually finishing as runners-up behind a steamrolling Bayern juggernaut that was now steered by Pep Guardiola. Add to this a nice cup run (Dortmund were unlucky to lose the final against Bayern, because a legal Hummels goal that would have given his team the lead wasn't allowed to stand) and a decent showing in Europe and the fans were quite happy with a season that went a lot better than expected, given Götze's departure and the Lewandowski transfer turmoil.

During the off-season, Klopp expertly addressed his problems. He signed the most prolific striker in Italy, Torino's Ciro Immobile, and one of the best forwards in the Bundesliga, Hertha Berlin's Adrian Ramos. Then he hit upon the inspired idea of putting right-winger Aubameyang up front. Twelve months after BVB didn't have a single stand-in for Lewandowski, there were suddenly no less than three potential replacements. What's more, all three were different types of forwards, meaning the team now had something it used to lack – stylistic flexibility. The same went for other parts of the pitch. Fan favourite Kagawa was rescued from his Manchester exile to bolster an offensive midfield that already included Gündoğan and the gifted but occasionally overly sensitive Henrikh Mkhitaryan. Dortmund could now attack with pace or patience, with skill or muscle, depending on the situation.

Which is why the fans were brimming with expectation when the new season began with a home game against Leverkusen. They were hoping their team was now in a position to give mighty Bayern a proper run for their money again. The South Stand was in particularly fine form on this Saturday, 23 August 2014, colourful and vociferous. The din was deafening, as Hakan Çalhanoğlu and Stefan Kießling were waiting to kick off. The two Leverkusen players avoided looking at the heaving, rolling sea of yellow for too long, instead eyeing each other or inspecting the grass growing between the white lines of the centre circle. Then Çalhanoğlu, standing to Kießling's left, turned his head and looked over his shoulder to observe Deniz Aytekin, the referee. Aytekin looked at the watch on his left wrist. It was exactly 3.30 p.m. He blew his whistle and Kießling nudged the ball over to Çalhanoğlu to start the game.

BVB still had a reputation for an ultra-aggressive approach, so Çalhanoğlu cannot have been surprised when there were immediately two opponents upon him. He quickly passed to his left, where his teammate Son Heung-min was trying to make a run. By the time the ball reached the South Korean, he too was facing two opponents. With the outside of his right foot, Son knocked the ball over to the left wing and into the path of his onrushing full back Sebastian Boenisch.

Dortmund's Greek centre-back Sokratis Papastathopoulos knew this could mean danger. He shifted over to Borussia's right flank and was just about to pick up speed and try to intercept the pass when he noticed that his midfielder Milos Jojić was running towards the point where Boenisch would make contact with the ball. Sokratis hesitated, hoping that Jojić could clear the situation with a sliding tackle. But he didn't. Boenisch got to the ball a fraction of a second before Jojić could and played a first-time pass back into the centre of the pitch.

This must have been the moment when Klopp sensed trouble. Surging forward with their customary gusto, three times his men had created two-on-one situations within the first five seconds of this game – without winning or blocking the ball. This could only mean one thing: they were now outnumbered at the back. More precisely, it was right back Piszczek who was outnumbered. As Boenisch's diagonal pass came sizzling across the grass, he had to mark both Kießling and Karim Bellarabi, not knowing which of the two would collect the pass. It turned out to be Bellarabi. With his first touch, the Leverkusen striker controlled the ball. With his second, he nutmegged Piszczek. With his third, he scored from ten yards out.

On the terrace behind the goal, the 24,500 fans fell abruptly silent. At the sidelines, Klopp smiled a sour smile, then looked at the ground and slowly shook his head. Before any of his players had touched the ball in the new season, his team had fallen behind. In the press stand, the reporters stared at the stadium clock, then consulted the record books. Nine seconds. It was the fastest goal in the history of the Bundesliga.

It was not the moment that derailed Dortmund's season and would lead to Klopp's stunning decision to step down – that had more to do with an uncanny injury curse – but it was emblematic of what was to come. For the next five months, what could go wrong did go wrong. In fact, even things that couldn't really go wrong somehow did.

On 14 December 2014, Jan-Henrik Gruszecki walked towards the door of his Dortmund flat with a heavy heart. The 30-year-old was returning from Berlin, where he had watched Borussia deliver yet another depressing and by and large inexplicable performance. The same players who not very long ago had thrilled an entire continent with daring attacking football, turning spectators into fans wherever they went, had stumbled across the pitch like shell-shocked soldiers. Klopp had watched it all from the sidelines with the body language of a man who was rapidly reaching his wits' end. A rather pedestrian Hertha team had won the game 1–0, sending Dortmund into a relegation spot.

Relegation. As Gruszecki grabbed the door handle, this most unthinkable of scenarios was no longer out of the question. In fact, Borussia had been in last place a couple of weeks earlier, for the first time in almost three decades. But back then, following another stinging setback in Frankfurt, most observers still felt that Borussia were merely unlucky. Ridiculous injury woes and a string of bad breaks had conspired against a team that was doing many things right. They played well, they put in the requisite effort, they created goalscoring opportunities. But now that was no longer the case. There had been just too many unlucky defeats and too many bad breaks for the players. Now they had begun to play like what the table said they were – candidates for the drop.

Gruszecki turned the handle and wondered how you could stop such a downward spiral. At every other club, the solution would have been obvious: sack the coach and bring in what Germans call a fireman, a manager who specialises in hopeless situations. But in Dortmund, this was not even a theoretical possibility. Gruszecki wondered if he could think of a precedent in Bundesliga history. Had there ever been a team that was supposed to challenge for the title and then hit rock bottom without eliciting calls for the manager's head? No, he concluded, this was a first. It made him proud of his club, but it didn't make the situation any less desperate.

Gruszecki opened the door to his flat and squinted. He turned his head to shield his eyes from the light. Then he looked again. There were heavy wooden tables, littered with steins of beer, in the middle of his living room. There were stag antlers on the walls. Cigar smoke hung in the air. And there were eighteen young men in dark three-piece suits and stiff collars milling about. Gruszecki knew what these men were doing in his flat. They were forming Borussia Dortmund. But that doesn't mean it didn't still blow his mind.

'I was stepping from December 2014 into December 1909,' he recalled. 'When I'd left my flat to go to Berlin, they had only just begun building the set. But when I returned I walked straight into a faithful reconstruction of the pub room in which Borussia was founded.'

Two years earlier, Gruszecki had started a crowdfunding project together with two friends. Their aim was to raise at least 120,000 euros to finance a film about Borussia's formative years. During the initial research, Gruszecki learned that the actual room where the club came into being would soon be auctioned off by court order. He put in the winning bid and now lives in what is literally his club's birthplace.

The three film-makers eventually collected 259,000 euros, a national record for such ventures. The money came from close to 3,000 individuals, among them Marco Reus, who sold one of his match-worn shirts, and Klopp, who held an autograph session and then donated the revenue. The club was very supportive, too, which is why Carsten Cramer was present when Gruszecki returned from Berlin to stumble into the filming of the moment when Borussia were founded.

At one point, Cramer turned towards Gruszecki and said: 'This makes you realise how big the club is – and how fleeting the present.' Gruszecki had a similar thought. 'I was watching the filming and realising that our problems in the league were nothing to worry about. I said to myself: if we go down, so what? This club is about much more than just winning or losing a few football games.' However, he was also convinced that if Borussia should not win the next two games, they would indeed go down.

Seven days later, Klopp was standing on the pitch in Bremen, staring into a relentless camera and looking at least four years older. 'The only good news today,' he said on this damp and dark and depressing evening, 'is that 2014 is over, that the first half of the season is over.' He wearily tilted his head to one side, indicating he was now referring to hosts Werder Bremen. 'In the dressing room next to ours they are already celebrating staying up, but all I can say is: I wouldn't write us off.'

His team, which had won each of the previous six games against Werder, scoring sixteen goals in the process, had just been beaten 2–1. It was Borussia's tenth defeat in the league since that day in August when Bellarabi had found the target after nine seconds. The loss meant that Dortmund, who had finished each of the last four Bundesliga seasons in first or second place, went into the winter break in seventeenth place. The 2013 Champions League finalists were thirty points behind Bayern Munich. They even trailed surefire relegation candidates Paderborn – the self-styled 'most hopeless team in Bundesliga history' – by four points. It was a meltdown of historic proportions. Not since Alemannia Aachen in 1969 had a reigning Bundesliga runner-up placed so low around Christmas.

Almost a year later, during the team's winter training camp under a new coach, I sat down with a few of the players to ask them if they had an explanation for what happened in Klopp's final season. They all shook their heads. 'Football has become so competitive that you can't take anything for granted any more,' Mkhitaryan, normally highly eloquent, said. 'That's football. Everything is possible.' Left back Marcel Schmelzer, one of those footballers Klopp had turned from a reserve-team player into an indispensable part of a championship-winning side, replied: 'Once you have fallen into a downward spiral, it's very difficult to get out of it again. You go into a game knowing you just have to win – and suddenly you're down a goal yet again. It becomes a vicious circle.'

The mental aspect certainly played a role. The string of injuries – things got so bad that Gündoğan, who had been sidelined for 430 days with a complicated back injury and who should have been eased in very slowly, was asked to go the distance again and again, because although he wasn't fit he was at least healthy – resulted in a few defeats and suddenly a group of players who were not used to losing went into games with losing on their minds.

It seemed to be a particular problem for Mkhitaryan. The Armenian was the most expensive player in Borussia's history, having been signed from Shakhtar Donetsk for 27.5 million euros, or £23.5m, in 2013. He was one of the most technically accomplished players in club history, not to mention one of the smartest, nicest and politest professional athletes you could ever hope to meet. But now he couldn't hit the broad side of a barn. As he told the BBC's *Football Focus*: 'At Dortmund, I was very stressed after a few games when we were playing really bad. Klopp showed me the way. He supported me and told me I had to keep my head up because good things were coming. I am thankful to Klopp. He worked on my personality and the psychological part.'

The loss of Lewandowksi also proved to be more of a problem than it should have. While Aubameyang was a revelation, Immobile and Ramos could not live up to expectations. Before the season, I had offered business manager Zorc a bet on behalf of a magazine. I said his team would score twenty goals less than the previous year, or exactly the number netted by Lewandowski. 'Normally I don't bet,' Zorc replied. But then he added he would even wager 500 euros to go to a good cause if the magazine would do the same. 'That's because we are absolutely convinced,' he explained, 'that we are well positioned in attack.' By Christmas, Borussia had scored eighteen goals, compared to thirty-eight a year earlier.

But there was another thing you heard again and again during those weeks that turned into months. As early as November 2014, Klopp was asked if his football had been 'decoded', meaning if the opposition had learned how to put what the coach liked to call his 'pressing machine' into neutral. The question never failed to annoy Klopp – 'Can you decode pace?' he once responded with thinly veiled sarcasm – but it may have been a valid one if rephrased only slightly. Of course football isn't a computer program you can easily infect with a virus once you know the code. But maybe, after seven years under the same coach, Borussia's game had become one-dimensional. Maybe the team needed a new impulse, a change of style.

When I discussed this with Mkhitaryan many months later, he came up with an unusual simile: 'Take as an example the restaurant business. If you have a good restaurant, there will be people coming to eat at your place every day. But if you have the same menu for five or six years, they will eventually grow tired of your restaurant. I think it's the same with football. Every once in a while, you have to change your style and show your supporters that playing in a different way can be fun, too.' (Mkhitaryan grew up in France, so he may know a thing or two about *la belle cuisine*.)

Still, the most amazing thing, perhaps even more surprising than the mess Dortmund were in, was that nobody demanded the manager's head. During the winter break, Watzke publicly stated: 'We will never sack Jürgen Klopp. The services he has rendered to this club are incredible. There will never arise a confrontational situation between us.' He added that he was optimistic the team would turn things around, but admitted: 'Reaching Europe through the league has become impossible.' The fans felt the same.

Even when Dortmund suffered yet another shock defeat at home, against Augsburg, and dropped into last place in early February, there were no demonstrations or blockades, as in 2004. There were actually fans who said they'd rather go down with Klopp than replace him with a great-escape expert and stay up. It turned out to be a moot debate, because the reversal of fortunes was already underway.

As was so often the case, a Klopp team improved after the winter break. By early March, when Schalke came to town for another Ruhr derby, Dortmund had managed to put a couple of points between themselves and the drop zone and could breathe more freely. It was a special occasion, because I was taking two English fans – Aston Villa supporters from Cannock, twenty miles northwest of Birmingham – to the South Stand. Three months earlier, Ryanair had introduced matchday specials from London Stansted to Dortmund because, as the company's spokesman Robin Kiely said, 'Borussia Dortmund have built up a sizeable fan base in the UK.'

Tony Collins and Jim Coney, the two Villains, did not support BVB, though. ('I don't care who wins,' Jim said as we were walking towards the ground, 'I just want to see a good game.') They were here to watch the football from what was now perhaps the most famous terrace in the world and then tell me what they thought for a *FourFourTwo* feature. Their tickets cost less than £12, which left them speechless. Truth be told, though, seeing Borussia for £12 is almost impossible, because tickets for the terrace are like gold dust in Dortmund, where many people actually prefer to stand. In fact, when you notice empty seats at Dortmund's ground, you shouldn't assume that those tickets weren't sold. What happens quite often is that someone pays a lot of money for a really good seat, but then tries to sneak past the stewards and onto the terrace.

Although Borussia were eight places below rivals Schalke in the standings, the hosts dominated the match and created an almost absurd amount of excellent chances. Under former Chelsea coach (and, ironically, future Villa manager) Roberto Di Matteo, Schalke had picked up a defensive style that was not easy on the eye but yielded results. They sat back and absorbed the pressure – until, with twelve minutes left, a Mkhitaryan pass was deflected into the path of Aubameyang, who poked the ball past the goalkeeper right in front of the South Stand. Without breaking stride, he picked up a small bag that was lying behind the goal and waved towards his good friend Marco Reus to join him. Then they put on Batman (Aubameyang) and Robin (Reus) masks and waved at the fans going bonkers on the terrace. The final result was 3–0.

'All-seater stadiums have ruined football,' Jim mused later that day. 'I've heard people say this before, but I was never convinced of this. Today I am.' Tony added: 'You don't know what you've missed until you see it. You'll never get an atmosphere like that in England now. Impossible.' He gestured towards his jacket. 'I was showered in beer when the first goal went in. Brilliant! I loved every second! It brought back memories of my youth on the Holte End.'

The derby win gave BVB another boost and soon the team was well on its way to doing what Watzke had deemed impossible, getting into Europe after all. Which made the events of 15 April 2015 even more stunning. During the morning of this Wednesday, a rumour began making the rounds that Klopp would step down at the end of the season. This forced the club to hastily arrange a press conference, as any company trading stock has to inform the public of any developments that could influence the share price. At 1.32 p.m., press officer Sascha Fligge welcomed the assembled media and announced that 'the subject of this press conference is one we all hoped would never come up'. Chairman Hans-Joachim Watzke, sitting next to Klopp, was ashen-faced and spoke in a halting voice when he said that the coach had decided it was time to leave the club. Compared to Watzke, Klopp seemed calm and composed. He explained: 'I have stated on numerous occasions in the last years that I would let everyone know as soon as I have the feeling to no longer be the perfect coach for this exceptional club.'

Klopp then answered many questions, but by and large could say little more than that he had a gut feeling something needed to change. He was still speaking when I received a text message from a well-known Dortmund fan. It read: 'God, I already miss this guy!' After 29 minutes, Fligge ended the press conference. He said: 'This is a sad day for BVB.'

Klopp's announcement sent shock waves through the city, even though there was a general feeling that he might have picked the right moment to move on. He was already the coach with the longest tenure in club history and many fans could see that he had a point when he hinted a fresh start would do both him and the club a lot of good. Having said that, Klopp had grown into such a titanic figure – without doubt the most popular coach Dortmund had ever had and probably just as important as Hitzfeld – that his departure was always destined to leave a gaping hole. Tickets for his last game as Dortmund coach, an entertaining 3–2 over Bremen, were as sought-after as tickets for a final and the ultras honoured him with a touching choreography. It read: 'Thank you, Jürgen' and, borrowing an aphorism from the Austrian writer Ernst Ferstl: 'We need many years to understand how precious moments can be.'

It bears repeating: while non-Dortmund supporters had long since tired of Klopp's antics – the jumping around and the hollering, the chest-beating and those arguments with the fourth official – BVB fans had never wavered in their loyalty and sympathy. And that meant Klopp's successor would always face an uphill struggle, no matter who he was. As it turned out he was the man who seemed perfectly qualified for the post – Thomas Tuchel, the coach who had followed Klopp at Mainz.

There were so many parallels between the two men, it was almost uncanny. A year before Klopp announced he was leaving Dortmund, Tuchel had shocked Mainz by saying he had taken the club as far as he could and would go on a sabbatical. Like Klopp in 2008, Tuchel had never won anything yet was regarded as the hottest coach in the country. During his sabbatical, he was linked with a bewildering array of teams, from Schalke and VfB Stuttgart to RB Leipzig. Before the World Cup in Brazil, there were reports that he might follow Joachim Löw as national coach and in March 2015, rumours suggested he might join Bayern Munich as assistant coach to take over from Pep Guardiola in 2016, when the Catalan's contract would run out.

And as had been the case with Klopp, the club that came closest to signing him were Hamburg. In fact, Hamburg must have been very sure of securing his services. When the club sacked their manager in late March, they did not replace him with a proper coach, despite being in a relegation fight, but instead asked director of football Peter Knäbel to stand in. It was a gamble, and Hamburg lost again. On the same day that Klopp gave his press conference, Knäbel was fired. In other words, Hamburg knew that Tuchel was so perfect for the vacancy that had suddenly arisen in Dortmund that the chase to get him was over.

But how perfect was Tuchel really? While he could be just as intense as Klopp, his passion was cerebral not instinctive. Like his great role model, Pep Guardiola, he had a reputation as only caring about the game as played between the white lines. Like Guardiola, he refused to give one-on-one interviews and rarely if ever mingled with the fans. Even though Tuchel did his very best to come across as more outgoing and less manic than during his years at Mainz, he never really lost this cold-fish stigma during his two truly astonishing years in Dortmund.

'As a person, and also as a coach, Klopp is probably more emotional than Tuchel,' Mkhitaryan told me in early 2016, during the club's winter training camp in Dubai. 'Maybe that's why Klopp's playing style was more about counter-attacks and pressing. Tuchel's philosophy is to keep possession and play very offensive football. He is a mentally strong person and has changed a lot in this team from the first day.'

During that camp, I also met Andre Arendsee, a fireman who

follows the club everywhere. It was his thirty-fifth training camp with BVB. I first asked him about the general feeling surrounding the club. 'Borussia have to be careful,' Andre said. 'They can't become too commercial or they'll be beaten round the head with that motto they have – real love. But they know this. Still, it will be difficult. They have won so many new fans. They have to stay true to themselves and remain who they are. But at the same time they have to move forward.'

Then I asked him about Tuchel. 'I think he's a good choice,' Andre replied. 'He has won over people quickly. Of course the results have helped, but it's also that he's turned out to be a lot more open and approachable than people thought.' The results were indeed very good. In Tuchel's first year, Borussia finished second and collected no fewer than 78 points, a new Bundesliga record for runners-up. (The previous record had been set by Schalke way back in 1972.) What's more, the team scored 82 goals, which was a new club record in the Bundesliga.

But there were some dark clouds gathering on the horizon. A few weeks after the team returned from Dubai, Tuchel and Mislintat came to blows. With hindsight, it was telling that their row had nothing to do with how they did their jobs. Both men respected and even admired each other in a professional capacity, but somehow could not get along as people. They stopped talking to each other and Mislintat even chose to stay away from Borussia's training centre. Also with hindsight, it spoke volumes that Borussia never considered replacing Mislintat, who had just urged the club to sign a talented kid from France called Ousmane Dembélé. Quite the contrary, the scout was even given more responsibilities.

The rift between the men who ran the club and the man who ran the team deepened in the summer of 2016. Three key players, who had only one year left on their contracts, were courted by other clubs: İlkay Gündoğan (Manchester City), Mats Hummels (Bayern Munich) and Henrikh Mkhitaryan (Manchester United). During a televised interview, Watzke said: 'I don't think we can get all three to extend their contracts, so I don't believe all three will be here next year.' Then he added: 'But it's utterly out of the question that all three will be gone next year.' However, that is what happened. By all accounts, the one man out of this trio Tuchel wanted to stay was Mkhitaryan, but when United agreed to pay 42 million euros (£32.5m), the Armenian was let go. It was a very lucrative summer for Borussia – but the selling spree appeared to put an end to the title ambitions Tuchel must have harboured. He cannot have been happy.

Then came the attack.

A few minutes after seven o'clock in the evening on 11 April 2017, Borussia Dortmund's players climbed onto their team coach with the kind of determined calmness that comes with routine. True, in ninety minutes the players were supposed to contest a Champions League quarter-final against AS Monaco. But although there were many young players in this Dortmund team, the core of the side had been together for a long time and had played many games as big, or even bigger, than this one.

Slowly, the coach left the parking lot of the team's hotel and spa in southeast Dortmund, five or six miles away from the stadium. At 7.15 p.m., the bus turned onto the hotel's driveway. Seconds later, it passed a hedge. Suddenly, there were loud bangs, almost like explosions. For a short moment, some players thought the coach was being pelted with stones. It wouldn't have been the first time. Sometimes, on particularly volatile away trips, opposing fans will attack a team's coach by throwing bottles or paint bombs. It's the reason some people think that team coaches should be allowed to have bulletproof glass. However, this is against the law because of security measures: if a coach has an accident, the passengers must be able to shatter the windows and climb out. And so the windows of Dortmund's team bus were not bulletproof.

They were made of safety glass, though, so the players knew that nobody was throwing stones when they heard the sound of breaking glass. Something must have hit the coach with unusual force.

Metal pins were flying through the air. Dortmund's Spanish defender Marc Barta was bleeding. A smell hung in the air that told the players there had indeed been explosions. 'Go, go!' they yelled at the driver. He accelerated, turned onto a busy two-lane road, and sped down the street until he was sure they were out of the danger zone. Then he stopped the bus to see what had happened.

But what exactly had happened? The police quickly found out that three roadside pipe bombs, filled with shrapnel, detonated when the coach passed by. Luckily for the players, the middle one had been aimed too high and missed the target, otherwise many of the passengers would have been seriously wounded, perhaps even killed. But who was behind the attack? In the immediate aftermath of the incident, most people assumed it was an act of terrorism. It was an easy assumption to make, especially for Germans. After all, suicide attacks near the Stade de France in Paris had killed three people during a friendly between Germany and France in November 2015, so the public was aware that football could be a target for terrorists. Dortmund's president Rauball, who had been in Paris, said 'our politicians and our society' had to find ways of dealing with the terrorist threat, while chairman Watzke told the players: 'Let's prove that our society will not cave in to terrorism.'

Ten days would pass before Rauball, Watzke, the club's players and fans found out that this had not been an attack on a society or a country. It had been an attack specifically aimed at Borussia Dortmund. And the motive was not terrorism – but money.

To understand all this – to the extent that an act of insanity can be understood by any sane person – you have to look at Dortmund's share price. By 2009, it had fallen to 0.93 euros, but the club's rise under Klopp found its reflection on the stock market. In 2014, the share price broke the 4-euro barrier. In 2016, it reached the 5-euro mark.

This seems to have planted a monstrous plan in the head of Sergei, a 28-year-old German born in Russia. He took out a loan and then purchased a sizable amount of so-called 'put options' on Dortmund shares. In layman's terms, these options amount to a bet: if the stock price suddenly plummets, put options earn you a large profit. Now Sergei had to find a way of making Dortmund's share price fall. According to the police investigation, he must have concluded that injuring or killing a few players would do the trick. He had been booked into the team's hotel on the day of the attack. After the bombs had gone off, most guests ran out of the hotel to see what had happened. Sergei went into the restaurant and ordered a steak. (Two weeks after the police had traced the put options back to Sergei and arrested him, Dortmund's share price climbed above 6 euros for the first time in fifteen years.)

The attack resulted in a much-publicised initiative by Dortmund's supporters. Since the match against Monaco was called off and rescheduled for the next day, many French fans were stranded in the city. Using the hashtag #bedforawayfans, locals offered them a meal and a roof over their heads. Even Real Madrid legend Iker Casillas, now playing for Porto, published a tweet that applauded the Dortmund fans' gesture. 'Those are the sort of supporters we have,' Sahin later said in a moving, emotional piece for *The Players' Tribune*. 'They knew that what had happened earlier in the day was bigger than football. That's just the way Dortmund fans are. I know, because I've been one my whole life.'

But the attack also resulted in a rapid deterioration of the relationship between Tuchel and almost everybody working for the club. A BVB team that everyone could see was emotionally unprepared to play a game of football lost the rescheduled Monaco match 3–2. On the next day, Tuchel harshly criticised the decision to give his players only twenty-four hours to get over an attack on their lives. He said a feeling of 'powerlessness' had gripped the team. His words were directed at UEFA, but they clearly implied that Tuchel felt let down by the club and thought Borussia, especially chairman Watzke, should have stood up to Europe's governing body. However, the members of the board, none of whom had actually been on the bus, maintained that the matter had been discussed with the coach and that none of the players was in any way forced to play. Regardless of the precise chain of events and no matter who said or did what, from that day on Borussia Dortmund's executives and their most important employee were for all practical purposes accusing each other of taking liberties with the truth to make the other look bad. Tuchel was now living on borrowed time.

But he kept winning. In late April, Borussia travelled to Munich for a spectacular cup semi-final against Bayern. Reus, who still hadn't won a trophy as a player, put Borussia ahead, but Martínez and Hummels, of all people, turned the game around. The hosts then missed many opportunities to score the deciding third goal and so it was still a close game when suddenly the stars smiled on 19-year-old Dembélé. The teenager had a tendency to drive fans crazy by habitually making the wrong decision. He dribbled when he should have passed, he passed when he should have shot, he shot when he should have dribbled. And yet the supporters loved him, and Tuchel rarely took him off, because he had the raw skills to make something happen every time he touched the ball. On 69 minutes, his floating no-look cross from the right flank found Aubameyang at the far post and the prolific striker, en route to winning the Golden Boot in the league, tied the game against the run of play. Five minutes later, Dembélé found himself in almost the exact same position, but this time he only feinted a cross. Surrounded by three defenders, he turned around and curled the ball into the top corner for the winning goal.

It was a sporting triumph and a public relations disaster. Dortmund had become the first German club to reach four cup finals in a row and although the first three had all been lost, against Wolfsburg and Bayern (twice), the team would be considered huge favourites for this one, against Eintracht Frankfurt. And yet the club had to gently prepare the public for the fact that there was no way Tuchel could continue as the first team's coach. Watzke publicly mentioned 'dissent' between Tuchel and the board and a few writers in the know tried to explain that the coach was at loggerheads with an astonishing number of people at the club. But it was too little, too late and rather wishy-washy. Most fans were simply bewildered when they realised their club was willing to part company with a highly successful coach who might even deliver the team's first silverware since 2012.

And of course he did. Dortmund won a scrappy, tense cup final in Berlin against Frankfurt 2–1, thanks to goals from Dembélé and Aubameyang. Three days later, Tuchel was fired. It was a decision that divided the club's support. In fact, there had been scattered catcalls after the cup final when Watzke's face appeared on the giant video screen. They were few and far between, but only months earlier it would have been utterly unthinkable for a Dortmund fan to boo the man who had been instrumental in saving the club.

Ironically, the whole Tuchel saga was a good example of the manifold dangers that lurk when you become the coolest club in the world. As always, BVB were trying to stay true to their ideals and serve their community, but it was becoming harder every day to define this community, as the club now had fans everywhere. In August 2016, Watzke coined a memorable expression to explain this dilemma when he said that the club's internationalisation amounted to 'a balancing act between Borsigplatz and Shanghai'.

In Shanghai, nobody could understand why anyone would sack the man who had earned more points per game than any Dortmund coach before him. It was a feeling shared by most BVB fans you would meet when you travelled from Shanghai to Dortmund, via, say, Ukraine and Poland and then Berlin. Yet the closer you got to Dortmund and to the Borsigplatz square, the spiritual home of the club, the more supporters you would encounter who said there was no alternative, as Tuchel had never understood what Borussia was all about and had alienated almost everybody working for the club.

But no matter whose side you chose to take in this baffling quarrel, BVB's total disregard for the bottom line – games and trophies won – indicated that 108 years after Franz Jacobi and his friends had stood up to the Catholic Church to form their own association, and seventeen years after Dortmund went public and issued shares to be traded on the stock market, Borussia had not become a sleek leisure brand but were still a stubborn old football club.

This book came to life during the most tumultuous, eventful and confusing period in Borussia Dortmund's long history: a period during which a club that had previously been coached by the same man for seven long years signed or sacked four managers from four countries in the span of twelve months.

As we have seen, the first, Thomas Tuchel, was relieved of his duties shortly after winning Borussia's first trophy in five years. The second, the Dutchman Peter Bosz, took Dortmund's offensive style to new heights. His team got off to a flying start, scoring nineteen goals in the first six league games, before suddenly going nine games without a win. In one of those matches – it was the derby, no less! – BVB became only the second team in league history to squander a four-goal lead.

The third coach, the Austrian Peter Stöger, took over in December 2017, having just been fired by Cologne after guiding this team to the worst start any Bundesliga club has ever had (a mere three draws from fourteen matches). Stöger well and truly turned his fortunes around by becoming the first BVB coach to go unbeaten in his first twelve league games. However, then his side conceded six goals against Bayern Munich and was embarrassingly knocked out of the Europa League by a smart but limited Salzburg team. Worse than the naked results was Stöger's dour, cautious style which the fans never warmed to. Despite securing Champions League qualification, he was replaced by the Swiss Lucien Favre after the end of the season. In Favre's first game in charge, Dortmund needed not one but two stoppage-time goals to beat a second-division side in the cup. In his first Bundesliga game, Favre saw Borussia fall behind after 31 seconds.

What in heaven's name was going on in Dortmund?

It was a question often asked during those uneasy times. There was an obvious answer, of course, but nobody could say it out loud. Club representatives, including the players and the coaching staff, couldn't say it because it would have been interpreted as a cheap excuse. And journalists couldn't say it because they would have been accused of lazy thinking. It was only in late 2017, when the court proceedings against Sergei began, that people woke up to the fact that the entire club was still in a state of shock. Gradually, as the players made their statements in halting voices, it dawned on more and more observers that these were individuals who, following a brief period of empathy and commiseration, had been treated as professional footballers, meaning they were expected to get on with business despite being victims of a traumatic experience. No one thought about what the psychological aftermath may have been. After all, nobody has any idea how a group of athletes would deal with being attacked by a disturbed individual (Sergei suffers from clinical depression and was, by his own admission, in a suicidal state when he planned the attack) who attempts to influence a share price by wounding or killing them. Who can imagine what effect it would have because nothing like this has ever happened before?

As a club, how do you manage such a situation? To this day, Borussia Dortmund are cautious about public statements relating to the attack, but can it really be a coincidence that in the fairly short span of time between late May 2017 and late August 2018, the majority of people who were on the bus left the club? We are talking about no less than twelve players here – Marc Bartra, Sokratis, Sven Bender, Matthias Ginter, Ousmane Dembélé, Pierre-Emerick Aubameyang, Nuri Sahin, Roman Weidenfeller, Gonzalo Castro, Mikel Merino, Emre Mor, Felix Passlack – plus an entire coaching staff. (Marco Reus and Mario Götze, who didn't leave, had not been on the coach when the bombs went off.)

Needless to say, those departures were not all instigated by the club. Weidenfeller retired, while Aubameyang and Dembélé more or less forced their high-profile transfers – to Arsenal and Barcelona, respectively – which netted the club roughly £190 million. But when Borussia's chairman Hans-Joachim Watzke spoke to 11Freunde magazine in December 2018, he finally admitted: 'After the attack, nothing was the same. Not just as regards the relationship between the directors and the manager. Especially the players who sat in the rear of the bus were of course no longer the same. It was a defining watershed for everyone.'

Yes, the attack had changed the squad. And it inadvertently ushered in Dortmund's next youth movement. When Watzke gave that interview during the winter break, a thoroughly overhauled BVB team was sensationally topping the league table, six points ahead of Bayern Munich. And at the centre of this whirlwind, which had the fans who formed the the Yellow Wall dreaming of the Bundesliga title, was a cheeky teenager who had learned a bag of tricks on the streets of Kennington, just south of the River Thames.

There has been a lot of speculation about the British influence at BVB – from the BAOR soldiers who adopted the club as home away from home, to Scottish fan favourites, such as Murdo MacLeod and Paul Lambert (not forgetting that Aberdeen's Scott Booth also wore black and yellow), to today's supporters who cross the English Channel on a regular basis to watch their football in Dortmund. But, amazingly, no Englishman had ever played for Borussia until Jadon Sancho made his Bundesliga debut as a substitute on 21 October 2017, at just seventeen years of age.

Sancho had joined Manchester City from Watford in 2015. Two years later, he terminated his scholarship deal with the Blues and turned down City's offer of a professional contract to join Borussia. When FourFourTwo later asked him why he had spurned the chance to earn riches, win trophies and play for Pep Guardiola in

order to move abroad at a tender age, Sancho replied: 'Why, Dortmund? It speaks for itself: youngsters get opportunities. You've got
to thank Dortmund, because it's unheard of for a team that gets
eighty thousand fans at every home game to put so much faith in
youngsters.'

If the young man figured he would get much more playing time
in Dortmund than at City, and could develop outside the media
glare and without too much pressure, he was right on the first
count but quite wrong on the others. Because after a few tentative
steps during his first year abroad – a couple of games for the first
team, some for the reserves and even the odd one for Dortmund's
Under-19s – Sancho became pretty much one of the first names on
the team-sheet as soon as the 2018–19 campaign was underway.

The main reason was that he possessed the one quality which
Germany's fabled Talent Promotion Programme had somehow
failed to instil in the country's youth. Although this programme
produced countless cultured midfielders who could thread lethal
passes through the eye of a needle, Sancho could *get past a defender*.
Or two. Sometimes three. In fact, he was so unstoppable that he
broke all kinds of offensive league records in his first full season
(for instance, he became by far the youngest player in history to
have a hand in thirty Bundesliga goals, either as scorer or a set-up
man) and won his first England cap as early as October 2018. So
much for avoiding the limelight. And as to no pressure, well, suddenly Sancho found himself in a title race. It's no exaggeration to
say that he and his team-mates felt not only the dreams of all Dortmund supporters on their shoulders but the hopes of an entire
footballing nation that had seen Bayern win six league titles in a
row and was longing for a change.

Of course Sancho wasn't the only reason for Borussia's resurgence. Maybe it all began as early as March 2018. First an old
hatchet was buried when Watzke revealed that Mathias Sammer
would return to Borussia as an external adviser. 'When his Bayern
time came to an end, and we'd became older, more mature and

sensible, we got closer again,' the chairman explained. Then it was announced that Sebastian Kehl was going to fill a newly created post, head of professional football. If those decisions were inspired by the template that has worked so well for Bayern over the years – involving former players to safeguard continuity – it yielded results astonishingly quickly. After a shaky start to the season, the young team delivered amazing attacking football, capped by an emotional home win against old and new rivals Bayern in which Dortmund came from behind twice to score the winning goal right in front of a delirious South Stand.

The famous terrace had been through an upheaval of its own during the difficult one and a half years in the wilderness following the bomb attack. Perhaps there were just too many controversial issues which divided opinion among the support, from Götze's return and the sacking of Tuchel, to the departure of firm fan favourites like Neven Subotić or Nuri Sahin. Add to this the questionable manner in which Dembélé and Aubameyang strongarmed the club into selling them, and you could understand why a feeling of disillusionment had set in.

A symbolic day was 26 February 2018. Dortmund recorded their worst attendance in twenty years, when only 54,300 fans showed up to watch their team against Augsburg. For a reason, of course. Earlier in the season, the Bundesliga had introduced Monday night games, ostensibly to give teams active in the Europa League more time to rest. However, many fans felt the clubs were trying to squeeze more television money out of the schedule at the expense of people who follow their team home and away (and would probably have to take two days off work to attend an away game on a Monday night). The 'South Stand Alliance', an umbrella organisation formed in 2014 which represents regular supporters, as well as ultras groups, to foster cohesion among the entire fan scene', called for a boycott of the Monday game against Augsburg. Not everyone felt this was an ideal way of expressing discontent, but 25,000 of those particularly committed fans who normally form the Yellow Wall did so and stayed away.

Just nine months later, the Yellow Wall yelled itself hoarse when local boy Marco Reus scored a brace against Bayern and Sancho ran rings round the Munich defence. Suddenly there was considerable daylight between Dortmund and the biggest club in the land in the standings. Barely two weeks after this memorable match, Sergei was convicted of 28 counts of attempted murder and sentenced to 14 years in prison by a Dortmund state court. At least in a legal and practical sense, the nightmare was finally over.

Dortmund's lead, however, would not be enough to break Bayern's dominance, as BVB couldn't carry their scintillating form into the second half of the season, while the Munich giants racked up an incredible winning streak. Dortmund still would have lifted the league title if it hadn't been for a highly heated and tumultuous derby down the stretch that featured two straight red cards for Dortmund players (a Bundesliga first for the club) and turned on a contentious decision by another controversial novelty – the video assistant referee.

If failing to hold Bayern at bay was a disappointing end to the season, this was not apparent from the scenes after Dortmund's final league game, away at Gladbach. The travelling support – more than five thousand fans – applauded their team and celebrated former captain Marcel Schmelzer, one of the few survivors of the Klopp era, who had been pushed to the fringes during the season but never sulked or complained. The players on the pitch were still rueing a missed opportunity at winning silverware, but the mood in the stands was, puzzlingly, almost festive. Maybe the reason was that the fans sensed this was not the end of a challenge but the beginning.

BIBLIOGRAPHY

Bäcker, Klaus and Schneck, Josef and Knust, Bruno: *Von Malta bis Turin (From Malta to Turin)*, Foto Dax, 1993

Baroth, Hans Dieter: *Jungens, Euch gehört der Himmel – Die Geschichte der Oberliga West 1947–63 (Lads, Heaven is Yours – The Story of the Oberliga West)*, Klartext, 1988

Bender, Tom and Kühne-Hellmessen, Ulrich: *Matthias Sammer – Der Feuerkopf (The Firehead)*, Sportverlag, 1998

Fligge, Frank and Fligge, Sascha: *Die Akte Schwarzgelb (The Black and Yellow Files)*, Lensing Wolff, 2005

Fligge, Frank and Fligge, Sascha: *Echte Liebe – Das spektakuläre Comeback des BVB (Real Love – BVB's Spectacular Comeback)*, Econ, 2016

Gehrmann, Siegfried: *Fußball, Vereine, Politik – Zur Sportgeschichte des Reviers 1900–1940 (Football, Clubs, Politics – The Ruhr Area's Sporting History)*, Reimar Hobbing, 1988

Harenberg, Bodo (Ed.): *Chronik des Ruhrgebiets (The Ruhr Area Chronicles)*, WAZ-Buch Chronik, 1987

Hesse, Uli and Schnittker, Gregor: *Unser ganzes Leben – Die Fans des BVB (Our Entire Life – The BVB Supporters)*, Werkstatt, 2013

Hesse, Uli: *Alles BVB (Everything BVB)*, Werkstatt, 2016

Heymann, Alfred: *Borussia Dortmund*, Droste, 1977

Hochstrasser, Josef: *Ottmar Hitzfeld – Die Biographie*, Argon, 2003

Justen, Hans-Josef and Loskill, Jörg: *Anstoß – Fußball im Ruhrgebiet (Kick-off – Football in the Ruhr Area)*, Gronenberg, 1985

Kolbe, Gerd (Ed.): *Wir halten fest und treu zusammen (We Stick Together Firmly and Faithfully)*, Global, 1977

Kolbe, Gerd: *Der BVB in der NS-Zeit (BVB During the Nazi Years)*, Werkstatt, 2002

Kozicki, Norbert: *Reinhard Stan Libuda*, Beluga New Media, 2007

Lehmann, Jens and Siemes, Christof: *Der Wahnsinn liegt auf dem Platz (The Madness is on the Pitch)*, Kiepenheuer & Witsch, 2010

Lindner, Rolf and Breuer, Heinrich: *Sind doch nicht alles Beckenbauers – Zur Sozialgeschichte des Fußballs im Ruhrgebiet (They Aren't All Beckenbauers – The Social History of Football in the Ruhr Area)*, Syndikat, 1979

Meek, David and Tyrrell, Tom: *Manchester United in Europe*, Coronet, 2002

Osses, Dietmar (Ed.): *Von Kuzorra bis Özil – Die Geschichte von Fußball und Migration im Ruhrgebiet (From Kuzorra to Özil – The Story of Football and Migration in the Ruhr Area)*, Klartext, 2015

Pramann, Ulrich: *Das bißchen Freiheit – Die fremde Welt der Fußballfans (That Little Bit of Freedom – The Foreign World of the Football Fans)*, Stern, 1980

Raap, Rainer (Ed.): *Die Fußballfans aus dem Revier (The Football Fans from the Ruhr Area)*, Strohhalm, 1993

Reckers, Bruno: *Vom Borsigplatz zum Fujiyama – Mein Leben mit dem BVB (From Borsig Square to Mount Fuji – My Life with BVB)*, Neue Buchschmiede, 2017

Schnittker, Gregor: *Revier-Derby – Die Geschichter einer Rivalität (Ruhr Derby – History of a Rivalry)*, Werkstatt, 2011

Schnittker, Gregor: *Die Helden von 66 (The Heroes of '66)*, Werkstatt, 2016

Schulze-Marmeling, Dietrich and Steffen, Werner: *Und du stehst immer wieder auf – Die Geschichte von Borussia Dortmund (And You Always Rise Again – The Story of Borussia Dortmund)*, Werkstatt, 1998

Schulze-Marmeling, Dietrich and Kolbe, Gerd: *Westfalenstadion – Die Geschichte einer Fußball-Bühne (Westfalenstadion – The Story of a Football Stage)*, Werkstatt, 2004

Schulze-Marmeling, Dietrich and Kolbe, Gerd: *Ein Jahrhundert Borussia Dortmund (One Hundred Years of Borussia Dortmund)*, Werkstatt, 2009

Viellvoye, Jo: *Borussia Dortmund – Die Geschichte einer großen Mannschaft (The Story of a Great Team)*, Copress, 1966

Wilson, Jonathan: *Inverting the Pyramid*, Orion, 2008

Wittke, Wilfried and Menn, Christian: *Borussiaaa – Auf dem Gipfel (On the Summit)*, Klartext, 1997

Wittke, Wilfied (Ed.): *So ein Tag – Die Original-Spielberichte der WR von 1963 bis heute (What a Day – WR's Original Match Reports from 1963 to Today)*, Edition Steffan, 2001

Wörner, Horst and Held, Sigfried: *Siggi Held – Rund um den Ball (Around the Ball)*, Gerhard Hess, 2013

INDEX